The Worlds of
the Seventeenth-Century
Hudson Valley

SUNY SERIES, AN AMERICAN REGION:
STUDIES IN THE HUDSON VALLEY

THOMAS S. WERMUTH, EDITOR

The Worlds of
the Seventeenth-Century
Hudson Valley

Edited by

Jaap Jacobs

and

L. H. Roper

excelsior editions

State University of New York Press
Albany, New York

Covert Art: *Nova Belgica et Anglia Nova* (1635) by William Janzsoon Blaeu, courtesy of the Boston Public Library ID# 10053

Published by State University of New York Press, Albany

Excelsior Editions is an imprint of State University of New York Press

For information, contact State University of New York Press, Albany, NY
www.sunypress.edu

Production by Jenn Bennett
Marketing by Kate McDonnell

Library of Congress Cataloging-in-Publication Data

The worlds of the seventeenth-century Hudson Valley / edited by Jaap Jacobs
   and L.H. Roper.
      p. cm. — (SUNY series, an American region : studies in the Hudson Valley)
   Includes bibliographical references and index.
   ISBN 978-1-4384-5098-8 (pbk. : alk. paper) 978-1-4384-5097-1 (hc : alk. paper)
   1. Hudson River Valley (N.Y. and N.J.)—History—17th century.   2. Dutch—
Hudson River Valley (N.Y. and N.J.)—History—17th century.   3. New
Netherland—History.   I. Jacobs, Jaap, 1963– author, editor of compilation.
II. Roper, L. H. (Louis H.) author, editor of compilation.

   F127.H8W95 2013
   974.7'3—dc23   2013022609

10 9 8 7 6 5 4 3 2 1

Contents

List of Illustrations

Preface and Acknowledgments

In September 2009, the Center for Regional Research, Education, and Out-reach (CRREO) at the State University of New York—New Paltz, as part of the four hundredth anniversary commemorations of the arrival of Henry Hudson in the river that today bears his name, invited thirteen scholars from Europe and the United States to participate in a symposium on "Henry Hudson, New Netherland, and Atlantic History." In addition to presenting papers on their respective areas of expertise, the academics participated in workshops, directed by Dr. Dennis Maika, which provided a rare opportunity for the educators who attended the symposium to interact intensively with professional historians and to discuss both substantive and pedagogical ideas for learning about the world from which Hudson came, the "new" world with which he and other Europeans interacted, and the settlement of the Dutch colony that ensued from his exploration of "his" river. This symposium was made possible through the good offices of New York State Assemblyman Kevin Cahill.

As part of this initiative, twelve of the participants have contributed essays to this volume that expand upon their symposium presentations. The contributors have also provided primary source materials from the work-shops that supplement their papers and provide further accessibility to the seventeenth-century history of the Hudson Valley. Our intention here is to provide teachers and others interested in this period of the region's past with an in-depth introduction and ready reference to the issues involved in the expansion of European interests to the Hudson River and the colonization of its environs.

To further these goals, we have arranged the volume in accordance with the symposium program by dividing the contributions into four parts with three essays in each. The first part, "European Worlds," provides insights into the European contexts, including cartographical, which gave rise to the career of Hudson and the early seventeenth-century exploration of North America. The second group of essays, "American Worlds," discusses the American Indian societies with which European explorers and African and European settlers came into contact and they track the history of contact between natives and newcomers in the Hudson Valley and the effects of interaction on American Indian, African, and European people. The third set of papers, "The Establishment of Colonial Worlds," analyzes the formation of and relations between the founded colonies by the Dutch, English, and French in New Netherland and the surrounding area. The final group of contributions, "The Formation of Atlantic Networks," considers social and economic developments in the seventeenth-century Hudson Valley from wider perspectives in order to provide a better understanding of the development and character of African-American and Euro-American communities and of the character of religious belief and practice in the area.

Although we intend this division to set out the contributions into coherent categories, it should not be regarded, however as a strict segregation. Many of the contributions share themes and analyses that transcend their placement here.

Joyce Goodfriend first published an expanded version of her symposium paper in volume 92, no. 3, of *New York History* (2011) and we acknowledge with thanks the kind permission of the New York State Historical Association to republish her paper here.

Abbreviations

CSPC   W. Noel Sainsbury, et al. (eds.), *Calendar of State Papers, Colonial: America and West Indies.*

DRCHNY   E. B. O'Callaghan and B. Fernow (eds.), *Documents Relative to the Colonial History of the State of New York*, 15 vols. (Albany, 1853–1887).

ERNY   *Ecclesiastical Records of the State of New York*, 7 vols. (Albany, 1901–1916).

JR   Reuben G. Thwaites (ed.), *The Jesuit Relations and Allied Documents: Travels and Explorations of the Jesuit Missionaries in New France, 1610–1791*, 73 vols. (Cleveland, O. 1896–1901).

NNN   J. Franklin Jameson (ed.), *Narratives of the New Netherland, 1609–1664* (New York, 1909).

NYCM   New York Colonial Manuscripts.

NYSA   New York State Archives, Albany, NY.

RNA   Berthold Fernow (ed. and trans.), *The Records of New Amsterdam from 1653 to 1674*, 7 vols. (Baltimore: Genealogical Publishing Company, 1976 [1897].

VRBM   A. J. F. van Laer (trans. and ed.), *Van Rensselaer-Bowier Manuscripts, being the Letters of Kiliaen van Rensselaer, 1630–1643, and Other Documents relating to the Colony of Rensselaerswyck* (Albany, 1908).

WMQ   *William and Mary Quarterly*, 3rd ser.

I

EUROPEAN WORLDS

1

The Seventeenth-Century Empire of the Dutch Republic, c. 1590–1672

Jaap Jacobs

*T*he overseas expansion of the Dutch Republic, culminating in the "First Dutch Empire," is a remarkable story of the quick rise to prominence of a small country in northwestern Europe. Much smaller in population than European rivals like Spain, England, and France, and without considerable natural resources, the Republic was able within a few decades to lay the foundation for a colonial empire of which remnants are still part of the Kingdom of the Netherlands nowadays. This First Dutch Empire, running roughly from the beginning of the seventeenth century until the early 1670s, was characterized by rapid expansion, both in the Atlantic area and in Asia. The phase that followed, the Second Dutch Empire, shows a divergence in development between the East and West. In the East, territorial expansion—often limited to trading posts, not settlement colonies—continued and trade volume increased, but in the Western theater the Dutch witnessed a contraction of territorial possessions, especially with the loss of New Netherland and Dutch Brazil. Even so, Dutch trade and shipping in the Atlantic was not solely dependent upon colonial footholds, not in the least because the Dutch began to participate in the Atlantic slave trade. This Second Dutch Empire ended in the Age of Democratic Revolutions, when upheavals in Europe and America brought an end to both the Dutch East and West India Companies and led to the loss of a number of colonies, such as South Africa, Sri Lanka, and Essequibo and Demerara on the Guyana coast. A Third Dutch Empire can be considered to encompass the increasing dominance of the Dutch over the East Indies, especially the islands that now form Indonesia, in the nineteenth and early twentieth century, ending with decolonization after the Second World War. The fourth phase is one in which the term "empire" may appear to be less applicable. Rather, it is the phase of continued decolonization, with the independence of Surinam in 1975 and the subsequent migration of many descendants of slaves to the Netherlands.

This very general periodization of Dutch colonial expansion and contraction in many ways runs parallel to that of other European countries. Yet, when we take a closer look at the first phase, certain features of Dutch expansion appear to be unique. Some of these are the direct result of differences between the Netherlands and the European monarchies surrounding it and can be traced back to the origins of the Dutch Republic.

By the mid-sixteenth century, the seventeen provinces of the Low Countries had gradually been brought under the rule of the Habsburg monarchs, first Charles V, and subsequently his son Phillip II, who also ruled territories on the Iberian Peninsula, among other domains. Yet from the 1560s onward, resistance toward these overlords began to increase, partly fuelled by antipathy toward the attempts to quell the beginnings of the Reformation, partly also in defense against centralizing efforts which encroached upon privileges previously granted to cities and estates. The Iconoclastic Fury of 1566, in which Roman Catholic churches were purged of images to be made suitable for reformed worship, triggered an escalation into what is now called the Dutch Revolt. By 1600 the seven northern provinces had de facto become independent, even though Spain—and other European countries—did not officially recognize this until the Peace of Westphalia in 1648.

The Dutch Revolt had a far-reaching impact on the seven provinces that constituted the Republic of the Seven United Netherlands, also called the United Provinces or the Dutch Republic—the term most commonly used by historians nowadays. The most obvious effect was the decapitation of the customary early modern sociopolitical pyramid. In the sixteenth century, sovereign power over each province had rested with a monarch in a personal union, meaning he combined the feudal titles of individual provinces, such as Duke of Gelderland, Count of Holland, etc. In the 1581 Act of Abjuration, a number of the rebellious provinces, combined in the States General, cast off their allegiance to Philip II and voided his sovereign powers. Interestingly, the ideological foundation of this decision was remarkably similar to that used in the American Declaration of Independence almost two centuries later, which has fuelled speculation that Thomas Jefferson used it as an example, even though there is no documentary evidence to boost that claim. Rather, I would suggest, it points to the persistence of underlying currents of philosophies of governmental authority. A striking difference with the popular tendencies of the American Revolution is that the States General after 1581 tried to bestow sovereignty on noblemen from France and England, before finally deciding in 1587 to stop such efforts. This left the Dutch Republic in a hybrid situation, with sovereignty becoming collective, partly residing in the States General and partly in the provincial estates.

If that was not sufficient cause for conflicts to come, the situation was muddied further by the position of the stadholder, usually filled by members of the House of Orange. This noble family, with its princely title deriving from the independent principality of Orange in the south of France, had played an important role in the Dutch Revolt. William of Orange had been stadholder—governor—of some of the provinces and acted as representative of the sovereign overlord. In that position, the stadholder in the sixteenth century held supreme military positions and also had the power to appoint local officials and supervise the meetings of provincial estates as well as the States General. Yet after the Dutch Revolt, the stadholder technically became the servant of the provincial estates, although foreign visitors often misunderstood his power. The locus of this byzantine state system was the Binnenhof in The Hague. This was, in the early decades of the seventeenth century, the place where both the stadholder, the States of Holland, as well as the States General, resided. Considering that much remained the same, with the exception of the concentration of sovereignty in a single person overlord, it might be better to describe the institutional changes between 1570 and 1650 not so much as the decapitation but rather as the collapsing of the top tier of the pyramid.

The Dutch Revolt caused another important socioeconomic change as well: the different role of the clergy. Prior to the Revolt, bishops, abbots, and parish priests were of importance at different layers in the socioeonomic structure. As a result of the Dutch Revolt, the Catholic Church lost its prominent position, as well as most of its property. Catholic churches were purged and turned into reformed houses of worship, while monasteries were confiscated and turned to other uses, for instance to financing universities that educated reformed ministers. Although the Reformed Church also instituted regional and provincial supervisory bodies, the Reformation did lead to a change in the relation between Church and State. The Reformed Church was not a state church, but rather a public church: the only denomination with a right to public worship. It did not encompass the entire population, but was confined to a vanguard consisting of its membership, which submitted voluntarily to ecclesiastical discipline. For many matters, including control over houses of worship, the clergy had to rely on secular magistrates. Their success depended on the extent to which they could sway local officials to act on their complaints.

The collapse of the top of the pyramid and the removal of the church brought more power to the middle class in Dutch society. These burghers—self-employed artisans, shopkeepers, farmers who owned their land—considered themselves the core of the local community. These men—always men—were their own masters, meaning they were not in anybody's employ, like servants, and they were of sufficient means, unlike the poor. They manned the local militia (*schutterijen*). The burghers formed quite a broad layer, showing considerable differentiation. At the top end we find the rich elite of merchants and magistrates. The Dutch Revolt had removed from power a number of the old Catholic families. New families obtained a place in the city councils of the cities of Holland and other provinces. In many cases, these regents combined their mercantile activities with a position in government, and they used their influence to implement economic policies that favored their own group. Nowadays we would call this abuse of power, but our conception of corruption is different from that in the 1600s. Once the Dutch Republic had consolidated its military position in the late-sixteenth century, the marriage between commerce and politics greatly added to its increasing eminence. Within an essentially conservative frame of mind that pervaded the seventeenth century, there was yet room for innovation, both technological (windmills) and mercantile (such as in matters of finance and banking), with the Amsterdam Exchange Bank, the Merchant Exchange, and improvements in the use of shareholding, for instance. It is notoriously difficult for historians to capture the atmosphere of any age, but when studying the early decades of the seventeenth century, a sense of boundless opportunities seems to have pervaded Dutch society, a mentality in which daring bred success. The fact that political power was in the hands of the mercantile elite certainly helped. This lasted until about the mid-seventeenth century, when we find the number of magistrates with a commercial background waning. While some sons of elite families went into government, and some went into trade, fewer and fewer combined the two. In addition, the elite became less accessible to newcomers. Dutch society as a whole was less dynamic in the second part of the seventeenth century.

Yet by that time the foundations for a colonial empire had been laid. Of course, it was not just internal factors that assisted the Dutch Republic in its remarkable rise to the status of world power; external factors also played a role. The imperial overstretch from which Spain (between 1580 and 1640 combined with Portugal) suffered allowed Dutch merchants to make inroads into Spanish trade and shipping in the Atlantic and the Asiatic theaters. Cutting off the colonial supply, so as to cripple the Spanish effort to reconquer the rebellious provinces that formed the Dutch Republic, was an important strategic consideration, and it was boosted by a virulent anti-Catholic mood. This is more obvious in the West India Company than in the East India Company, but in the first part of the seventeenth century it played a major role in both. Privateering in the Caribbean Sea and attacking Spanish settlements along the coast of South America was a favorite pastime of West India Company operatives. Yet the biggest result came with the capture of a Spanish silver transport in the Bay of Matanzas on the northern coast of Cuba in 1628. West India Company admiral Piet Heyn took eight Spanish ships carrying over 170,000 pounds of silver. The proceeds allowed the Company to set up the expedition that captured the northeastern part of Brazil in 1630.

Northern European rivals, like England and France, in the first half of the seventeenth century, suffered from internal struggles that hampered their ability to counter Dutch expansion. The English economy was not very strong circa 1600 and soon afterward religious strife and political struggles combined to produce the disruptive English Civil Wars (1642–1651). France similarly underwent a couple of decades of problems: partly peasant revolts, partly economic stagnation. Yet by the 1660s both countries had emerged as strong competitors to the Dutch. The rise of increasingly powerful monarchies in France and England had resulted in a unity of purpose and a determination by its royal leaders to counter these Republican upstarts who had appropriated a larger share of the world's economy than they had a right to. Faced with such opposition from centralized governments, the Dutch decentralized state system became a disadvantage rather than an asset. Whereas it had previously allowed an extent of flexibility beneficial to expansion, decentralization now made it more difficult to achieve a unified response to external threats.

In a way then, the Dutch Republic's phenomenal colonial expansion could not have taken place at any other time than the first half of the seventeenth century, wedged in between the Dutch Revolt and the rise of absolutism in European states. In assessing this development, the difference between the Atlantic and Asiatic theaters is striking. Initially, Dutch merchants focused on Asia, where valuable spices could be obtained. Here, they encountered relatively powerful Indigenous states, in which the economies were well developed and the density of the population usually was high. Partly because of these factors, the trading posts in the East remained small. Territorial expansion, with the objective of establishing colonial settlements, was difficult in the East, and it was rarely the intention, at least initially.[1]

On the other hand, there were opportunities for expansion in the New World. Here, resistance was not so much to be expected from the Indigenous populations, whose numbers declined due to the European diseases previously unfamiliar to them, but from other European nations, who had established colonies earlier. The objectives of the two great Dutch trading companies expressed this difference. Trade was the main objective of the *Verenigde Oost-Indische Compagnie* [East India Company or VOC], and gaining footholds was a means to this. The principal objective of the *Geoctroyeerde West-Indische Compagnie* [West India Company or WIC] on the other hand was to inflict damage on the colonial resources of the Iberian enemies. In pursuit of this objective the WIC tried its hand at the conquest of enemy colonies and privateering on its shipping. But the combination of business enterprise and instrument of war ultimately proved unsuccessful.[2]

The format the Dutch employed for overseas expansion—privately funded companies with a state monopoly—shows the decentralization that characterized the Dutch Republic, especially in its organization in local chambers. For a number of years in the period prior to 1621, Dutch merchants had been sailing to areas of the Atlantic other than New Netherland. To *patria* they carried sugar from Brazil, the Canary Islands, São Tomé, and Madeira, and salt, essential to the Dutch fishing industry, from the Cape Verde Islands, the coast of Venezuela, and islands in the Caribbean. Dutch ships also sailed to the coast of West Africa to obtain pepper, ivory, and gold. Even before the Twelve Years Truce with Spain (1609–1621) there had been plans to amalgamate the separate ventures into a single chartered company, as had been done in the East India trade.

Almost immediately following the resumption of hostilities with Spain at the end of the Twelve Years Truce, the States General issued the patent for the West India Company. Colonization scarcely played a role in the patent, whereas privateering and trade, which in the eyes of the merchants offered better opportunities for profit, were principal objectives. The political situation in the Atlantic demanded a belligerent company. But financiers in the Dutch Republic were not particularly enthusiastic, most likely because they perceived the West India Company, to a far greater extent than the East India Company, to be a privately financed weapon in the fight against Spain. The most lucrative areas had already been in the hands of Spain and Portugal since the beginning of the sixteenth century. To create an Atlantic empire, the Dutch Republic would have to wage war. So trade and war were allies in the formation of the West India Company. It remained to be seen, however, whether it would be a particularly fortunate combination. As long as the Company's activities were limited to privateering and to carrying out attacks on Spanish colonies, private and state interests coincided to a great extent. But the establishment of Dutch colonies, especially settlement colonies, was another matter.[3]

Dutch colonization proceeded under the auspices of the States General, the central government of the Dutch Republic, in which each of the sovereign provinces was represented. The States General issued charters for the East India Company and the West India Company. Like the East India Company, the WIC was a public-private partnership in the form of a joint-stock company with shipping and trade monopolies. Both companies exercised powers that we associate with states, such as the power to conduct treaties and engage in warfare against Spain and Portugal. The East India Company managed to sustain its commercial rights for over two centuries. In contrast, the West India Company soon lost most of its trade of shipping monopolies. The emphasis in its activities shifted to colonial government in the Atlantic world and de facto it became a hybrid institution of colonial government rather than a commercial company. The West India Company was subdivided into five chambers: Amsterdam, Zeeland, Maze, Noorderkwartier, and Stad en Lande. Its central administration, which was in charge of general policy, consisted of the *Heren XIX* [Lords Nineteen], in which Amsterdam had eight votes, Zeeland four, and each of the other chambers two. One vote was reserved for the States General, ensuring that the government's interests were represented at the highest level within the Company.[4] The presidency of the *Heren XIX* rotated between the chambers of Amsterdam and Zeeland. In principle, meetings were held in the place where the presiding chamber was established, but sometimes the States General called meetings of the *Heren XIX* in The Hague.[5] Since most of the voyages to New Netherland had been organized by Amsterdam merchants, New Netherland was supervised by the Amsterdam chamber, which had twenty directors. These were elected with a tenure of six years from the *hoofdparticipanten* [large shareholders], each of whom had to invest a minimum of six thousand guilders. Committees within each chamber were charged with specific executive duties, such as the management of the wharves, the equipping of the ships, and the sales of the cargoes brought in by those ships.[6]

At the height of its power, around 1640, the West India Company controlled several colonies in the Atlantic: northeastern Brazil, a number of islands in the Caribbean, forts on the West African coast, Congo, Angola, and New Netherland. New Netherland was supervised by the Amsterdam chamber which instituted a separate committee to conduct the correspondence with New Amsterdam. In all formal documents, the highest authority in New Netherland carries the title "director-general and council." Exact titles were important in the seventeenth century and in this case it indicates the relatively unimportant position of New Netherland among the Company's possessions. Petrus Stuyvesant was not a governor-general, like Count Johan-Maurits van Nassau-Siegen in Brazil. A step further down in the hierarchy were regular directors and vice-directors. In New Netherland, vice-directors, reporting to director-general and council, were positioned at Fort Orange [Albany] and on the Delaware. The highest official at Curaçao was also a vice-director. In the same way, the exact designation for the members of the council was *"raden,"* councilors, not High Councilors, as in Brazil. When in 1654–1655 the councilors in New Netherland assumed the title of High Council, they were sternly reminded by their superiors in Amsterdam that they had no authority to do so: "You will do well to abstain therefrom in the future and be satisfied with the title belonging to each office."

Governance by council in a Dutch colonial setting meant that the responsibility for decisions was shared by a collective body. Councilors were not just there to give advice, which could be followed or discarded by the director-general at will. They actually shared power. In most cases, the council in New Netherland was composed of West India Company employees, such as the vice-director, the *fiscaal* (the chief law enforcement officer), and the secretary. The power to appoint councilors lay solely with the Amsterdam chamber. In some cases, colonial councils made provisional decisions on matters of succession, subject to later approval from the Dutch Republic. An example is the appointment of Stuyvesant as director of Curaçao in 1642. During Stuyvesant's time as director-general of New Netherland, the council usually consisted of four men, including himself. In his seventeen years in the job, Stuyvesant had a total of twelve different councilors.[7] Only in two or three cases was he able to exert any influence on the choice, so this was not a hand-picked council as is sometimes suggested. Apart from the early years, when conflicts arose between Stuyvesant and both his vice-director and the *fiscaal*, the director-general cooperated very well with his councilors.

The task of the council was to give advice and work together with the director-general in running the colony. The director-general and council had legislative tasks, discussing and promulgating ordinances on several issues, as well as executive duties, with the director-general as CEO. Stuyvesant entrusted his councilors with several assignments, both within New Netherland, as well as in the contacts with the surrounding English colonies. Its third task was to act as a High Court, trying capital cases, and as a court of appeal.

The meetings of the council took place in the meeting room in the fort and were chaired by the director-general. He convened the meetings, decided on the agenda, proposed policy decisions and put matters to a vote. In the case of a tie, the director-general had a deciding vote. So he had a position of considerable influence, but even a strong personality such as Stuyvesant was outvoted on occasion. An example is the appointment of a new commissary for Fort Orange in 1647. Stuyvesant had suggested Michiel Jansz, but only vice-director Dinclage agreed with him. The other councilors voted for Carel van Bruggen—actually an Englishman; Charles Bridges was from Canterbury, but his name was Dutchified. So Stuyvesant was outvoted and Van Bruggen was appointed.[8]

Majority rule also applied in special situations when members of the city government of New Amsterdam were added to the council, as happened a number of times. It is a sign of the good collaboration of Stuyvesant with the city government. In numerous cases a vote was taken and the individual opinions were recorded, but in many other cases of less importance the decision to be taken was obvious; thus, after a brief discussion all agreed, and the council minutes reveal unanimity.[9] When important issues were at stake and when time was available, the procedure was different. Let me give an example: on 10 November 1655, Stuyvesant asked the council whether the Indian attack on New Amsterdam two months earlier should be avenged by declaring war. He submitted a paper to the council with various questions:

a) what were the military options;

b) how the war should be paid for;

c) would it be a just war; and

d) would the risk not be too great?

Stuyvesant's paper was read aloud in the meeting and all councilors received a copy. They were asked to submit their opinion in writing prior to the next meeting. The aim of the procedure was also indicated:

> We earnestly request the honorable councilors for their written opinion on the foregoing propositions, [to be] given either collectively or individually. The latter is preferred to avoid partiality. For our part we [meaning Stuyvesant] shall not fail to place our opinion on the table beside those of your honors, so that the lords superiors in the fatherland may be all the better informed concerning the state of affairs, and so that we may arrive at a salutary resolution.[10]

So the purpose of the procedure was twofold: to come to the best possible decision, and to justify it to the superiors back in the Dutch Republic. Individual opinions are recorded quite frequently in the New Netherland council minutes. They can also be found in records of other Dutch colonies. The quote above provides the explanation. The colonial officials could be called upon to account for their decisions by their superiors in the Dutch Republic. They could even be charged with neglect or mismanagement, and this actually happened to both Stuyvesant and some of his predecessors, as well as in the case of Frederick Coyett, who was in charge of Dutch Formosa (Taiwan) when it was conquered by the Chinese.

By the 1650s communication had become quite frequent. In the correspondence with New Netherland each letter covers several topics. Usually, the letters are ten to twenty pages long. There were other ways in which the directors in Amsterdam, housed in the West India House, were kept informed. Several people sent letters to the directors in Amsterdam. For instance, in a letter of 27 January 1649, the Amsterdam directors informed director-general and council that they had received four letters from the vice-director on Curaçao, a letter from the schoolmaster on that island, a letter from commissary on Fort Orange (Carel van Bruggen), three letters from the New Amsterdam minister, and a letter from the fiscal.

The Amsterdam directors had other sources of information as well. Returning ship captains and company officials provided information orally. All this communication gave the Amsterdam chamber a detailed view on what was happening in New Netherland. It allowed the directors to give specific instructions to their officials in the colony.

Usually, the letters to and from New Amsterdam are ten to twenty pages long, which is actually quite short, when compared to the correspondence with Batavia in the eighteenth century, which ran into hundreds of pages per letter. The correspondence consists of two categories: general letters, sent to the highest official and council, and private letters (*particuliere missiven*), sent only to the CEO. This distinction has been overlooked by the nineteenth-century translators who worked on the Dutch documents of New Netherland. The translations of the correspondence give the impression that the directors corresponded solely with Director-General Stuyvesant. Actually, most of the letters are direct at director-general *and* council.

We may presume the general letters from the directors in the Dutch Republic were read aloud in the colonial councils by a secretary. Unfortunately, we know little about those sessions of the council. As no decisions were taken, they left no trace in the council minutes. Likewise, there is almost no information about the procedure via which the letters from director-general and council to their superiors were drawn up; it would seem that the highest official (i.e. Stuyvesant) composed drafts, which were then read in the council. After suggesting changes the council approved the final version, which was then written out by the secretary or one of the clerks, before being signed by the chief executive officer (again, Stuyvesant). Also, copies had to be prepared to be expedited by later ships. In some cases the whole process had to be done very speedily, as a sudden change of weather could hasten the departure of the ships. On the whole, the administrative setup of colonial government provided a system of checks and balances against abuse of power or of the highest officials acting autocratically, which is not to say that conflicts and corruption were completely absent, of course.

This brief overview indicates that some of the most important characteristics of the Dutch Republic, such as its economic structure, its mercantile mentality, and its governmental setup, were replicated in Dutch trading posts and colonies. The most important characteristic, though, was flexibility. As the Dutch encountered divergent situations around the globe, they seem to have been better capable and more willing than other European nations to work with what they found, rather than impose their own scheme of things. It was this ability that allowed the Dutch to maintain a presence in Japan, to the exclusion of all other European nations, and it was this ability that allowed the Dutch to shift from company-controlled shipping and trade in the Atlantic to private merchant-controlled, when the Dutch Republic found itself unable to counter the quest for territorially based colonization by other European powers.

Notes

1. J. van Goor, *De Nederlandse koloniën: Geschiedenis van de Nederlandse expansie 1600–1975* (The Hague: SDU Uitgevers, 1994); E. van den Boogaart, *Overzee: Nederlandse colonial geschiedenis, 1590–1975* (Haarlem: Fibula-Van Dishoeck, 1982); C. R. Boxer, *The Dutch Seaborne Empire, 1600–1800* (New York: Knopf, 1965).

2. Wim Klooster, *The Dutch in the Americas: a narrative history with a catalogue of rare prints, maps, and illustrated books from the John Carter Brown Library* (Providence, RI: John Carter Brown Library, 1997); H. J. den Heijer, *De geschiedenis van de WIC* (Zutphen: Walburg, 1994); Johannes Postma and Victor Enthoven (eds.), *Riches from Atlantic Commerce: Dutch Transatlantic Trade and Shipping, 1585–1817* (Leiden: Brill, 2003), in which the introduction provides an overview of recent literature on Dutch expansion in the Atlantic.

3. Den Heijer, *De geschiedenis van de WIC*, pp. 26–34; Willem Frijhoff, *Wegen van Evert Willemsz.: een Hollands weeskind op zoek naar zichzelf, 1607–1647* (Nijme-

gen: SUN, 1995), p. 494. Frijhoff's magisterial book is now also available in translation, Frijhoff, *Fulfilling God's Mission: the Two Worlds of Dominie Everardus Bogardus, 1607–1647* (Leiden: Brill, 2003). References here are to the Dutch version.

4. Cf. Frijhoff, *Wegen*, p. 494. That the States General had only one vote does not imply that only one representative was present. In 1638, the whole of the committee of the States General, nine men strong, was present at the meeting of the Heren XIX: Nat. Arch., The Hague, Archive States General, loketkas WIC, inv. no. 12564.6 (28 February 1638–1 May 1638).

5. For example, with reference to the discussion on the opening of trade with Brazil in 1638, Nat. Arch., Archive States General, loketkas WIC, inv. no. 12564.6 (28 February 1638–1 May 1638).

6. Den Heijer, *De geschiedenis van de WIC*, pp. 31–3, 83; *VRBM*, pp. 86–135.

7. Not including skippers in 1647 and occasional members. The twelve are Johannes La Montagne (1638–1656), Lubbert van Dincklagen (1647–1651), Brian Newton (1647–1653), Paulus Leendertsz van der Grift (1647–1651), Hendrick van Dijck 1647–1651), Adriaen Keyser (1647–1651), Cornelis van Tienhoven (1652–1656), Cornelis van Werckhoven (1653–1654), Nicasius de Sille (1653–1664), Cornelis van Ruyven (1659–1664), Pieter Tonneman (1657–1659) and Johan de Deckere (1658–1664).

8. NYSA, NYCM, 4:347–348 (6 November 1647; Arnold J. F. van Laer (trans. and ed.), *Register of the Provincial Secretary, 1638–1642. New York Historical Manuscripts: Dutch, vol. 1.* (Baltimore. Md.: Genealogical Publishing Co., Inc., 1974), 4:460–461).

9. NYSA, NYCM, 6:19 (2 March 1655; Charles T. Gehring (trans. and ed.), *Council Minutes 1655–1656*, New Netherland Documents Series, vol. 6, Syracuse; Syracuse University Press, 1995, pp. 21–22), 15 (2 March 1655; Gehring, *Council Minutes 1655–1656*, pp. 16–17).

10. NYSA, NYCM, 6:149 (10 November 1655; Gehring, *Council Minutes 1655–1656*, pp. 130–132).

2

The Seventeenth-Century English Empire

L. H. Roper

*A*s the proverbial schoolchildren know, the Englishman Henry Hudson (c. 1570–1611) conducted his 1609 exploration of the river that bears his name on behalf of the Dutch East India Company. We also know that the English government took a dim view of Hudson's enlistment by foreigners and limited his future voyages to domestic employers. This subsequent career, though, came to naught as the explorer's crew, fearful that their master's obsession for a navigable northerly passage to the Indies would bring about their deaths by freezing, mutinied and cast Hudson, his son, and a handful of loyalists adrift in the Arctic. In terms of eponymous bodies of water, then, the Hudson River has translated, on the one hand, into a vital economic ligament which, to a large degree, created the modern "Empire State" while, on the other, the frozen wasteland of Hudson's Bay still brings a shudder when we consider the fate of its discoverer. This stark present-day dichotomy reminds us that Hudson's career illustrates the ambiguous and hesitant character of early seventeenth-century English overseas exploration, trade, and colonization and the correspondingly fitful early development of what came to be the British Empire. It also reminds us that we obtain the clearest view of the early history of the English overseas interests—including the establishment and formation of Anglo-American colonies and, ultimately, the English takeover of New Netherland and creation of New York—from a transatlantic perspective.[1]

The English, as we know, became involved relatively late in the expansion of European commercial and political interests overseas. It can, though, be interesting to speculate what might have happened had Henry VII (reigned 1485–1509) sponsored the voyages of Christopher Columbus rather than the

Castilian Queen Isabella (reigned 1479–1504). Would the subjects of the Tudors have established themselves, as their counterparts did, in the Caribbean? And might some hypothetical Englishmen, having followed Columbus to Cuba and Hispaniola, substituted for the *conquistadores* Hernán Cortes and Francisco Pizarro and conquered the powerful and wealthy Mexican and Inca Empires? Would those endeavors then have given rise to an English empire that wound up governing much of Central and South America and funneling the "wealth of the Indies" to London (rather than Seville)?

In the end, of course, this did not happen although, on the face of things, nothing in the respective political, economic, and social situations of England and "Spain" (which did not exist in the modern sense in the early modern period) gave the latter any advantage in an imperial "race." Rather, the accident of Columbus "discovering" a "New World" created a colonial base for the initiatives taken by Cortes and others, the success of which, in turn, depended upon circumstances involving Indigenous populations, especially their sociopolitical political circumstances, and the effects of European disease upon those populations. The English, as we shall see, followed a similar colonial-led prescription for territorial expansion when they finally established their own American footholds a century later; but the Indians whom they encountered neither lived in fabulous cities like Tenochtítlan nor possessed the wealth of the Mexica or the Incas. Correspondingly, the English "invasion of America," as some have styled it, transpired in a rather lengthier, more fitful way than its Spanish counterpart.[2]

Instead, while the Spanish advanced seemingly inexorably across the map of the Americas and even around the globe over the course of the sixteenth century, the English empire actually receded. The calamitous loss of Calais in 1558, which marked the end of an English continental presence that dated back to the eleventh century, underscored the increasing impotence of England as a force in European affairs as did repeated failure to dictate matters in Scotland and Ireland. These imperial setbacks reflected, to contemporary minds deeply affected by the Reformation, a fundamentally serious turn in the state of affairs. On the one hand, Catholic Spain moved from strength to strength: its acquisition of overseas territory and wealth enabled it both to spread "popery" and to thwart the advance of Protestantism in the Low Countries, France, Hungary, and Germany as well as to subvert church and state and re-establish "popery" in England. Indeed, English observers had no difficulty conceiving of Spanish plans to establish a "universal monarchy" that would place liberty-loving practitioners of "True Religion" under the "yoke" of "popish tyranny."[3]

To the consternation, then, of these champions of English advancement, the subjects of the Portuguese and Castilian crowns had plied the oceans for over a century and a half while mariners in French service had visited the North American coast and the St. Lawrence River from 1524 and the Dutch had embarked on the aggressive voyaging that laid the foundation for their seventeenth-century "Golden Age." By 1609, when Hudson first saw Manhattan, Europeans had established outposts in such far-flung places as Angola, Brazil, Florida, Goa, Java, Macau, Manila, and Québec. The Spaniards, of course, had subjugated the great American Indian empires of Mexico and Peru; correspondingly, the Habsburg rulers of the Iberian Peninsula derived substantial revenues from Asian commerce and from "New World" plantations and mines. None of these successes, as contemporary commentators, such as the cleric Richard Hakluyt, lamented, involved the English, who with the exception of a clutch of privateers, such as Sir Francis Drake, and a handful of traders to Russia and the Middle East, remained conspicuous by their general absence from the global scene prior to the death of Elizabeth I (reigned 1558–1603). Indeed, despite the completion of Drake's circumnavigation of the globe in 1581 and the celebrated defeat of the "Spanish Armada" in 1588, English efforts to muscle in on the Iberian interests had proven dismal up to this point: the litany of their failure includes the "Lost Colony" at Roanoke on the coast of present-day North Carolina (1585); the Spanish defeat of the "English Armada" (1589); the efforts of Sir Walter Raleigh to find "El Dorado" in Guiana in South America (1595); and the death of Drake himself in the botched attempt to sack the Spanish city of Cadíz (1597) during the course of the Spanish war. Small wonder, then, that an ambitious English seafarer such as Henry Hudson would look to other countries, especially the burgeoning Dutch Republic, for better prospects.[4]

Hand-wringing over this situation generated a further concern over the unwillingness of the Elizabethan government to provide more vigorous support for the Dutch rebels in their war of independence (1568–1609, 1621–1648) against the "dearest son of the Scarlet Whore of Rome," the Spanish king Philip II (reigned 1556–1598), as well as for the Huguenots in the French Wars of Religion (1562–1598). According to advocates of more aggressive anti-Spanish foreign policy, unless and until those in charge of the English ship of state changed tack and assumed their proper leadership role, including promotion of overseas exploration, trade, and settlement, in the advancement of reformed religion, tyranny and slavery would surely result for the English people and their fellow Protestants.

Unfortunately for the adherents of this policy, the continually parlous fiscal state of the early modern English state, as Elizabeth, for one, well knew, did not allow for much involvement in matters that we would regard today as governmental policy. Prior to 1651, when the civil wars (1642–1651) that had convulsed the British Isles ended, expensive "public" ventures, such as overseas colonization, proved invariably beyond the fiscal and administrative reach of English governments dependent upon habitually inadequate "ordinary" income derived from customs revenue and Crown lands to maintain themselves. The best efforts, which were not consistently applied, of monarchs and their advisors, failed to achieve reform of the traditional system of taxation and finance even as governmental needs expanded with the population: neither the sufficiency of revenue nor the means of assessing and collecting funds was adequate to support policies that the Tudor and Stewart monarchs hoped to undertake on overseas fronts. The liberality of Elizabeth's successor, James I (reigned 1603–1625), toward his favorites, especially George Villiers, duke of Buckingham (1592–1628) aggravated the gap between revenues and expenditures.[5]

Thus, these monarchs habitually lacked sufficient money to equip and maintain substantial armies and fleets or to support directly voyages of "discovery" (although privateering, which generated revenue, was another matter) and this enduring shortcoming was underscored by the indifferent results achieved in Scotland and Ireland noted above and in the disastrous ones suffered in continental wars: English armies won no significant victories between the capture of Boulogne (1547) and the defeat of the Scottish army at Dunbar (1651).

Given these fiscal and institutional realities, English governments relied continually on "private" mechanisms to carry out "public" projects and these entities also enabled well-placed individuals to carry out their own initiatives with governmental approval. The joint-stock corporation, a device which came into being in the latter half of the sixteenth century, proved an especially useful early example of this sort of public operation. For instance, the East India Company, which received its charter, in essence, to take charge of all English interests and affairs east of Cape Horn in 1600 and which remained in existence until 1858, and the Virginia Company, created in 1606, which underwrote the colonization of Jamestown, relieved the government of financial responsibility for these ambitious and extensive undertakings. To protect their investments, the men behind these ventures had their liability limited to the extent of their investment in case of shipwreck or other calamity. The joint-stock corporation fell out of fashion by the 1640s due to its unwieldiness and a perception that its form bore too close a resemblance to a republic. Yet, the English continued to prefer to create colonizing rights by chartered proprietary rights to individuals, such as William Penn, founder of Pennsylvania (1682), and groups, such as the Trustees who founded Georgia in 1732, well into the eighteenth century.[6]

The state of English society during the lifetime of Henry Hudson cast even greater shadows on the nation's prospects for the explorer lived during a time identified by modern scholars as the worst to be alive in England for the next four hundred years. The population did continue to grow throughout the sixteenth century, but it did so by outpacing the devastation wrought by regular outbreaks of epidemic disease, such as smallpox and the plague. On the political front, various factions battled each other for power as they waited, with varying degrees of impatience, for their old queen to die; this situation culminated in the madcap rebellion and execution of the earl of Essex in 1601. On the economic front, the Dutch Revolt (punctuated by the 1585 sack of Antwerp, the longtime center of English trade with the continent) and hostility with Spain severed important medieval commercial lifelines while regular periods of dearth and the endless wars with Spain and in Ireland placed a great drain on the exchequer, kept prices high, aggravated factional behavior in the political nation, and contributed to the general malaise.[7]

Despite the lack of institutional support, though, a clutch of merchants and political figures, in conjunction with Hakluyt, maintained their interest in long-range trade and colonization as manifested in the chartering of the East India Company in response to Dutch penetration of the Indian Ocean and in a 1602 voyage, sponsored by a group of London notables, including the Lord Mayor Sir Thomas Smyth, and led by George Weymouth, which investigated several potential colonization sites along North American coast. These green shoots received a fillip with the beginning of the new reign of James I which brought the Irish and Spanish conflicts to an end, as well as noticeable improvement on the economic front.

While the new king, who famously styled himself *Rex Pacificus*, took great pains throughout his reign to avoid antagonizing the Spaniards; the Treaty of Westminster (1604) that ended the Spanish war provided, in the eyes of the monarch, a legal and geographical outlet for English settlement north of Florida. Thus, Smyth, Hakluyt, and a clutch of associates in the form of a Virginia Company of London received a charter to colonize North America between modern-day Philadelphia, Pennsylvania and Spanish territory while a counterpart, the Virginia Company of Plymouth, received identical powers to lands north from Delaware Bay. These colonizers envisioned these endeavors—the presence of women (or lack thereof as here) providing the telling indicator of intent—as military adventures to find a water route to the Pacific Ocean (the enduring and fatal quest of Henry Hudson) and the greater wealth of the East Indies, to find and conquer fabulously wealthy indigenous empires, and to establish a base for preying on Spanish shipping "beyond the line" of peace established by the peace treaty.[8]

These dreams, of course, quickly soured. The wretched colonists of the Plymouth group settled at Saghedoc where the effects of the Maine winter reportedly caused them to resort to cannibalism before they abandoned the endeavor. In Virginia, despite "evidence" of trade with China and reports of vast bodies of water, a passage to the Pacific remained stubbornly undiscovered and while the neighboring Indians, especially the Powhatans, exercised substantial power they neither possessed the mines nor the other wealth of their South American counterparts. Moreover, although Hakluyt stressed, in his prescription for colonization, the importance of maintaining good relations with Indigenous people, the Powhatans and their sachem, Wahunsonacock, greeted the newcomers to Chesapeake Bay with hostility and suspicion. The outbreak of dysentery (the "bloody flux" to contemporaries) within a few months after the arrival of the colonists in May 1607 ravaged and demoralized them. The securing of what proved to be the first permanent English settlement in North America remained an open question in the immediate term.

Their inability to get along with each other exacerbated the precarious situation of the Jamestown settlers. Famously (and surprisingly), the Virginia Company had appointed Captain John Smith, a veteran of the Dutch and Hungarian wars, as the first president of the colony but the selection of a man lacking a gentry background rankled with those colonists, such as Edward Maria Wingfield, who claimed a higher social rank and, correspondingly, a greater title to authority. While Smith's character, and his ceaseless self-promotion, captured the affections of many inhabitants of the United States looking back at the "genesis" of their country from modern perspectives, his qualities aggravated tensions between himself and other contemporaries. Indeed, for all of the attention subsequently paid to Jamestown—2007 constituting the quadricentennial anniversary of the colony—its early history remains shrouded in mystery and controversy.

The military character of the enterprise contributed to the obscurity of its record. As relics of the fighting in the Low Countries—where allegiances could become blurred to the point of non-existence and where, correspondingly, treachery and spying became watchwords—Wingfield, Smith, and other Jamestown leaders readily resorted to accusations, counter-accusations, and justifications (both private and public) about what was transpiring. Yet, we do have brief glimpses of this world of finger-pointers through the documentary murk: the execution of George Kendall, a member of the council, as a Spanish spy; the jailing of Wingfield by Smith; and the "accident" suffered by Smith when a bag of gunpowder (unwisely placed around his midriff) exploded obliging his return to England in 1609.

Smith took the opportunity provided by this enforced retirement to write a series of histories of Virginia and "New England" and joined the Reverend Samuel Purchas as the heirs to Hakluyt's role as chief promoter of English overseas colonization. In his accounts, he took pains to emphasize the importance to the survival of Jamestown of his carrot-and-stick dealings with Wahunsonacock that obtained necessary food from the Indians and reduced their antipathy, his "no work, no eat" policy that purportedly aggravated "gentlemen," and his insistence that the colonists follow the Indian example and disperse to the interior during the summer. Even so, the English foothold in North America remained precarious for more than five years after the arrival of the first cohort. In 1610, it became so dire that the Virginians made plans to abandon and torch the place; only the timely arrival of a party led by Thomas West, Lord De la Ware (and also a military man), forestalled this attempt.[9]

By 1614, though, these dark clouds had begun to clear. Although De la Ware died en route back to England, the vigorous government of his successor (and yet another Low Countries veteran), Sir Thomas Dale, brought the colony to administrative heel. On the imperial front, the shipwreck of Sir Thomas Gates's fleet on Bermuda enabled the founding of a second English colony on that island in 1612 while Jamestown had begun to serve as a base of operations for incursions further afield: in 1613, an expedition led by Samuel Argall attacked a French settlement in Acadia. Argall also oversaw the kidnapping of Wahunsonacock's favorite daughter, Pocahontas.

This act, coupled with Wahunsonacock's renewal of hostilities with the Susquehannocks to the north, brought a halt to the first Anglo-Powhatan War (1609–1614) as it enabled the marriage between Pocahontas and the mysterious, but very important, John Rolfe. In addition to helping to engineer peaceable relations with the Indians, Rolfe served as a chief engineer of the transformation of Jamestown from a military venture to a plantation. This change provided a platform for the establishment of a permanent English presence but one that mandated the creation of a colonial society (rather than a garrison) and, correspondingly, a different approach to colonization, and Rolfe played a key role here as well. Moreover, while the search for riches in the older exploratory and military sense continued (notwithstanding, for instance, Hudson's dismal Arctic end), the creation of colonial Virginia signaled a fundamental change in the Anglo-American imperial approach.

Rolfe's prime responsibility for this stems, first, from his famously successful introduction of tobacco cultivation to the Chesapeake by 1614. For the first time in its history, Virginia offered an economic lifeline and a means to achieving social and political prominence in accordance with early modern English understanding as the "sot-weed" provided the ready means for delivering landed income, the recognized platform of individual status and social formation on both sides of the Atlantic. The prospects for establishing this foundation, which was required to attract any respectable quantity of migrants, had been problematic in the colony until Rolfe's intervention (he introduced the commodity through his contacts in present-day Venezuela). At the same time, the establishment of a valuable colonial commodity generated more direct governmental interest in overseas activity or, at least, in deriving revenue from the economy generated by that activity. Perhaps most importantly, Rolfe's example may well constitute the first example of Anglo-American success. In addition to pursuing landed income, he also used his patronage contacts in the metropolis to advance both himself and his locality, an essential element in the pursuit of ambition all over the early modern English-speaking world and in establishing the political, economic, and social points of contact between the metropolis and colonies.[10]

Although Rolfe remains a frustratingly mysterious figure in the record, it is clear that he maintained close connections with men who, perhaps not coincidentally, became leading lights in the Virginia Company at the same time as tobacco was becoming entrenched at Jamestown. Dissatisfaction with the leadership of Sir Thomas Smyth began to appear as the colony seemed enmeshed in an unending cycle of disaster—Indian war, shipwreck, dysentery, factionalism—with no result in sight. By 1614, other leading investors led by Thomas Wriothesley, second earl of Southampton, had had enough and wrested control of the company from Smyth. Although it remains unclear who took the initiative here, the Southampton group, especially Sir Edwin Sandys, who assumed direct oversight of the company's affairs, shared with Rolfe an imperial vision that involved cultivation of commodities, recruitment of settlers, and a correspondingly settled colonial government.[11]

The execution of this vision, though, required, first and foremost, the revitalization of the Virginia Company and Rolfe and Pocahontas became deeply involved in this effort returning to England to conduct a publicity tour in 1616–1617. Although, unfortunately, Pocahontas died at the end of the trip, the appearance of the Virginian couple proved a great success: their appearance at court, Pocahontas' reunion with Captain John Smith, and their personification of a new, happier era of Anglo-Powhatan relations, as well as the good news of tobacco, triggered the requisite renewed investment and interest in moving to Virginia. To capitalize on this enthusiasm, Sandys and his associates replaced the martial law that had been in effect in the colony since Dale's assumption of the government with a series of reforms designed both to promote migration and, in typical English fashion, to ensure the protection of the liberties of the colonists. The most important and longest lasting of these initiatives included the creation of local governmental institutions such as the House of Burgesses, a derivative parliament, permission for the settlers to own their own land, and the derivative device of indentured servitude. This latter phenomenon allowed poorer migrants to make their way to America via contracts that paid the costs of their trip in exchange for a term of labor of four-to-five years and that stipulated, in accordance with the practice of servitude as it existed in early seventeenth-century England, that masters provide food, shelter, clothing, and other necessaries during the term of the indenture. Provided they completed their service, servants received "freedom dues": land, tools, and tobacco seed to get themselves started.[12]

This revival, however, became rather too successful. The "tobacco boom" did bring a relatively massive influx of English people to Virginia between 1618 and 1622. Yet, while, on both the face of things and, indeed, over the long term, this number of arrivals secured the future of Jamestown; in the shorter term, it generated a number of serious issues. First, the capacity of the colony to accommodate the arrivals comfortably remains, at best, unclear. At the least, allegations of mistreatment or neglect—even to the point of starvation and other horrors—for the newcomers, provided fuel for another battle—this time between Robert Rich, second earl of Warwick, and his clients and the Southampton-Sandys group—over control of the Virginia Company. At the same time, the population increase and the increased demand for land and other resources it created damaged relations with the Powhatans: in 1622, led now by the English-hating sachem and half-brother of Wahunsonacock (who had died in 1618), Opechancanough, the Indians surprised the colonists killing about one-quarter of them. The intensity of the battle over the company, the horror stories emanating from the colony over the fate of migrants, and, finally, the report of the "massacre" led James I to quash the company's charter in 1624 until cooler heads could prevail.[13]

This "royalization" of Virginia is often regarded as a benchmark in the histories of both the colony and of the Anglo-British Empire as, seemingly for the first time, the Crown had taken direct control of a colonizing venture. In reality, however, the government regarded its termination of the Virginia Company's rights as a short-term measure and anticipated reconstituting a successor company in the fairly near future; indeed, several plans to do so appeared over the next fifteen years, but failed due to the opposition of colonists concerned about their land titles and the distractions of other events. Even more pertinently, many of the same people who had administered Virginia, on both sides of the Atlantic, during the company period, such as Edward Sackville, fourth earl of Dorset, continued to do so after the royal takeover.[14]

Nevertheless, "royalization" did permit the Crown to continue its efforts to bring order to the tobacco trade albeit more directly. Another of the unwanted results of the "tobacco boom" had been the arrival of a continuous stream of Dutch vessels at Point Comfort, Virginia's port. The Virginians maintained generally friendly relations with their Dutch neighbors; merchants based in New Netherland generally provided a better price and a readier market for the "staple" than those in England did. But of even more importance for a perennially cash-strapped government, the customs revenue from the importation of tobacco into England that should have augmented the royal treasury was instead conveyed to Amsterdam by these interlopers.

The Crown tried, on several occasions, to devise plans to keep the Dutch out but, due to a combination of colonial resistance and its own inability to follow through on its ideas, it never succeeded in implementing them. As early as 1619, the lord treasurer Lionel Cranfield, earl of Middlesex, debated various ways of regulating and taxing tobacco imports as part of his general attempt at reforming the government's financial system although these efforts—and Cranfield's career in public service—crashed in 1624 on the resistance of Buckingham to any significant change—or any significant enquiry into his complete control of patronage. After royalization and the death of James, Charles I (reigned 1625–1649), in 1632, appointed the diplomat Sir William Boswell and an obscure Huguenot gentleman, the Sieur de Licques, as receivers-general for all of the tobacco produced by the English colonies in America under the Great Seal in anticipation of collecting as much as £50,000 per annum. This plan, however, fell by the wayside when Boswell became ambassador to the Dutch Republic and the king went to Edinburgh for his Scottish coronation in 1633.[15]

Unlike his father, Charles I tried to work with the Virginians to bring order to tobacco production and these efforts demonstrate particularly the ironic political character of the early English Empire in America. Due to distance between the metropolis and the colonies, the generally accepted proposition that local people "of quality" should have charge of local affairs (as underscored by the creation of the House of Burgesses), and the historical preoccupation of the Crown with other matters, successful planters like Rolfe established their preeminence in Virginia and its counterparts almost immediately after their situations became settled. While Rolfe had died before Opechancanough's attack, the disruption caused by that attack, coming as it did on the heels of the tobacco boom, created the opportunity for a first generation of planters to succeed to his position.

Thus, William Claiborne, most especially, became a preeminent inhabitant of the Chesapeake between his arrival at Jamestown as surveyor for the Virginia Company in 1621 and his death in 1677. His long career marks Claiborne as an exemplar of seventeenth-century Anglo-America. First, using his position (and the salary it provided), he acquired substantial lands and the servants required to turn those lands into income-producing estates. Then, he became involved in the Indian trade and built a thriving trading post on Kent Island (named for Claiborne's home county in England) in northern Chesapeake Bay. Ultimately, he extended his economic interests to West Africa and to the Caribbean where he received the island of Roatán off of the Nicaraguan coast.[16]

Claiborne, of course, translated this socioeconomic situation into political preeminence. He and his allies in Virginia, notably Samuel Mathews, developed a deep personal enmity for Sir John Harvey, appointed by Charles I as governor of the colony and charged with settling the tobacco trade with its House of Burgesses. Harvey, who seems to have held an overly optimistic view of the support that the government would offer him, regarded himself as a vice-gerent entitled to the complete deference of the king's subjects. The Virginia planters, perhaps needless to say, did not share this view and took every opportunity to thwart Harvey's attempts to place their commerce under regulation. When, in a fit of pique, he tried to arrest them, they turned the tables and "thrust him out," sending him back to England to try and salvage his position. Tobacco production remained unregulated until the enactment of the first Navigation Acts as a specifically anti-Dutch measure by the new (and short-lived) English Republic in 1651 after the execution of Charles and the end of the Civil Wars. Even then, smuggling remained rampant. Only the English takeover of New Netherland in 1664 put a damper on this lucrative commerce.[17]

In the meantime, Virginia provided the platform for the political and geographical extension of the English Empire. As noted above, as early as 1609 a relief fleet for Jamestown led by Sir Thomas Gates was wrecked on Bermuda. While Gates and most of the survivors later made their way to the mainland, some of the company remained behind to establish England's second American colony under the auspices of the Somers Islands Company, which was closely related to the Virginia Company. In 1624, another Jamestown-bound ship wound up on the Caribbean island of St.

Christopher (today, St. Kitts), which became the first permanent English toehold in the Caribbean followed by Barbados (which became the most important, in terms of population and wealth, of the English colonies in the seventeenth century) in 1627.

Virginians also maintained a keen and constant interest in expanding their territory: they also sought to increase trade with the Indians and the quest for a water route through North America to Asia never disappeared from adventurous minds. In addition, they had to negotiate the arrival of other Europeans in North America: Argall's sortie against the French manifested an early intent to carry out offensives against offensive establishments. Moreover, Claiborne and others made rather later forays north to the Delaware River, south to the present-day Carolinas, and westward to the Cumberland River. Ironically, though, the success of Virginia gave rise to the 1632 grant by Charles I to his former Secretary of State George Calvert, Lord Baltimore, of a colony along northern Chesapeake Bay to serve as a haven for Roman Catholics. This grant inadvertently included, to Claiborne's fury, Kent Island and sparked a nasty 45-year feud between the Virginian and the Calverts finally resolved in favor of Maryland.[18]

In the midst of the establishment of the island colonies, another wayward ship bound for Virginia arrived, rather more famously, in what was already called New England in 1620 (although no English people lived there at the time). This ship carried a community of Separatists from Scrooby, Nottinghamshire who had removed, in the face of general hostility to their views on religious government, to the relatively tolerant Netherlands. But, after a time, they wished to relocate to an English-speaking place and used their connections in the Virginia Company to secure the right to cross the Atlantic. Whether by a contrary wind, by design, or divine providence—as these "Pilgrims" claimed—they wound up many hundreds of miles away from Jamestown without any legal authority to be there. This extra-legal reality compelled them to enact hastily a "compact" to the effect that they had assumed the right to constitute a settlement where they were. A decade later, they were engulfed, to their annoyance, by the unprecedented movement of some 10,000 people in the "Great Puritan Migration" that created the colonies of Massachusetts Bay, Connecticut, New Haven, and Rhode Island during the 1630s—famously without the support of the Crown which frowned upon the religious and political orientation of the migration's leadership. Unlike their Chesapeake counterparts, the New Englanders maintained a rocky relationship with New Netherland, notwithstanding a common theological understanding, as competition for the fur trade and the further movement of the English to Long Island and other Dutch-claimed territory put pressure on the government of the Dutch West India Company (as discussed in the essay by Lauric Henneton below). "Puritans" also founded the Caribbean colony of Providence Island in 1630, the same year as Boston, but this experimental mixture of godliness and slavery fell victim to the Spanish (yet another example of the English reach exceeding its grasp) in 1641.[19]

Yet, for all of the attention (then and later) that has been lavished on these "Puritans," in the larger scheme of things they tended to have rather less importance in the seventeenth century. First of all, while adherents of their particular socioreligious view moved to all parts of the English-speaking world, they occupied a minority position in those colonies (as they did in England and Ireland). Moreover, the nature of migration to New England rendered that region of the early seventeenth-century English Empire quite distinctive: the nature of the godly worldview meant that people tended to move as gathered or covenanted churches with, of course, women and children while migrants to the Chesapeake and the West Indies tended to be young, single males and the very mass of migrants meant a larger population density than elsewhere. Moreover, gender imbalance and the continuing effects of disease and warmer climates, along with the general pursuit of estates in land in other colonies meant that while towns proliferated, relatively, in New England, they were rarer farther south.

The nature of migration to the Chesapeake and the West Indies, coupled with the pursuit of the sort of estates that were unavailable in England, also meant a perennial labor shortage in those places in the first half of the seventeenth century. The explosive popularity of Virginia tobacco after 1618 and, about twenty years later, West Indian sugar created a greater demand for labor. Even the attractions presented by "freedom dues" proved inadequate in luring sufficient servants to the mainland while the geographical limits of the islands restricted opportunities for advancement there quite early.[20] Moreover, the abusive treatment reportedly accorded to servants for running away, getting pregnant, and other offenses deterred migration (not to mention the hazards of a transatlantic voyage—tempests, pirates, sour beer, etc.). On the other hand, the recourse, at least in the abstract, afforded by English society to those abused meant that masters could not exercise the sort of control they wished over the behavior of their workers. Thus, an alternative had to be found.

As early as 1616, the historical record discloses the presence of African slaves on Bermuda, which indicates that the planters there had both an awareness of American-style slavery and connections with the Atlantic slave trade. Slavery, though, did not exist (famously) in England itself at this time and, thus, English colonists had no familiarity with the concept unless, like

Rolfe, they had visited the Spanish or Portuguese colonies where it had long been entrenched (especially in Portuguese Brazil, which remained the largest and most important slave society in the Americas for almost four centuries). It remains unclear who introduced slavery into the English colonies or why but it is clear that the advantages it presented for masters—lifelong servitude, no recourse to law for those excluded from society by virtue of their status and skin color, the prospect of enslaving the children of slave mothers—meant that it readily translated from Bermuda to the North American mainland.

By 1619 (but probably earlier), the first Africans had appeared at Jamestown. While the status of these people seems to have been initially unclear—we have evidence of a community of free people of African descent living on the Eastern Shore of Chesapeake Bay as early as the mid-1620s (which suggests that were treated as servants)—by the middle of the seventeenth century, all of the English colonies had come to equate African ethnicity with enslavement. Certainly, the development of sugar production on Barbados (where land and opportunities were especially limited for servants and where the climate, both meteorological and social was particularly harsh for them) created a hitherto unprecedented demand for slaves in the English-speaking world after the 1630s. At the same time, the enslavement of Indians captured in war (such as the Pequot War of 1636) had become an important aspect of the history of slavery in the English Empire and would continue to be so for another eighty years.[21]

The attempt to recreate a metropolitan-style landed hierarchy as the proper means of constructing a society entailed the pursuit of commercial and personal connections between colonies and with the metropolis. The particular success of the staple-slave variation of this theme on Barbados insured its introduction, to varying degrees in other English colonies. By 1660, a derivative aristocracy had been established throughout the Anglo-American world: intermarriage between members of the elite, land acquisition, maintenance of status through landed wealth (the cultivation of staple crops), metropolitan connections (political and commercial), and control of a labor force (generally enslaved) translated into Anglo-American success on every front. While the colonies that came into existence north of Maryland may not have had enslaved populations of the same magnitude as Virginia, let alone Barbados, slaves played an important economic role and these societies devised similar means for keeping the enslaved in "their place." Moreover, the continuing commerce among all of the colonies, including the provision of foodstuffs and other essentials for maintaining slaves, insured that all parts of the English Empire maintained a significant stake in this transatlantic world that propelled, albeit haphazardly, the English colonization of the Americas.[22]

Yet, emphasis must remain on "haphazardly," for the spread of the English Empire in the Western hemisphere—not to mention the Eastern—before 1651 did not extend very far despite periodic visits to the interior of North America. By this time, the English had only settled along the coast of New England, along the Connecticut River, and on the shores of Chesapeake Bay, as well as on Barbados and part of St. Christopher. More pointedly, English efforts to establish colonies in Guiana, a primary target of imperial efforts since the efforts of Sir Walter Raleigh (c. 1552–1618), habitually failed in the face of Spanish opposition.[23]

In Asia, meanwhile, the East India Company had fought off Portuguese resistance and received a *firman* (trading license) from the Mughal emperor to trade at Surat on the west coast of India in 1608, but it proved difficult to build on this success. In terms of the subcontinent, Mughal power necessarily restricted the scope of the company's operations until the eighteenth century. In terms of the Spice Islands, English merchants did not have concerns, of course, about a vast territorial authority, but they did have to deal with Dutch determination to monopolize the trade in cinnamon, cloves, mace, and other exotic, rare, and desirable commodities. The Dutch had first arrived in present-day Indonesia in the 1590s during their revolt against Habsburg authority, and their conflict with the Portuguese in the islands continued for some fifty years (as discussed in the essay on the "Dutch Empire"). When the English appeared in the Indian Ocean, the *Vereenigde Oost-Indische Compagnie* (VOC) was chartered in 1602 and its more efficient structure enabled the successful expulsion of the newcomers from Banda and, in 1623, most notoriously, in the "Amboyna massacre." These violent incidents, along with the continuing Anglo-Dutch commercial competition in North America, the Baltic, and the Mediterranean as well as a growing sensibility among certain English leaders that the governmental and social character of the Dutch Republic presented a problematic example led, in turn, to a growing view during the first half of the seventeenth century that the Netherlands, rather than Spain, constituted the greater threat to English interests. This comprehension fuelled the three Anglo-Dutch Wars (1652–1654, 1665–1667, 1672–1674).[24]

These wars, while they failed to produce a decisive result in terms of the combatants, manifested several halting, yet significant developments, all arising from the changes in the nature of the English state brought about by the Civil Wars (1642–1651), in terms of the history of the English Empire. For while the governments that came into existence following the triumph of the forces opposed to Charles I continued to grapple with the financial, religious, and related constitutional issues that had plagued the early Stuart monarchy, the English Republic (1649–1653), and, especially, the Cromwellian Protectorate (1653–1659) benefited from the relatively efficient system of levying and collecting revenue that was created through the exigencies of war, from the existence of a professional army imbued with a sense of purpose, and from a leader, in the form of Oliver Cromwell (1599–1658), determined to make England a leading player in the wider world.

This combination resulted in English conquests of Scotland and Ireland and the incorporation of those nations into a Great Britain. It also resulted in the subjugation of royalist resistance in American colonies and the establishment, the capture of Jamaica, and the threat of an attack on New Netherland, clear examples of a new capacity of the metropolis to impose—and the desire to impose—its will. This shift was naturally accompanied by a new proclamation of a self-confident "Britannia."[25]

Yet, despite unprecedented military success and purposefulness and the addition of new colonies between 1620 and 1650, the nature of the English Empire had not changed that dramatically. First and foremost, imperial behavior remained largely dependent on the behavior of colonists, although those Anglo-Americans—such as the government of the New Haven colony who threatened to invoke metropolitan force upon the Swedish colony on the Delaware River—knew that the character of the Cromwellian government gave teeth to this warning.[26] This reality also meant that the grandest plans of the Protectorate—the "Western Design" against the nerve center of the Spanish Empire in America, Santo Domingo—fell to dust when sulking Barbadian royalists declined to lend either men or material support to the endeavor. As a result, the "Design" failed miserably; having to settle for Jamaica, a distinctly consolation prize at the time, the Cromwellian aura of providential invincibility that had grown since the destruction of the royalist cavalry at Naseby (1645) began to dissipate with extraordinary rapidity: the greater advance of the British Empire (as it came to be after the 1707 Act of Union between England and Scotland gave Scots legal access to English colonies) was still yet to come.[27]

Notes

1. The analysis here draws upon the extensive one offered in L. H. Roper, *The English Empire in America, 1602–1658: Beyond Jamestown* (London: Pickering & Chatto, 2009).

2. John H. Elliott, "Cortés, Velázquez, and Charles V" in Anthony Pagden (trans. and ed.), *Hernan Cortes: Letters from Mexico* (New Haven, CT and London: Yale University Press, 2001), pp. xi–xxxvii; cf. Jorge Cañizeras-Esquerra, *Puritans and Conquistadors: Iberianizing the Atlantic, 1550–1700* (Stanford, Cal.: Stanford University Press, 2006); Francis Jennings, *The Invasion of America: Indians, Colonialism, and the Cant of Conquest* (New York: W. W. Norton, 1976).

3. Pagden, *Lords of All the World: Ideologies of Empire in Spain, Britain and France, c. 1500–c. 1800* (New Haven and London: Yale University Press, 1998).

4. Peter C. Mancall, *Hakluyt's Promise: An Elizabethan's Obsession for an English America* (New Haven: Yale University Press, 2007).

5. John Cramsie, *Kingship and Crown Finance under James VI and I, 1603–1625* (Woodbridge, Suffolk and Rochester, NY: The Boydell Press for the Royal Historical Society, 2002).

6. E.g., James O'Neil Spady, "Bubbles and Beggars and the Bodies of Laborers: The Georgia Trusteeship's Colonialism Reconsidered" in L. H. Roper and Bertrand Van Ruymbeke (eds.), *Constructing Early Modern Empires: Proprietary Ventures in the Atlantic World, 1500–1750* (Leiden, Neth. and Boston, MA: Brill Academic Publishers, 2007), pp. 213–68.

7 On the "nasty nineties" in England, John Guy, "The 1590s: The Second Reign of Elizabeth I?" in idem (ed.), *The Reign of Elizabeth I: Court and Culture in the Last Decade* (Cambridge: Cambridge University Press, 1995), pp. 1–19.

8. Joyce Lorimer, "The Failure of the English Guiana Ventures 1595–1667 and James I's Foreign Policy," *Journal of Imperial and Commonwealth History* 21 (1993), pp. 1–30.

9. The various and predictably conflicting accounts of the first years of Jamestown include John Smith, *A True Relation of Such Occurrences and Accidents of Noate as hath Hapned in Virginia since the First Planting of that Collony* [London, 1608]; Smith, *The Proceedings of the English Colonie in Virginia* [London, 1612]; Smith, *The Generall Historie of Virginia, New-England, and the Summer Isles* [London, 1624]; Smith, *The True Travels, Adventures, and Observations of Captaine John Smith* [London, 1630], George Percy, "Observations Gathered out of a Discourse of the Plantation of the Southerne Colonie in Virginia," [1606/7]; Percy, "A Trewe Relaycion of the Proceedings and Ocurrentes of Momente which have Hapned in Virginia" [1612]; Edward Maria Wingfield, "A Discourse of Virginia" [1608], all in James Horn (ed.), *Captain John Smith: Writings and Other Narratives of Roanoke, Jamestown, and the First English Settlement of America* (New York: The Library of America, 2007), pp. 5–40, 35–118, 199–670, 671–770, 920–934, 1093–1114, 950–966; Thomas West, baron De la Ware, *Relation of Lord De-La-Ware* [1611] in Lyon Gardiner Tyler (ed.), *Narratives of Early Virginia, 1606–1625* (New York, 1907), pp. 209–14.

10. Joyce Lorimer, "The English Contraband Tobacco Trade from Trinidad and Guiana, 1590–1617" in K. R. Andrews, N. P. Canny, and P. E. H. Hair (eds.), *The Westward Enterprise: English Activities in Ireland, the Atlantic, and America, 1480–1650* (Detroit, MI: Wayne State University Press, 1979), pp. 124–150.

11. E.g. John Rolfe to Sir Edwin Sandys, January 1619/20 in S.M. Kingsbury (ed.), *Records of the Virginia Company*, 4 vols. (Washington, D.C.: Library of Congress, 1906–35), 3:241–249. All dates from the sources are rendered Old Style, which was followed in England at this time, unless otherwise indicated.

12. The Southampton-Sandys takeover of the Virginia Company occurred in conjunction with what proved to be a reemergence of the faction in government. This maneuver entailed, ironically, the successful introduction of George Villiers as the new favorite of James I, L. H. Roper, "Unmasquing the Connections between Jacobean Politics and Colonization: The Circle of Anna of Denmark and the Beginning of the English Empire, 1614–1618," in Carole Levin, Jo E. Carney, and Debra Barrett-Graves (eds.), *High and Mighty Queens of Early Modern England* (New York: Palgrave Macmillan, 2003), pp. 45–59. For English servitude, see Ann Kussmaul, *Servants in Husbandry in Early Modern England* (Cambridge: Cambridge University Press, 1981).

13. Roper, *The English Empire in America*, pp. 81–90.

14. E.g., "The Humble Representation and Petition of your Majesty's Commissioners for your Plantation of Virginia," [1641], MS Bankes 8/2, Bodleian Library, University of Oxford; "Declarations against the Virginia Company," 1 April 1642, in Warren M. Billings (ed.), *The Papers of Sir William Berkeley* (Richmond, VA: Library of Virginia, 2007), pp. 40–44. For 1625 as a benchmark, e.g., Karen Ordahl Kupperman, *The Jamestown Project* (Cambridge, MA: Harvard University Press, 2007); Peter Mancall (ed.), *The Atlantic World and Virginia, 1550–1624* (Chapel Hill, N.C.: University of North Carolina Press, 2007).

15. For Cranfield's consideration of the tobacco problem, e.g. "Reasons why a Free Trade for Tobacco wilbee more Benefitiall unto his Majestie then the Sole Importation to bee Graunted unto any Particular Company," [1623], U269/1 Ov62, Sackville Papers, Centre for Kentish Studies, Maidstone, Kent. For Cranfield's difficulties, Menna Prestwich, *Cranfield: Politics and Profits under the Early Stuarts* (Oxford: Clarendon Press, 1966), pp. 423–468. For the Boswell-de Licques venture, "Proclamation by the King," 12 April 1632, Colonial Office records 1/7, The National Archives of Great Britain, Kew; Sir William Boswell to James Hay, Earl of Carlisle, 25 September 1632, Egerton Mss. 2597, ff. 84–85, British Library; State Papers 84/144 ff. 162–169, The National Archives.

16. For Claiborne's career, e.g., "Claiborne v Clobery," *Maryland Historical Magazine* 27 (1932), pp. 17–28, 99–114, 337–353; 28 (1933), 26–43, 172–195, 257–265; Robert Brenner, *Merchants and Revolution: Commercial Change, Political Conflict, and London's Overseas Traders, 1550–1653* (London: Verso, 2003 [1993]), pp. 122–135, 161–193.

17. L. H. Roper, "Charles I, Virginia, and the Idea of Atlantic History," *Itinerario* 30, no. 2 (2006), pp. 33–53. For the persistence of Dutch involvement in the Chesapeake, notwithstanding the Navigation Acts, [Report to Secretary of State Thurloe], [June 1656?], MS Rawlinson A 38, ff. 703–706, Bodleian Library; Victor Enthoven and Wim Klooster, "The Rise and Fall of the Virginia-Dutch Connection in the Seventeenth Century," in Douglas Bradburn and John C. Coombs (eds.), *Early*

Modern Virginia: Reconsidering the Old Dominion (Charlottesville, Va. and London: University of Virginia Press), pp. 90–127.

18. "The Humble Petition of Coll: Wm: Claiborne a Poor Old Servant of your Majesty's Father & Grandfather," 13 March 1676/7, Archives of Maryland Online, at http://www.aomol.net/html/index.html, 4:157–239; Roper, *English Empire in America*, pp. 121–126. For Virginian exploration, see, e.g., [Edward Williams], The Discovery of New Brittaine (London, 1650) and Francis Yeardley to John Ferrar, 8 May 1654, both in A.S. Salley (ed.), *Narratives of Early Carolina, 1650–1708* (New York: Barnes & Noble, 1967 [1911]); L. H. Roper, "New Albion: Anatomy of a Colonisation Failure," *Itinerario* 32, no. 1 (2008), pp. 39–57.

19. For the "Pilgrims" and the Virginia Company, Sir Edwin Sandys to John Robinson and William Brewster, 12 November 1617, Robinson and Brewster to Sandys, 15 December 1617, and Robinson and Brewster to Sir John Wolstenholme, 27 January 1617/18, all in [William Bradford], *Bradford's History "Of Plimoth Plantation,"* S. E. Morison (ed.) (Boston, 1928), pp. 40–44. For Providence Island, Karen Ordahl Kupperman, *Providence Island, 1630–1641: The Other Puritan Colony* (Cambridge: Cambridge University Press, 1993).

20. Even so, the 166 square miles of Barbados contained some 50,000 inhabitants—30,000 Africans and 20,000 Europeans—in 1680, Richard S. Dunn, "The Barbados Census of 1680: Profile of the Richest Colony in America," *WMQ* 26 (1969), pp. 4–30.

21. For the appearance of Africans at Jamestown, John Rolfe to Sir Edwin Sandys, January 1619/20, in Kingsbury, *Records of the Virginia Company*, 3:241–248 at 243; Engel Sluiter, "New Light on the '20. and Odd Negroes' Arriving in Virginia, August 1619," *WMQ* 54 (1997), pp. 395–398. For free Africans, J. Douglas Deal, "A Constricted World: Free Blacks on Virginia's Eastern Shore, 1680–1750," in Lois Green Carr, Philip D. Morgan, and Jean B. Russo (eds.), *Colonial Chesapeake Society* (Chapel Hill: University of North Carolina Press, 1988), pp. 275–305; William Thorndale, "The Virginia Census of 1619," *Magazine of Virginia Genealogy* 33 (1995), 155–170.

22. L. H. Roper, "Big Fish in a Bigger Transatlantic Pond: the Social and Political Leadership of Early Modern Anglo-American Colonies" in Claire Laux, François-Joseph Ruggiu, and Pierre Singaravélou (eds.), *At the Top of Empire: European Elites in the Colonies (16th–20th Centuries)* (Brussels: Peter Lang, 2009), pp. 141–166.

23. Lorimer, "The Failure of the English Guiana Ventures."

24. Jane F. Merritt, "Power and Communication: Thomas Wentworth and Government at a Distance during the Personal Rule, 1629–1635" in idem (ed.), *The Political World of Thomas Wentworth, Earl of Strafford, 1621–1641* (Cambridge: Cambridge University Press, 1996), pp. 109–131 at 117–118; Karen Chancey, "The Amboyna Massacre in English Politics, 1624–1632," *Albion* 30, no. 4 (1998), pp. 583–598; Vincent C. Loth, "Armed Incidents and Unpaid Bills: Anglo-Dutch Rivalry in the Banda Islands in the Seventeenth Century," *Modern Asian Studies* 29 (1995), pp. 705–740.

25. David Armitage, "The Cromwellian Protectorate and the Language of Empire," *The Historical Journal* 35, no. 3 (1992), pp. 531–555; Karen Ordahl Kupperman, "Errand to the Indies: Puritan Colonization from Providence Island to the Western Design," *WMQ* 45, no. 1 (1988), pp. 70–99. Michael J. Braddick, *State Formation in Early Modern England, c. 1550–1700* (Cambridge: Cambridge University Press, 2000).

26. Theophilus Eaton and New Haven Court to Johan Risingh, 6 July 1654, Handel och Sjöfart, vol. 194, Riksarkivet (The National Archives), Stockholm, Sweden (the documents in this collection are unfoliated and are available on microfiche; this letter appears in fiche 15 of volume 194) reprinted in C. A. Weslager, *The English on the Delaware: 1610–1682* (New Brunswick, NJ: Rutgers University Press, 1967), pp. 265–266.

27. Larry Gragg, *Englishmen Transplanted: The English Colonization of Barbados, 1627–1660* (New York: Oxford University Press, 2003), pp. 53–55, 156–157; Armitage, "The Cromwellian Protectorate," at 546–553.

3

———

Dutch Cartography and the Atlantic World at the Time of Henry Hudson

Kees Zandvliet

Cartography and a New Dutch Self-Image

*J*n 1604 Amsterdam's official organist Jan Pietersz Sweelinck travelled to Antwerp to order a new harpsichord for Amsterdam's town hall from the famous Ruckers family. Shortly after the instrument arrived in Amsterdam, the city council commissioned Pieter Isaacsz to paint the woodwork at the inside of the lid. For the theme of the decoration, they turned to the painter and author Karel van Mander.

The painting shows a personification of Amsterdam. Two female figures offer her a ship and a string of pearls, symbols of sea power and wealth. Her left hand rests over a celestial globe. To her right, two sailors holding nautical instruments are consulting the globe. In the center of the picture are three ships, one of which is being unloaded. The stern of the largest ship bears the arms of Count Maurice of Nassau (from 1618 onwards Prince of Orange), stadholder of most of the provinces of the Dutch Republic. Below right, Isaacsz clearly based his depiction of Asians, sculptures, and temples on prints in Jan Huygen van Linschoten's *Itinerario*, the book that guided Dutch merchants and sailors in the last decade of the sixteenth century to the riches of Asia. An American Indian stands behind the tablet with an inscription. An unusual pattern can be seen in the background showing areas of green interspersed with areas of blue on which miniature ships appear. This represents the world projected onto a flat surface. The view is taken from high up somewhere north of Norway looking down at an angle at the entire known world. Because of the perspective, Africa and America appear contracted and the Mediterranean resembles a thin sea arm.

35

Figure 1. Pieter Isaacsz and Carel van Mander, "Personification of Amsterdam: center of world trade" (ca. 1604–ca. 1607). *Image courtesy of the Amsterdam Museum.*

The clue to Isaacsz's illustration is enclosed in a Latin verse on a tablet leaning against an obelisk, which reads in translation: "Did you think that, barred from the Spanish West, I would be lost? Wrong: because with God's help I opened the way to Africa and India, to where exotic China stretches out, and to a part of the world that even the Ancients did not know. Continue to favour us, God, and pray that they learn of Christ."[1]

Together, the illustration and the verse reveal the object of Isaacsz, Van Mander, and the city's design. The painting celebrates Amsterdam's newly acquired status as the center of world trade, despite the opposition of the combined kingdoms of Spain and Portugal. At the same time, the allegory honors the knowledge and courage of Dutch sailors, promises to spread the Protestant faith across the globe, and pays respect to the stadholder who, as captain- and admiral-general, led the struggle of the United Provinces against the Habsburgs. Undoubtedly the harpsichord, with its decorations that claimed Amsterdam's world status and its alliance with the stadholder Maurice, was admired by hundreds of visitors during the following years. Perhaps Hudson was familiar with the new harpsichord and its decoration in the city hall. His clients certainly were.

The imagery inspired printmakers and merchants alike. Only a few years later Pieter Bast produced a beautiful profile view of the city of Amsterdam. In the center of this view a woman, the personification of Amsterdam, is seated, holding a ship and the coat of arms of the city in her hands. Europeans, Africans, Americans, and Asians bring their most precious products to her and to the city. In the border of the print we see the newly built Stock Exchange. It is this stock exchange and the exchange bank that turned Amsterdam into the most important financial and commercial center of the seventeenth and a large part of the eighteenth century. Another print, published in 1613 by Abraham de Koninck, pays tribute to Amsterdam in yet another way. The central and large view depicts the city. Smaller views are added that show Middelburg, Rotterdam, Enkhuizen, and Flushing. To these views portraits of famous navigators are added, like Willem Barentsz who explored the northeastern route to Asia in the 1590s and wintered on the Arctic island Nova Zembla. The view of Flushing shows the portrait of Prince Maurice, stadholder but also admiral-general and thus officially the most important Dutch mariner of the day. This was not just a formality: stadholder Maurice was really a mighty figure in the Dutch Republic and very much interested in Dutch travels and in fighting the Portuguese and the Spanish overseas. The Amsterdam city government and Amsterdam merchants were eager to befriend him. Topographical paintings of naval battles and decorative wall maps were presented to him in order to strengthen the friendship.

One of Maurice's Amsterdam allies in the related fields of the world overseas, the military, and politics was Albert Coenraetsz Burgh (1593–1647),

Figure 2. Werner van den Valckert, "Soldiers of the civic guard company of Captain Albert Coenraetsz Burgh and Lieutenant Pieter Evertsz Hulft" (1625). *Image courtesy of the Amsterdam Museum.*

a regent who has left his mark on various paintings and printed maps. In 1625, Werner van den Valckert painted the civic guard company of the so-called Wael district which borders on the eastern side of Amsterdam harbor, today part of Amsterdam's Red Light District. Seated at the table are Captain Burgh and Lieutenant Pieter Evertsz Hulft (1578–1638). Burgh, whose name means castle or fortress, is holding a compass, symbolically connecting a map of the district with a plan of a fortress (Burgh or *burcht* in Dutch; castle or fortress in English). This gesture points to the duty of Burgh and his militia company to provide security for the area and their ability to read and use plans and maps. The man standing in the center is the ensign. The company's loyalty to the prince is evident from its standard, which sports Maurice's arms. Both Burgh and Hulft owed their appointment to the town council in 1618 to Maurice. The stadholder died in 1625. It may have been his death that led to the commission for this group portrait; a group portrait that underlines loyalty to the House of Orange and underlines that the city elite should be proud and disciplined defenders of the city and the country.

From 1618 until his death Burgh was one of the 36 members of the city council, but only in 1638 and 1643 was he one of the four burgomasters of the city. The year 1638 was thus a glorious and honor-filled year for Burgh. It was also a special year for the city: in September 1638 the French queen mother Marie De' Medici came to Amsterdam. Her son Louis XIII had exiled her and she was seeking support for her return to France. She was the first foreign royal person ever to visit the Dutch Republic and was given an enthusiastic reception. Especially in Amsterdam her visit was considered as an opportunity to underline the important and independent position of the city in the Dutch Republic and in the European theatre. Thus, in 1638 a one and only painting was made of the four Amsterdam burgomasters. The painting depicts the announcement of Marie dé Medici's arrival to the four seated burgomasters Abraham Boom, Burgh (second from the left), Pieter Hasselaer, and Anthony Oetgens van Waveren.

The civic guards played an important role in the reception of the French queen mother. According to Bas Dudok van Heel, the visit and the honor bestowed on Amsterdam was one of the reasons that the Harquebusiers Guard, of which Burgh was one of the four governors, decided that their Great Hall should be decorated with new group portraits of the civic guards and of the governors.[2]

The group portrait of the governors was finished in 1642 by Govert Flinck. Burgh is sitting on the right. The other governors are Jacob Willekens (1564 Werner van den Valckert, "Schutters van de compagnie van kapitein Albert Coenraetsz," 1649), Jan Claesz Vlooswijck (1571 Werner van den Valckert, "Schutters van de compagnie van kapitein Albert Coenraetsz," 1652), and Pieter Reael (1569 Werner van den Valckert, "Schutters van de compagnie van kapitein Albert Coenraetsz," 1643). Govert Flinck depicts the moment when the landlord brings in the ceremonial drinking horn. On the right is a heraldic shield showing a bird's claw, the Harquebusier (*clauwenier*) symbol. The portrait was displayed on the chimneypiece in the great hall of the Harquebusier Civic Guard.

Between 1640 and 1645 the other five pieces showing civic guards were completed. Put together they could be admired as one large panorama, surrounding the seventeenth-century spectator. One of them, isolated from its original context, is now known as the Night Watch, generally considered Rembrandt's masterpiece and the highlight of Dutch seventeenth-century painting. In Van den Valckert's militia painting, Captain Albert Burgh is shown as a man of maps, holding a pair of calipers in his right hand. More examples can be pointed out in which cartography and the Dutch self-image of global power are interrelated and where Burgh is present.

In the 1630s Willem Jansz Blaeu and his son Joan Blaeu published new editions of their world atlas. A number of maps were dedicated to wealthy and powerful Amsterdam regents. The map of the Caribbean was dedicated to Burgh, because he was an important regent but also because he was one of the directors of the Dutch West India Company, a member of the committee that took care of the matters of New Netherland and because as a business partner he was involved in the patroonship Rensselaerswijck.

Another occasion where we meet up with Burgh and maps took place in 1647. In that year Burgh travelled to Russia as the Dutch ambassador to Tsar Alexei Michailowitz. It was his second journey to Russia; fifteen years earlier he had been one of the two Dutch ambassadors to Alexei's father.

Figure 3. Willem Jansz and Joan Blaeu, *"Insulae Americanae in Oceano Septentrionali"* (1635). *Image courtesy of the Amsterdam Museum.*

Dutch Cartography and the Atlantic World / 39

The most important present that Burgh carried with him in 1647 was an enormous hand-painted copper globe. It was the ideal present to impress a foreign ruler. Such a globe showed the skills of Dutch geographers, painters, and coppersmiths and such a globe was the ideal conversation piece with which the ambassador could illustrate the range of Dutch trade, travels, and power. Similar globes were made in the 1640s for the King of Makassar, the ruler of one of the major trading ports in the Indonesian Archipelago, and for the Japanese shogun. Only the Russian globe is preserved and is now on display in the Moscow Historical Museum. Alas for Burgh, he never made it to Moscow. He died in Novgorod. His son Coenraedt succeeded him as an ambassador and as a member of the city council in Amsterdam.

Burgh did not live to see the completion of the building in the middle of the seventeenth century of the new Town Hall in Amsterdam, in itself a majestic celebration of the Peace of Westphalia of 1648. The "global" decorations of the new Town Hall could not be missed. The floor of the Great Hall, named The Burghers Hall and open to citizens and visitors, was inlaid with an enormous marble map of the two hemispheres. On one end stood Atlas carrying the globe, and on the outside, facing the most important square in town, the tympanum was decorated with a female figure, representing Amsterdam, receiving trade goods from all over the world.

There is no documentary evidence as to who received the commission for the design of the marble maps; but we can be sure that it was Joan Blaeu, the most prominent geographer of the day and a member of the city council from 1651 onward, who was given the job. The appointment can be considered as his official entry to the closely knit elite of the city. Thus, maps and globes, both independent and as integrated parts of other works of art, played a vital role in creating the self-image of Amsterdam, the Dutch Republic, and the most important statesmen as global players.

Now, before we turn to Dutch cartography and the Atlantic, we have to look once more to what extent individual players looked at themselves and geography. Was geography a separate undertaking and a goal in itself or did they see geography and maps as an integrated part of other arts and sciences, and did they consider cartography as vital for economic and military purposes?

Clearly, the Dutch self-image was one of integration. Numerous portraits attest to such a self-image. Perhaps the prettiest and most impressive one to support this idea is the portrait of Gerard Hulft (1621–1656) by Govert Flinck of 1654. Gerard Hulft, the son of Pieter Evertsz, mentioned earlier, was a member of a prominent patrician family of Amsterdam. Having graduated in law in 1645, he was appointed secretary of the city council. As

Figure 4. Govert Flinck, "Portrait of Gerard Hulft" (1654). *Image courtesy of the Amsterdam Museum.*

such he attended the council's deliberations and drew up the minutes. During the First Anglo-Dutch War (1652–1654) he volunteered to command 24 units paid for by himself. On 16 January 1654 the VOC Directors passed a resolution appointing Hulft councilor-ordinary of the Dutch East Indies. He left on 26 April of the same year for Batavia in the East Indies.

Flinck painted this portrait to mark Hulft's departure. He is depicted against a sea illuminated by the red morning sun, suggesting his destination in the East. The portrait is enclosed in an oval medallion crowned by two angels holding an anchor beneath the wings of a dove of peace. The oval is surrounded by symbols of Hulft's professional career. On the left, above, are various theological, historical, and legal tomes suggesting Hulft's status as a scholar. Depicted to the right of the oval are writing materials, a pile of parchment volumes, a book of accounts, and various loose papers and documents. These attributes represent Hulft's work as secretary and international merchant. Among the apparently disordered stack of papers, destinations such as *La Rochelle, Venetia, Londres,* and *Danzich* can be discerned.

Another bundle of documents (also to the left of the oval) is headed *Secrete Resolutie 27 Janu 1654*. This may refer to the confidential letter of commission that he carried with him when he left for the East Indies, appointing him to replace Governor-General Carel Reiniersz, who had been ill for many years, if the latter was still alive and active. In fact, by the time

Hulft arrived in Batavia, Reiniersz had died and Joan Maetsuycker had been appointed to succeed him by the Council of the Indies. This appointment was ratified by the directors in October 1654, thereby annulling their previous secret plans for Hulft. He had to make do with the rank of director-general, which Maetsuycker had held before.

On a ledge beneath the oval are various attributes relating to Hulft's prospective career in the East. On the far left are a globe in front of a cane and a short Japanese sword (*"wakazashi"*). Beside this lie calipers and draft designs for fortresses. To the right of the hourglass are various nautical instruments: a compass, an astrolabe and a cross-staff. These are tools that an East India Company employee would have needed on the voyage to the East and when governing trading posts.

In the center foreground lies a sheet of paper showing a caterpillar transforming into a butterfly. Accompanying this is the motto *Nil adeo fuit unquam tam dispar sibi* (nothing was so unlike itself). The motto appears to reflect the sudden turn in Hulft's career, bringing the former secretary of the city council to an adventure in the East. The drawing also reflects that in the world overseas the art of drawing is a necessary skill. In the Netherlands all people involved in overseas trade were to a large or at least to some extent geographers, producing and using maps for their business interest and using maps to clarify their status.

Dutch Cartography in the
Second Half of the Sixteenth Century

The Atlantic world became integrated into Dutch trade and Dutch cartography from the sixteenth century onward. Until 1585, Antwerp and Louvain were the main centers of printing, trade, and science in the Netherlands. Hence, these were also the centers of mapmaking in the Netherlands. The revolt against the Habsburg rulers, the blockade of the Scheldt in 1585, and the ban on foreign ships to come to Spanish harbors in the same year, caused a shift in economic activities. Overseas merchants moved to the North and merchants in the North who wanted to trade on an international scale were forced to find alternatives. But the growth of Dutch overseas trade was not only a reaction to political changes; it was also to a large extent the result of economic growth.

Flemish cartographers already working for an internationally oriented market followed the merchants to the North and mapmakers from the North returned. Cartographers already living in the North started to produce maps for a growing international market. The first major example in Dutch cartography symbolizing the development of international trade from the Northern Netherlands was the publication of the pilot guide of Lucas Jansz Waghenaer from Enkhuizen in 1584–1585. The guide covers the Atlantic coasts of Europe between the Canary Islands and North Cape. It made a strong impression. The fame of the Waghenaer guide is well known; the name Waghenaer even developed into a standard term. In England maritime guides as such were coined Waggoners. The area covered by the guides is limited to the area with which Dutch merchants had been familiar for a long time.

After 1585 Dutch merchants rapidly developed an independent and global attitude in their enterprises. The first cartographic response to this attitude was the production in Amsterdam of a pair of globes by Jacob Florisz van Langren in 1586. Two years later, the Amsterdam mathematician Nicolaus Petri published a book in conjunction with these globes. His instruction for the use of the celestial and the terrestrial globe was directed to the audience of international merchants for whom, as he says, the handling of globes is both of great pleasure and of great use.

One of these first Dutch global players was Balthasar de Moucheron. De Moucheron, the man who fitted out a fleet in 1584 to trade in the White Sea, was the driving force behind a number of fleets to sail or to try and sail to Asia via a Northern route in the two decades following 1584. During the preparations for the expedition of 1584 to the White Sea cartographical expertise was sought. De Moucheron consulted Russian and Portuguese charts. He also travelled to Duisburg where he consulted the famous geographer Gerard Mercator. Both De Moucheron and Mercator agreed that the Polar Sea would always be open for ships. De Moucheron also speculated that it would be possible to reach Asia after rounding the Cape Tabin. The expeditions failed to reach Asia, but trade with Russia through the harbor of Archangel was developed.

In 1585 because of the blockade of the Scheldt, De Moucheron moved from Antwerp to Middelburg in Zeeland. From there he continued his trade with Archangel. In the small Russian settlement the trading houses of the Antwerp merchant Gillis Hooftman (until 1590), De Moucheron, and the Amsterdam merchant Dirck van Os (from 1599 onward) stood practically side by side.

De Moucheron continued to think about possibilities of reaching Asia via the North Pole. In 1593 he consulted different learned friends, among whom Van Linschoten who afterward sailed on De Moucheron's ship. In the end of 1593 a meeting was arranged in The Hague with the stadholder and other prominent government officials to discuss government support for an expedition. In the planning stage De Moucheron, however, came into conflict with the minister and geographer Petrus Plancius (1552–1622) about the routes to be taken. Plancius was in favor of a route north of Nova Zembla. In the end it was decided to try various different routes. The ship that was financed by Amsterdam merchants, among whom Van Os was the most prominent, would follow the route of Plancius. The ship of Van Linschoten sailed south of Nova Zembla into the Kara Sea. The participation of the government in this expedition was remarkable and was partially due to the fact that a northern route could have territorial and military consequences. From an early date fortification of the straits between Nova Zembla and the mainland was considered.

After the return of the expedition in the autumn of 1594 the results were discussed in The Hague. The skippers and pilots were of the opinion that beyond Nova Zembla there was indeed open sea through which China could be reached. Stadholder Maurice and other statesmen inspected the logbooks and other documents. The stadholder ordered "a chart and description be made and have these documents deposited in the archives of the state, in order that further research can be done."[3] Some influential people in Holland were critical about the results of the expedition. It made De Moucheron turn for scientific help to the English geographer Richard Hakluyt the younger. He delivered a memoir in which he supported the ideas of an open sea as discussed by Mercator, Plancius, and De Moucheron. Geographical information also must have reached De Moucheron through Bernardus Paludanus, who corresponded on the issue of the Northeast Passage with Abraham Ortelius.

A new expedition of De Moucheron sailed in 1595. Due to its late departure, the fleet failed to sail through the ice in the Nassau Strait. For De Moucheron and the States General the disappointing results of the expedition were sufficient argument not to plan a new expedition. An additional argument was that by this time Dutch ships had set sail on the route to Asia via the Cape of Good Hope. However, merchants, statesmen, and pilots did not give up speculating about possible northwestern and northeastern routes to Asia, which explains why Henry Hudson was hired in 1609. Yet on a more practical level they focused instead on the Mediterranean, Asia (via the Cape of Good Hope route), and the Atlantic coasts.

In 1592 a new wall map of the world was published by Cornelis Claesz in Amsterdam. The States General granted him a privilege of twelve years for this map, which had been designed by the minister and geographer Plancius. Plancius and his map played a pivotal role in Dutch expansion overseas. Plancius would live to see the foundation of both the East India

Company (VOC, founded in 1602) and the West India Company (WIC, founded in 1621), and his maps and charts were of importance within the context of these companies and also in the early years before Dutch expansion was institutionalized.

In 1592 Claesz received a monopoly from the States General for the production of a number of crucial maps and charts for navigation overseas. Plancius was involved in the monopoly for one set of charts and one individual map. The set of charts consisted of 25 charts of the Portuguese chartmaker De Lasso; the individual map is the wall map of the world designed by Plancius. We do not know which arrangements Claesz and Plancius made with regard to the profit of the "1592 maps." It is beyond doubt though that Claesz paid Plancius for every copy sold, printed, or hand drawn; Plancius was not only a minister and a mathematician, he was also a rich man who was accustomed to speculation, investment, and trade.

On 12 September 1594 Plancius acquired another privilege from the States General, when he obtained a monopoly to produce charts in Mercator's projection in the Dutch Republic. Plancius received this privilege on the basis of the wording of his request and because nobody before him had received a similar privilege: he did not have to show copies of the charts to the States General. This does not imply that Plancius was not able to make such maps. The model for this chart had been produced by Mercator in 1569, and an exact explanation on the production of such charts had been published in the same year 1594 in an excerpt of Edward Wright in the *Exercises* of Thomas Blundeville. The acquisition of the monopoly is typical of both the influential position of Plancius and of his mercantile foresight.

Between 1587 and his death in 1609 Claesz was the dominant printer and merchant in the Dutch Republic for printed and hand-drawn maps, charts, rutters, and atlases in relation to overseas trade. Little is known about his personal life. He was a child of rich parents living in Louvain, probably born in or before 1551. Being a Calvinist he fled from the Southern Netherlands to Emden in Germany during the Dutch Revolt. From there he moved to Enkhuizen and afterward to Amsterdam. The last move, in 1578, was made just after Amsterdam had chosen the Calvinist side. After his arrival in Amsterdam, Claesz worked feverishly to fill his warehouse. In order to maximize his business he also ordered many books from Plantijn in Antwerp. His printing activities started in 1581. Atlases, journals of travels overseas, and geographical books were printed by Claesz. He conquered a dominant position on the market for exploration and expansion overseas. As Van Selm puts it: "His publications were not meant for the traditional buyers of books like scholars and clerics, but for citizens who dominated the economy of Holland. For them he produced books at great speed that often contained new information for overseas trade."[4]

In the nine years between 1582 and 1590 he published an average of six titles per year, but in the decade between 1591–1600 he raised his output to an average of thirteen titles per year. This increase can be explained by his involvement with Dutch overseas expansion and his partnerships with all the important mapmakers of the day.

Merchants and sailors were able to buy all the books, maps, and charts relevant to overseas navigation and trade in the store of Claesz, both printed and manuscript, as we can see in the catalogue of his stock of 1609. This catalogue gives us an excellent impression of the available printed maps and charts relevant for overseas trade. The most relevant in the Atlantic context are listed below, with the headings, the arrangement, and authors as given by Claesz:

Geographical Maps

- World map Plancius in 19 sheets with French, Spanish, Dutch, English, Latin, or German text

- World map Luis Teixeira in 22 sheets with Latin, Italian, Spanish, French, English, Dutch, or German text

- World map Jodocus Hondius in 8 sheets with Latin, Italian, Spanish, French, English, Dutch, or German text

- Europe, Asia, Africa, and America, each map on 8 sheets

Charts of All Navigations (with French and German text)

- World map of the circumnavigation of Olivier van Noort in 4 sheets with 26 prints

- Map of the Dutch journey to Nova Zembla with 33 prints

- Map of the Dutch journey to the Gold Coast of Guinea with 22 prints

- The "Spanish tyranny" with the map of the West Indies and the history of Bartolomeo de las Casas and 16 prints

- The maps of the East and the West Indies bound together in a book with the prints and maps of Jan Huygen van Linschoten

Maps on One Sheet

- Asia, Africa and America

- Canary and Flemish islands by Van Linschoten

- Guinea

- North Pole by Willem Barentsz

- River of Archangel by Mouris Willemsz

- Terra Nova (Newfoundland)

Charts

- Chart of the West Indies and Angola in four sheets

Not all originals of these maps and charts can be traced today, but the titles and the recognizable maps and charts are more than sufficient to conclude that Claesz could help both the interested public and the practical businessmen and pilots with all the relevant maps and charts in relation to territories overseas. This conclusion gets even more weight when we read in the same catalogue that Claesz could deliver manuscript charts of all kinds of "the East Indies, the West Indies, Guinee, Terra Nova, all made by the best mapmakers (*caertschrijvers*)." Chartmakers working in small towns like Edam must have sold a considerable number of their charts through Claesz' shop.

But the supply of Claesz was even larger. In the same catalogue he mentions the business partners from whom one could buy maps and charts in his store: Hondius, Willem Blaeu, the Antwerp publisher Vrient, Pieter van der Keere and Joris Muytinck. Claesz's ambition to be a more or less "national" supplier for fleets sailing overseas can be illustrated by a dedication in one of the books he printed in 1598: a book by Emanuel van Meteren containing the journals of the expeditions of Thomas Cavendish and Francis Drake. It is dedicated to De Moucheron, Van Os, and their associate merchants of the high seas.

The Atlantic Theatre before 1621

When Plancius prepared a memoir with instructions for Dutch pilots to sail to Asia in 1599, he said that he would only deal with the route from Brazil onward; the Atlantic voyage to Brazil was well-known to Dutch pilots according to Plancius. Even before 1584 some Dutch merchants had already sailed to more distant regions than the European coasts. Dutch merchants, often together with Portuguese merchants, sailed to Brazil, the Caribbean, and the Northern coast of South America. Some Dutch pilots became familiar with the Atlantic Ocean because of their experience in English, French, Spanish, or Portuguese service. Working on foreign ships brought them in contact with rutters, maps, and charts used aboard. Undoubtedly these Dutch pilots handled according to the advice in the manual *A Regiment for the Sea,* published by Bourne in 1574, who knew that "your cardes (charts) be most commonly made in Lishborne, in Portugal, in Spayne, or else in France (meaning Dieppe)."[5]

Dutch pilots did not have to go abroad to buy their charts of the Atlantic abroad for very long. Independent Dutch trade on the coasts of Africa and America developed quite rapidly after 1590. From 1592 onward, Van Linschoten, in close cooperation with the medical doctor and collector Paludanus (Berent ten Broecke, 1550–1633), worked on the *Itinerario* (1596) and the *Rheys-geschrift* (1595). He consulted almost all of the relevant works published in France, England, Spain and Germany.

Early Dutch charts for navigation in the Atlantic were produced by chartmakers in Edam and other cities in North Holland. Cornelis Doetsz of Edam made a chart of the Atlantic that covers the coasts of South America as far as Rio de la Plata, the entire west coast of Africa and the coasts of Europa and North America as far north as Norway and Newfoundland. The earliest and only copy known is from 1600. The Doetsz chart is based on Spanish and Portuguese models. It is also a chart that can serve as an example for the exchange of cartographical knowledge between the Netherlands and England. Charts of the English mapmaker Gabriel Tatton (active 1586–1612) of approximately the same period are very similar both in cartographic content and decorations. It is likely that Doetsz and Tatton knew each other as they had an association with Claesz in common. For a while Tatton was employed by Claesz in Amsterdam. In the beginning of the seventeenth century he designed maps for Claesz. While in Amsterdam he also produced a manuscript chart of the Pacific. In Amsterdam Tatton worked closely together with another Englishman, Benjamin Wright, who worked there between 1599 and 1611, and afterwards went to Italy.

The charts of Tatton and Doetsz were even sold as pairs: on a chart of Doetsz of the western part of the Indian Ocean of circa 1600—now in the National Library in Florence—is written "West Indien Tatton." They were ones bought as a pair by the well-known cosmographer Robert Dudley.

Indeed, the chart of Tatton can still be found in the same library. The charts of Doetsz and Tatton found their way to Florence as part of a bold scheme that involved Dutch merchants and maybe stadholder Maurice himself on one side and the Grand Duke Ferdinando de' Medici, assisted by Dudley, on the other side. The proposal for this scheme was written by a Dutchman living in Portuguese Brazil. Ferdinando wanted to establish an overseas commercial colony in Brazil. With Dutch assistance a small fleet was fitted out under the English captain Robert Thornton. The expedition set sail in 1608, got as far as the Amazon, and then lost its way. The fleet returned empty-handed to Livorno one year later; Ferdinando was dead by then.

Even though Dutch pilots knew their way in the Atlantic well before 1600, large parts of the American coasts had hardly been explored. Some Dutch merchants directed their attention in part to those less exploited coasts: gaps between the areas already known and cultivated by Spanish and Portuguese. On their voyages they undertook mapping which, overall considered, refined the world map. Roused by Walter Ralegh's stories of El Dorado, Dutch merchants in 1598 fitted out an expedition to the "wild" coast of Guyana. In his account of the voyage, A. Cabeliau claimed that between the Amazon and Trinidad, 24 rivers, many islands, and several ports had been discovered which were entirely unknown and which until then no one had visited. Such claims seem somewhat exaggerated even though Spanish knowledge of this coastal area was indeed limited. During this expedition maps were drawn by Pieter Cornelisz van Petten. Two of these maps, depicting parts of the island Trinidad, have been preserved.

On other expeditions in this period various stretches of coastlines were explored.

In 1609 Henry Hudson explored, in the service of the VOC, the coastal area near present-day New York and sailed up the river that was later named after him. The VOC had no interest in the American coast but was, in those early years, still looking for a Northeast Passage to Asia.

Dutch publishers quickly responded to the expansion of sea voyages and the flow of incoming information. Within two decades suppliers like Claesz, Blaeu, and draughtsmen of charts like Doetsz were able to supply rutters and large- and small-scale charts of the entire Atlantic area that were continuously improved. Descriptions, maps, town plans, and views—in combination and sometimes in print—supplied logistical information to interested merchants and skippers, which were necessary for efficient trade and sailing. For each region, Dutch merchants collected information concerning the history, inhabitants, flora, fauna, minerals, location, accessibility, climate, and fortifications. Most likely the Spanish *Relaciones Geograficas* on colonial territories from the second half of the sixteenth century served as a model.

The makers of maps were also prepared to use non-cartographic sources and this practice was not limited to overseas areas. A 1628 letter by Hessel Gerritsz, the first official mapmaker of the VOC, informs us that he compiled a map of Scandinavia from a combination of maps and written descriptions. This was not a Dutch invention; for example, the Portuguese map that locates the nations in northeast Africa—the land of the priest-king João—was obviously compiled with the aid of local informants. On the coasts of the Americas and Africa, Dutch merchants were largely dependent on local tribes, with whom it was important to develop good relations in coastal areas to generate knowledge of trade products, the topography, and the population in the interior.

Good examples of such maps are those that were made of the coasts and the interior of the colony New Netherland, one of them made shortly before the founding of the WIC. For the production of such maps, explorers were important. They can be compared with the Brazilian *Paulistas* or French *coureurs du bois*. Dutch explorers made contacts with tribes and thus established a trade network. A number of them learned Native languages to facilitate trade and in the process acquired a detailed knowledge of the area in which they were operating.

On Dutch maps we can see how indigenous knowledge has been incorporated. Both on hand-drawn and printed maps of New Netherland, of which we assume Hessel Gerritsz was the (co-)editor, we see very explicit attention being paid to the locations of native tribes. Gerritsz provides a rare attestation in the legend of a 1616 manuscript map giving an impression of how conscientiously he tried to combine information of Dutch explorers and Indians:

> Of that what Kleyntjen (a Dutch explorer) and his companion have indicated to me about the location of the rivers and the places of the nations which they have found on their outward trip from the Maquaas to the inland along the New River down to the Ogehage, enemies of the above mentioned Northern nations, I can at this point only find two concepts of drawn maps partly in the final version. When I speculate how this and the other concepts of descriptions should be combined, I conclude that the locations for the nations of the Sennecas, Gachoos, Capitanasses and Jennecas should be drawn in quite a bit further to the west.[6]

Figure 5. Adriaen Block and Hessel Gerritsz, "Map of New Netherland" (1616). *Image courtesy of Amsterdam Museum.*

Publishers, Willem Blaeu for instance, also continued to develop activities in the field of maps and charts of the Atlantic region. In 1608, Blaeu published a new seaman's guide of the European waters, the *Licht der Zeevaert*, also available in other languages. In the introduction Blaeu promised that this guide would be expanded with additional volumes, of which one would cover the "many lands, islands and places of Guinee, Brazil and East and West Indies." At that time the volumes dealing with the East and West Indies were not published. Yet, a different cartographic product than the seaman's guide made by Blaeu was completed about 1608: a chart in Mercator's projection for crossing the Atlantic Ocean.

Patrons, Scholars, and Collectors

Maps for walls and cabinets could be found in the meeting rooms of governmental bodies, in the houses of merchants participating in overseas trade, of politicians involved in expansion overseas, of skippers and pilots, and of interested scientists and other burghers who combined education with the possession of some money. The interested circle for maps of overseas territories consisted of at least a few thousand people, if we accept that the first registers of shareholders of the VOC give a good indication of the number of buyers of globes and maps of the world overseas.

In their conception maps were "mirrors" of the world. Maps were seen as treasure chests with opportunities to offer a wide variety of information.

With the help of maps it was easier to understand the Bible and contemporary, medieval, Greek, and Roman history. Maps were a glorious depiction of God's creation and they helped scholars to understand sciences and phenomena with geographical components: natural history, the art of war, navigation, politics, et cetera. In particular, early world maps, decorated maps, atlases, and books about the world overseas give lively impressions of this encyclopedic use of maps.

In relation to the world overseas the attention given to natural history in relation to maps and geographical texts deserves special mention. This focus on natural history was the result of a combined scientific and economic interest. The economic interest is obvious. Dutch merchants went to areas overseas in order to buy a wide range of agricultural products. These products were used for the preparation of food and medicines.

Overseas merchants and scientists in the field of medicines and natural history had more or less the same concerns when it came to knowledge of tropical flora and fauna. Geographical descriptions and maps were useful to understand the flora and fauna in their context.

An important scholar in this field was Carolus Clusius (1526–1609). In 1564 Clusius, studying the flora of Spain, combined his work with cartographic recordings. Ortelius included Clusius's map of Spain in his atlas. For Clusius—one of the caretakers of the *Hortus Botanicus* founded at the University of Leiden in 1585—and for his contemporaries the combination of natural history, medicine, and cartography was obvious; local herbs were studied in the context of local climate and regional diseases. Therefore, in the *Ambulacrum* of the *Hortus* in Leiden, a gallery parallel with the garden, several maps were displayed as aides for natural history research. To a certain extent we could say that the *Hortus* in Leiden with its ambulacrum and maps—such as the map *Orbis Terrarum Typus* (1594) by Plancius on which in the four corners the four parts of the world are figuratively and allegorically depicted—were interchangeable. We can regard the *Hortus* and the map as an encyclopedia of the world, a microcosmos. As mentioned, natural history studies also had a direct economic importance. Clusius's studies were important for the trade in non-indigenous crops. In 1602, commissioned by the VOC, Clusius made an instruction as to how servants should describe the flora and fauna of newly discovered areas. The same servants were requested to make descriptions and drawings of overseas plants and animals. The VOC explicitly supported research, as the prominent director Van Os confirmed in a letter to Clusius of December 1601. A first account by Clusius of overseas knowledge collected by Dutchmen can be found in his *Exoticorum Libri Decem* (1605). It also contains information on the South American fauna, which Clusius derived from Spanish authors. Numerous pilots, captains, and colleagues in the Netherlands are mentioned who had helped Clusius in the compilation of his book.

For a number of governmental bodies and people, maps were essential. Their maps served a number of purposes: planning of expeditions and settlement, evaluation of developed strategies, information about the areas involved, recording contemporary overseas history, propaganda, and accentuating the status of the bodies and people involved. In the early years of Dutch expansion globes and maps were crucial tools for merchants and politicians who were involved in decision making and planning. One might say that Dutch merchants used maps and globes with information of overseas territories before these maps and globes were handed to their personnel: skippers, pilots, and merchants. Nicolaus Petri made his book on the use of the Van Langren globes of 1585 for the group of merchants interested in global trade. Hooftman even inspired Ortelius to compile his atlas.

The correspondence and the collections of crucial decision makers like stadholder Maurice and Johan van Oldenbarnevelt, Grand Pensionary of Holland, also show how the elite held the strings of cartography. From the correspondence of the Leiden professor of anatomy and biology Pieter Pauw with Jan Orlers, an employee of Claesz between 1591 and 1596, we gain further insight in the popularity of world maps. In November of 1594 Pauw wrote to Amsterdam that he would like to get a world map printed in England. Pauw said that he had seen such a map on the wall in the office of the secretary of the city of Leiden, his father-in-law Van Hout. He remarked that if Orlers did not know how to get the map, he should consult Hondius who had lived in England for a long time. Pauw also gave specifications as to how he turned maps on paper into wall maps. He used large pieces of wood ("*wagenschot*") prepared depending on the size of the map. On the wood a piece of wet cloth was pasted. Once the cloth had dried the map was pasted onto it. Subsequently the map could be colored by hand and framed.

Throughout the seventeenth century printed wall maps of the world and of the four continents separately were found in many Dutch houses. Impressions of Dutch houses with maps on the wall can be seen in the paintings of famous masters like Johannes Vermeer and Pieter de Hooch. Framed, large wall maps and framed, hand-drawn and colored maps on parchment decorated the houses of the rich.

Many Dutchmen at the time owned beautiful hand-colored wall maps. Undoubtedly, the chart of Gijsbertsz of 1599, now in the State Library of New South Wales, was produced to decorate the house of one of the wealthy directors of one of the companies that traded with the Far East before 1602. The chart, enriched with illustrations taken from the *Itinerario*, covers the oceans and coastlines between Guinea in the West and Japan and New Guinea in the East.

Already, before the end of the sixteenth century, stadholder Maurice had a set of beautifully decorated charts at his disposal to inspire him to participate in expeditions overseas, both militarily and commercially. Four beautiful hand-drawn charts, illuminated and heightened with gold, probably once decorated the walls of one of the stadholder's residences. Three charts of this set are described in an eighteenth-century manuscript catalogue of maps belonging to the House of Orange. Today, of the original four only two are preserved, one of these showing the eastern coasts of Africa and parts of the Middle East and India and the other showing the Americas. The set was most probably made in 1596 or somewhat earlier by the Edam mapmaker Evert Gijsbertsz.

Evert Gijsbertsz, "Manuscript chart of America" (c. 1596). *Image courtesy of Amsterdam Museum.*

Company Mapmaking after 1602 and
Publishing Maps and Atlases

Few charts for oceanic navigation seem to have been produced in Amsterdam before 1595. Such charts, both printed and manuscript, were made by mapmakers in some small towns along the Zuyderzee coast north of Amsterdam, especially Enkhuizen and Edam, of whom Cornelis Doetsz is the most important.

After 1595 Amsterdam became the center of overseas trade and mapmaking. Many mapmakers and map merchants moved there. The most famous ones—Plancius, Hondius, and Claesz—came from Flanders. The shift of mapmaking, especially in respect to printed maps, from Antwerp to Amsterdam is one of the hallmarks in the history of cartography. But the shift of mapmaking from the North Holland cities Edam and Enkhuizen to Amsterdam has remained overlooked.

In 1617 Hessel Gerritsz was appointed as mapmaker of the VOC. His appointment was based on the fact that Augustijn Robaert had died. Even though Robaert was not an appointed mapmaker, he delivered maps and charts to companies for overseas trade from 1599 onward. From circa 1611 onward he can be considered the exclusive supplier of maps and charts to the VOC. During his life important steps toward institutionalized mapmaking took place and the center of the production of oceanic charts moved step-by-step from North Holland to Amsterdam.

Oceanic navigation brought both wealth and sorrow to the city of Edam. The growing number of widows and orphans gave the burgomasters reason to the following complaint in 1614: "Because of the recently developed navigation to distant countries of our fellow citizens great problems have arrived. Many of them are put into prisons or used as slaves in Barbary or one of the other nations of the Great Turk. Due to their long absence or death in the Turkish nations, East and West India their wives and children are faced with enormous financial burdens."[7] These "oceanic navigators" furnished the chartmakers in Edam and later in Amsterdam with updated charts.

In 1592 Robaert lived in Edam, receiving financial support from his niece Catharina Robaert (Trijn Roberts), also from Edam. Catharina had lived in Edam but moved to Enkhuizen in 1585. That year she was married to Paludanus, one of the most famous scholars in natural history in the Netherlands of his time. His cabinet of rarities was visited by thousands of people, coming to Enkhuizen from the Netherlands and abroad. When the first university in the Northern Netherlands was founded in Leiden, the curators called on Paludanus in 1591 to accept the post of professor of natural history and to design a botanical garden. Paludanus regretted not being able to accept this offer; his wife did not want to move to Leiden. Paludanus, though, befriended his fellow citizen Van Linschoten. He helped Van Linschoten in editing his *Itinerario* and even wrote parts of the text, especially those on America and Africa. For the *Itinerario*, Paludanus translated parts of books of various authors and interviewed Dutch sailors who had sailed the Atlantic coasts, among them Barent Ericksz of Enkhuizen.

With his relationship to Paludanus, Robaert had an influential and learned friend to help him to further his career. Most probably he learned his cartographical skills in the last decade of the sixteenth century while living in Edam. Paludanus, Van Linschoten, Doetsz, and Plancius may have helped him. We do not know when Robaert moved away from Edam. In 1606 he is mentioned for the first time as living in Amsterdam. His move is symbolical of the shift which made Amsterdam *the* center of overseas trade and thus also the center for mapmaking. Already, in 1602 Robaert had acquired such a steady income from his deliveries of charts that he was able to buy 600 guilders worth of shares in the newly founded VOC.

Although living in Amsterdam, his contacts with his hometown Edam continued. Robaert probably ran a "front office" in Amsterdam: Robaert likely acquired commissions for maps and charts of areas overseas in Amsterdan, while a number of these maps and charts were produced in Edam. All of this also means that many charts must have been produced by mapmakers working together, in a way similar to painters, by sharing the workload in a studio. The relationship of Augustijn with Edam continued to the very end. After his death Robaert's corpse was transported from Amsterdam to Edam. He was buried there in 1617.

The growing scale of Dutch chartmaking and an open eye to innovation of overseas areas also resulted in the development of new routines. One was recordkeeping in a logbook. In these logbooks profiles of coastlines and sketch maps of estuaries and islands were included. A next step was to furnish pilot-hydrographers with blank sheets of paper on which compass lines were drawn. Pilots could make a sketch on these sheets without having to bother about the preparation of a cartographical basis.

At the same time the education of oceanic navigators for the Companies was more or less standardized at the turn of the century: candidates could go to schools, learn from standard textbooks, and take an exam before they would enter into service of the VOC and after 1621 into service of the WIC. Davids points out that after 1610, in the major ports of Holland and Zeeland, private schools existed where pilots were trained. Already, before that year such schools could be found in Amsterdam (1586) and Flushing (before 1609). A number of these schools were run by experienced navigators. Most of these schoolmasters in one way or the other were involved with the West or East India Companies: as examiner of Company pilots, as a pilot and mapmaker, as an engineer, et cetera. Davids also points out that the training of the schools must have been complemented by training with professional pilots.[8]

Because of experience and training, the rarity of Dutch pilots changed at the end of the sixteenth century. In 1598 two different Dutch companies, one of De Moucheron and one of the Southern Netherlanders, had to hire English pilots for expeditions to Asia. In 1601, however, there were enough Dutch pilots to be hired for the ships of the Zeeland *Company of Ten Haeff*. On 20 September 1601, the directors in Zeeland requested their counterpart Pieter Lintgens in Amsterdam to hire two or three pilots from the ships that had just returned from Asia. Lintgens was authorized to hire these people "without any limitation in price."

After 1600 we can speak of a reversal of "rarity": in the late 1610s the Spanish king asked authorities in the Southern Netherlands to contract Dutch pilots for oceanic navigation. In one case the request was specified to the point that the pilot should be familiar with navigation through the Strait of Magellan.

The VOC made use of the services of the official mapmaker for more or less fixed prices. In the production and management of the charts the mapmaker was subject to the supervision of the directors or of their deputies. Furthermore, just as other Company employees, he was sworn to secrecy. However, in practice, the mapmaker to the VOC carried out the production and correction of charts fairly independently. The obligation to secrecy was at odds with his production for the free market. Willem Blaeu (1633–1638) and his son Joan (1638–1673) exploited their somewhat hybrid position to the full.

In 1617 the political situation worked against Blaeu; therefore he had no chance to become the mapmaker of the VOC. His former servant Hessel Gerritsz was given the job. When Gerritsz died in 1632 the situation was quite different. Calvinist hardliners like Reinier Pauw had been replaced in Amsterdam by regents like Bas, Huydecooper, Burgh, and Reael. Plancius died in 1622. Blaeu must have felt very honored when the VOC Directors Voet, Van Loon, and Reael visited him to ask if he would become their mapmaker on the same terms as Gerritsz. Blaeu accepted without hesitation and was officially appointed. The contract of Gerritsz was copied. The continuity of VOC mapmaking was guaranteed through the stipulation that the four assistants of Gerritsz were contracted by his successor Blaeu; besides,

Blaeu received all the VOC papers and maps that had come out of Gerritsz' house through the good offices of Reael.

Reael must be considered as the key figure in getting Blaeu appointed and in strengthening his position. Not only was he in the right position in Amsterdam politics and as a VOC director, he was also a personal friend of Blaeu, sharing the same interest in mathematics and geography. Reael helped Blaeu to get another honorable position—that of examiner of the pilots, next to Lastman and a few specially assigned directors. The examination of the pilots must have been an enjoyable meeting of mathematical experts. Reael was the director who joined in these meetings. It was also Reael who was asked to check the quality of Blaeu's charts.

Blaeu used VOC and WIC maps to extend his own atlas into a publication in two volumes. Due to the more liberal climate of the 1630s, Blaeu was able to do so. The same atlas with the newly added maps, a number of them based on Gerritsz's maps or even designed by Gerritsz, was used by Blaeu in 1635 as a political statement. Blaeu did so by dedicating a lot of the maps to crucial decision makers. These dedications illustrate both Blaeu's group of friends and political and commercial allies, and the alliance between the stadholder Frederick Henry, who took a more liberal stand than his brother and predecessor Maurice, and the new political elite of Amsterdam.

Reael and Blaeu must have discussed thoroughly which persons should be honored with a dedication. Of the circle of Frederick Henry we find Jacob Wytz (Flanders, army commander) and Constantijn Huygens (Strait of Magellan, secretary of the stadholder and a leading figure in the world of the arts). The Amsterdam circle and their friends are represented by:

- Dirk Bas (China, political leader of the Amsterdam libertine faction)

- Simon van Beaumont (Zeeland, Remonstrant pensionary of Rotterdam and amateur poet)

- Andries Bicker (Rhine, influential Amsterdam politician, leader of the so-called Bicker *ligue*)

- Albert Burgh (Caribbean, a "converted" follower of Pauw, whose son Coenraedt married Christina, the granddaughter of Cornelis Pietersz Hooft)

- Pieter Hasselaer (Genoa, supporter of the Remonstrants, whose father-in-law was Hooft, also an important relative for Blaeu)

- Cornelis Pietersz Hooft (World: Blaeu already dedicated his world map of 1606 to Hooft in whose office he started his career)

- Reael himself (East India)

- Dirck Tholing (Persia, who belonged to the circle of Hooft and Blaeu); and

- Nicolaas Tulp (Guinea, sometimes pro-, sometimes Contra-Remonstrant)

With the help of dedications on maps published by Willem (and his son after 1635), like the one dedicated to the staunch Calvinist Willem Backer (North Pole, married to a daughter of the Christian humanist Laurens Jansz Spiegel), one can deduce the developments in the circle of friends and allies in the field of literature and politics of the Blaeus, usually libertine and sometimes Calvinist politicians with a humanist perspective. The dedication to the army commander Wytz is perhaps the most exceptional and the most typical one. With this dedication Blaeu showed his sympathy for the alliance between the libertine faction and stadholder Frederick Henry. Wytz was a political friend of Hooft at the court of Frederick Henry. He made himself popular with the libertine faction when he came to Amsterdam in the 1620s to restore law and order when the possessions of Remonstrants were plundered.

The Atlantic Theatre after 1621

From 1621, Dutch trade in the Atlantic fell under the authority of the West India Company, which employed mapmakers, land surveyors, and engineers in the Republic and overseas. But the founding of the WIC did not make the Atlantic Ocean an exclusive area for the company, as was the case in some parts of Asia. The relative openness of the Atlantic to international shipping resulted in WIC mapmaking agencies facing fierce competition in the production of charts. Chart production remained largely in the private sector; nevertheless, steps toward institutionalized mapmaking were taken after 1621.

Like the VOC, the WIC did not leave the collecting and editing of information concerning maritime issues to the initiative of skippers and publishers alone. Skippers and pilots were instructed to make maps of anchorages, coasts, and ports and to turn these over to the Company's board of directors, the *Heren XIX*, under penalty of three months' wages. In addition, the WIC had its own mapmaker, or, more correctly, its own exclusive supplier of maps. Between 1621 and his death in 1632, Hessel Gerritsz was the WIC's map supplier. The organization of the cartographic production at the WIC was almost identical to that at the VOC. In both cases the mapmaker remained active in the private sphere, where he used the name of the Company to enhance his reputation.

In 1627, Gerritsz began the compilation of a navigation manual with detailed maps and coastal views. He first evaluated the overseas information of foreigners. Next, he made a critical compilation from available journals, coastal views, and maps in the WIC and the VOC archives. He spoke to dozens and possibly hundreds of skippers and pilots. Gerritsz recorded observations directly from returning pilots in a book (*remonstrantieboek*), sheets of which can be found in what remains of the WIC's cartographic archives.

So, whereas the Dutch had been behind the Spanish and Portuguese in possessing cartographic information at the end of the sixteenth century, in 1632 a WIC official announced with pride that they had caught up: "All ports are known to us and he [the Spanish enemy] cannot change or disguise his course without us discovering it."[9] Indeed, one year earlier, Spanish authorities had ordered Dutch books on the art of navigation to be translated into Spanish. The newly available detailed information was subsequently used for the production of engraved small-scale charts, the so-called *overzeilers*, for long-distance ocean voyages.

After its capture by the Dutch in 1630, Recife in Brazil became the WIC's overseas administrative center to coordinate military and exploratory expeditions and hydrographic surveys; the admiral was responsible for hydrography in Brazil. One of the first admirals working there was Johannes van Walbeeck, who, for two years beginning in the spring of 1630, was involved in various cartographic activities including coordinating the survey of the coast of Brazil. Van Walbeeck gave the pilots the following instructions for a chart of the Brazilian coast in October 1631: "The commander will leave port in the shallop and set course for Rio Grande, remaining close to the shore, accompanied by the yacht, which is more seaworthy, and will as closely as possible inspect, in passing, all entrances, harbors, and bays to collect all pertinent information, and will drop anchor every evening at sunset, and only continue his voyage at daybreak."[10]

After 1632, under the guidance of Admiral Jan Cornelisz Lichthart, a new and more detailed chart was made of the Brazilian coast after a seven-year survey. A few manuscript copies of this chart, made by Johannes Vingboons, have survived. The title of one of the copies mentions that it was sent to the Netherlands by the governor-general, Johan Maurits van Nassau-Siegen, who arrived in Recife in 1637.

In 1631, Hessel Gerritsz completed two charts of the Caribbean and Atlantic as a pair, meeting at Cape Nassau on the north coast of South America. The Atlantic chart, showing the crossing from Africa to Brazil was published after his death in 1632 by the brothers Joannes and Philips Vingboons. This *Brasilysche paskaert* (1637) provided pilots with information about the prevailing winds and ocean currents during the various seasons. In crossing from the African coast, the captain used not only the wind, but also the east-west ocean current. Ships crossing from Africa aimed at Cape Augustine, the most easterly point of South America (where the current splits and travels southwest and northwest), and from there headed for Recife a few miles to the north while remaining safely within sight of the coast. On the home voyage they made use of the current that travels northwest, sometimes stopping off in the Caribbean.

For a long time, the *Brasilysche paskaert* was the most advanced chart available. It formed the basis of the map of Brazil in Joan Blaeu's atlas, first published in 1642. After 1637 there was little that was new in hydrographic charting of Dutch Brazil, mainly because from 1637 to 1644 hydrographic charts and land maps of Brazil were combined to form a general map. There are indications that Blaeu and Vingboons worked together on the production of large-scale prototypes for the new chart of the coast of Brazil (c. 1639) compiled in Recife under the direction of the Admiral Lichthart.

The charts of the Atlantic and of the entire Caribbean became very popular and were reprinted several times. The *West-Indische paskaert*, which Blaeu's father had first published around 1629 and Blaeu had reprinted in 1639, was revised and reprinted well into the eighteenth century and was copied by the publishers Jacob Aertsz Colom, Anthonis Jacobsz Lootsman, Hendrik Doncker, Pieter Goos, Johannes van Keulen, Huych Allard, Jacob Robijn, and Johannes Loots.

The WIC director Samuel Blommaert was a leading geographical expert. He wrote that he took much more care than others to obtain detailed knowledge of whatever happened within the limits of the chartered area of the WIC as well as continuously taking information from anyone who came from that region. Blommaert's geographical interests and his activities as both a WIC director and agent of Sweden resulted in the monumental three-volume manuscript atlas by Joannes Vingboons preserved in the Vatican. This atlas once belonged to Queen Christina of Sweden (reigned 1632–1654) and is connected to Swedish overseas activities that developed on the coasts of North America and Africa after 1635. A number of the maps in the atlas give details about Swedish settlements.

The Christina atlas gives an excellent impression of the level of the WIC's hydrographic knowledge at mid-century. The atlas includes a collection of 56 manuscript charts that together form the WIC's *padrón real* of the Atlantic Ocean, as well as a small-scale index chart of the entire chartered territory. All the information from the overseas explorations collected by Gerritsz and Vingboons was used for creating this *padrón real*, the only complete version of which is in the Christina atlas.

All 56 charts forming this *padrón real* were drawn at the same scale (1:500,000) and, if connected, would form a general map more than 8 meters in length. The *padrón real* provides an image of the coasts of North and South America, from Newfoundland down the east coasts, through the Strait of Magellan, and up the west coast as far north as the southern point of California; it also provides an image of the west coast of Africa from the Senegal to the Cape of Good Hope. These maps can also be regarded as a model for a navigation manual, which had already been promised to the public in 1608 by Willem Blaeu and for which Joan Blaeu had great expectations. For various reasons, the Blaeu/Vingboons manual never materialized; Blaeu probably wanted a manual of grandiose proportions, while the WIC had no intention of financing such an expensive book.

Shortly after 1650, the WIC lost its leading role in the production of its charts. There are few indications that skippers still obeyed the instructions to hand over maps showing new explorations to the Company. The WIC's retreat in the field of maritime cartography was completed in 1674 with the founding of the second WIC, after the first had gone bankrupt. Dutch shipping in the Atlantic was liberalized. Private mapmakers then took over the cartographic task completely, which was a return to the situation prior to 1621.

The Middelburg WIC Chamber inspired the local mapmaker Arent Roggeveen to move forward with his own manual for the Atlantic rather than wait for Blaeu or other Amsterdam mapmakers. In 1668, Roggeveen obtained the privilege for his *Burning Fen*, to be published in Dutch, English, French, and Spanish. The *Burning Fen* was an important breakthrough: it was the first printed navigation manual with large-scale charts accompanied by coastal profiles and descriptions of the entire Atlantic territory, and it reached a broad international market.

Soon after, other publishers followed with more extensive navigation manuals. In 1680, the Amsterdam publisher Keulen and his partner Claes

Jansz Vooght obtained a privilege for a competing navigation manual, the *Zee-fakkel*, a commercial product that fit well with the creation of the free-trade area in 1674, the year the WIC was dissolved and a new WIC, with a more limited scope, was founded. Keulen's *Zee-fakkel* gives detailed information on the entire Atlantic region and was published in Dutch, Italian, and Spanish; a planned English edition never materialized. Keulen's work distinguished itself from the works of Dutch and foreign competitors by its large number of coastal views, enlarged views of estuaries, and dense shading showing coastal relief.

All-in-all cartography was of great importance for Dutch expansion in the Atlantic area. Contrary to the situation in Asia, though, the production of maps and charts was not controlled by a governmental or semi-governmental body. The VOC was much more in control over cartographical information compared to its counterpart the WIC. In the Atlantic theatre, Company mapmakers and publishers working for the open market were in close contact, at least in the field of small-scale maps and charts.

In Dutch society as a whole maps were considered as vital means for the practice of overseas expansion, such as trade and navigation. They were also considered as works of scholarship and art and they were very much seen as symbols of modernity. Therefore maps—multi-volume atlases, globes and wall maps—decorated the interiors of a new and confident elite.

Further Reading

Svetlana Alpers, *The Art of Describing: Dutch Art in the Seventeenth Century.* (Chicago: University of Chicago Press, 1984).

Jaap Jacobs, *New Netherland: A Dutch Colony in Seventeenth Century America* (Leiden: Brill Academic Publishers, 2005).

Norbert Middelkoop and Tom van der Molen, *Amsterdam's Glory: The Old Masters of the City of Amsterdam* (Busseum: Thoth, 2009).

Günter Schilder, *Monumenta Cartographica Neerlandica, VII: Cornelis Claesz: Founder and stimulator of Dutch cartography* (Alphen aan den Rijn: Canaletto/Repro-Holland, 2003).

Benjamin Schmidt, *Innocence Abroad: The Dutch Imagination and the New World, 1570–1670* (Cambridge: Cambridge University Press, 2001).

Kees Zandvliet, *Mapping for Money: Maps, plans and topographic paintings and their role in Dutch overseas expansion during the 16th and 17th centuries* (Amsterdam: Batavian Lion International, 2002).

Kees Zandvliet (ed.), *The Dutch Encounter with Asia, 1600–1950* (Zwolle: Waanders and Amsterdam, Rijksmuseum, 2002).

Notes

1. *Exclusam hesperia perituram Hispane putasti / Me? Frustra: nam cura Dei mihi pandit ad Afros / Primo iter, atque Indos, et qua patet extima China / Quaque etiam priscis non cognitus Orbis in Orbe. / Perge favere Deus, daque his agnoscere Christum.*

2. B. Dudok van Heel, "The Night Watch and the Entry of Marie de' Medici: A New Interpretation of the Original Place and Significance of the Painting," in *The Rijksmuseum Bulletin* 57 (2009), pp. 5–41.

3. J. H. de Stoppelaar, *Balthasar de Moucheron: Een bladzijde uit de Nederlandsche handelsgeschiedenis tijdens den Tachtigjarigen oorlog* ('s-Gravenhage, 1901), p. 105.

4. B. van der Selm, *Een menighte treffelijcke boecken: Nederlandse boekhandelscatalogi in het begin van de zeventiende eeuw* (Utrecht: HES, 1987), p. 182.

5. Quoted in E. G. R. Taylor, *The Haven-Finding Art: A History of Navigation from Odysseus to Captain Cook* (London: Hollis and Carter, 1956), p. 203.

6. Map of New Netherland by Cornelis Hendricks, annotated with comments, The Hague, National Archives Collection 4.VEL nr. 519; in my opinion this concerns a comment by Hessel Gerritsz of a somewhat later date. I assume Gerritsz may have made these observations for the New Netherland Company.

7. D. Brinkkemper et al., *Register van het Burgerweeshuis te Edam, 1558–1634* (Purmerend: Streekarchief Waterland, 1991), p. 73.

8. C. A. Davids, *Zeewezen en wetenschap: De wetenschap en de ontwikkeling van de navigatietechniek in Nederland tussen 1585 en 1815* (Amsterdam: Dieren, 1985).

9. J. H. J. Hamelberg, *Documenten behorende bij "De Nederlanders op de West-Indische eilanden." 1. Curaçao, Bonaire, Aruba* (Amsterdam, 1901–1909), pp. 10–11.

10. The Hague, National Archives, West India Company Archives, inv. nr. 49, f. 166.

II

AMERICAN WORLDS

4

Avenue of Empire

The Hudson Valley in an Atlantic Context

Timothy J. Shannon

*T*here is no romance or adventure to be had in recounting New York's colonial origins. New England had its hardy Pilgrims with their heads full of democratic ideals and hearts full of pietistic devotion while Virginia had Captain John Smith, the Elizabethan James Bond, outwitting foreign enemies and seducing their women. But what can the Empire State offer to its school children? According to the most complete eyewitness account of Henry Hudson's historic 1609 voyage up the river that bears his name, the local Natives greeted the newcomers with tobacco, shell beads, grapes, pumpkins, corn, and animal pelts, for which they received in return knives, hatchets, glass beads, and "trifles." At several points in the voyage, violence flared between the ship's crew and Indians, especially when the latter pilfered items from the ship or approached it armed with bows and arrows.[1] When Hudson and his crew sailed for home, they left behind no cross or banner claiming the land for God or king. It was hardly an auspicious start for a colonial enterprise. Henry Hudson has remained ever since a foggy figure in the pantheon of early American explorers, and his disappearance at the hands of mutineers during a subsequent voyage hardly inspires veneration.[2]

What about the Dutch merchants and administrators who followed in Hudson's wake? Despite the triumphalist tale told by Russell Shorto, the names of Adriaen van der Donck and Petrus Stuyvesant barely rate recognition, never mind admiration, among modern Americans. Other colonies had explorers and planters, heroes and villains, idealists and knaves. New Netherland had stockholders. The Dutch West India Company was the forerunner of today's faceless multinational corporations, a global presence but also a shadowy one.[3] Plenty of other North American colonies—including Massachusetts and Virginia—originated in joint-stock companies that secured charters, raised capital, and recruited settlers—but more so than any other, New Netherland is remembered in our national mythology as a product not of adventurers, but of venture capital.

This reputation is captured visually in Alfred Fredericks's 1910 painting *The Purchase of Manhattan Island* (Figure 7). The painting does its best to ennoble what has become known as one of history's great real estate swindles: the purchase of Manhattan from local Natives for a parcel of trade goods. The painting is a wildly inaccurate depiction of a long misinterpreted event. Judging from their dress, the Indians in the scene have wandered in from the Great Plains, and like modern Times Square tourists crowding around a three-card monte dealer, they listen too eagerly as West India Company agent Pieter Minuit makes his pitch. Fredericks based this scene on a nineteenth-century historian's claim that local Indians parted with Manhattan for $24 worth of beads and trinkets, an interpretation of the available evidence that has long since been debunked by modern scholars.[4] The ersatz feel of Fredericks's painting is compounded by the fact that he borrowed wholesale from Benjamin West's more famous *William Penn's Treaty with the Indians* (Figure 8), which depicted William Penn's arrival in Philadelphia in 1682 and enshrined the Quaker colony's founder as the embodiment of European fair-dealing with American Indians.

Figure 7. Alfred Fredericks, "Peter Minuit purchasing Manhattan from the Lenape" (1910). *Greenwich Village History*, accessed 19 February 2013, http://gvh.aphdigital.org/items/show/1465.

Figure 8. Benjamin West, "William Penn's Treaty with the Indians," (1770–1772) http://en.wikipedia.org/wiki/File:Treaty_of_Penn_with_Indians_by_Benjamin_ West.jpg, accessed 19 February 2013. Fredericks borrowed generously from this famous painting for his *The Purchase of Manhattan Island* (see Figure 7), but while William Penn entered the history books as an honest-dealing friend to the Indians, Minuit's transaction for Manhattan Island is remembered as a great swindle.

But wait a minute . . . don't the two paintings depict the same thing, a transfer of real estate in exchange for a treasure chest of goods? Then why have Minuit and the West India Company gone down in history as con artists while Penn and his Quaker associates are revered as paragons of virtue and kindness? West was certainly a better painter than Fredericks, but more to the point, he was a better public relations man. When West completed his painting in 1772, he was working for William Penn's sons, who were trying to reverse their own poor reputations as proprietors of Pennsylvania by elevating their father as a sort of patron saint of Anglo-Indian relations. In 1910, Fredericks merely wished to depict what everyone already thought they knew about New Netherland: the Dutch bought it for a string of beads.

A more nuanced interpretation of the European-Indian encounter in the Hudson region is provided by the Iroquois oral tradition of the Dutch arrival in their homeland. At treaty conferences during the colonial era, the Iroquois often recounted the origins of the Covenant Chain, the alliance that connected them to their colonial neighbors.[5] At Lancaster, Pennsylvania in 1744, the Onondaga orator Canasatego told this version:

Above One Hundred Years ago the *Dutch* came here in a Ship, and brought with them several Goods, such as Awls, Knives, Hatchets, Guns, and many other Particulars, which they gave us: And when they had taught us how to use their Things, and we saw what sort of People they were, we were so pleased with them, that we tied their Ship to the Bushes on the Shore; and afterwards, liking them still better the longer they stayed with us, and thinking the Bushes too slender, we removed the Rope and tied it to the Trees; and as the Trees were liable to be blown down by high Winds, or to decay of themselves, from the Affection we bore them, again removed the Rope, and tied it to a strong and big Rock . . . And not content with this, for its further Security, we removed the Rope to the big Mountain . . . and there we tied it very fast . . .

"During all this Time, the New-comers the *Dutch*, acknowledged our Right to the Lands and solicited us from time to time, to grant them part of our Country, to enter into League and Covenant with us, and to become one People with us.

"After this, the *English* came into the Country, and as we were told, became one People with the *Dutch*. . . .

"Indeed, we have had some small Differences with the *English*, and during these Misunderstandings, some of their young Men would, by way of Reproach, be every now and then telling us, that we should have perished, if they had not come into the Country, and furnished us with Strouds, Hatchets, Guns, and other Things necessary for the Support of Life: But we always gave them to understand, that they were mistaken; that we lived before they came amongst us, and as well or better, if we may believe what our Forefathers have told us: We had then Room enough, and Plenty of Deer, which was easily caught; and though we had not Knives and Hatchets, and Guns, such as we have now, yet we had Knives of Stone, and Hatchets of Stone, and Bows and Arrows, and these served our Uses as well then, as the *English* ones do now: We are now straightened, and sometimes in want of Deer, and liable to many more Inconveniences, since the *English* came among us."[6]

Unlike Fredericks's painting of the purchase of Manhattan, Canasatego's account of the Dutch arrival describes an encounter between Natives and newcomers from which each side derived benefits and obligations. By taking hold of the Covenant Chain, the Dutch (and their English successors) received security and customers for their colonial venture; in return, the Iroquois received tools, weapons, clothing, and other valuable trade goods. At the end of this story, Canasatego's language evokes a melancholy nostalgia for a time before the arrival of the Dutch and English, when the Indians made due with "Knives of Stone, and Hatchets of Stone, and Bows and Arrows" of their own manufacture, but overall, his speech is about the mutual interests of two independent peoples, not the canny exploitation of one by the other.

Whether told by Indians or Europeans, the story of the colonization of the Hudson Valley has trade at its center. What the story lacks in piety, fortitude, and bravery, it makes up for in wampum beads and woolens. The fur trade provided the foundation upon which the Dutch built New Netherland. Without it, the region would not have interested the Dutch much more than as a supply stop in their global maritime trade. Assessing the significance of the Dutch presence in North America, therefore, requires placing the Hudson Valley into the wider context of the three Atlantic empires—Dutch, French, and British—that jockeyed for trade and power within it.

The Dutch in New Netherland

The best place to begin is with the river itself. Rivers were the avenues of empires in seventeenth-century North America. They provided routes for exploration and the fastest and most convenient way for transporting resources from the interior to coastal seaports and beyond. We often imagine the early European settlements in North America as beachheads from which colonists slowly and uniformly advanced westward, but in fact the penetration of the interior varied considerably from one region to the next depending on the ease of inland navigation. In tidewater Virginia, tobacco planters dispersed quickly along the James, York, Rappahannock, and Potomac Rivers until encountering the fall line, where rapids, waterfalls, and rising elevations stopped ocean-going vessels from proceeding further. In New England, some colonists used the broad gateway provided by the Connecticut River to establish inland settlements at Hartford, Connecticut, and Springfield, Massachusetts at a time when their contemporaries were mostly clustered in coastal communities.

All rivers were not created equal. The Susquehanna is one of the longest rivers in eastern North America, but its fall line is not far from the head of the Chesapeake Bay and its shallowness makes it ill-suited for large watercraft. For most of the colonial period, it served as an obstacle rather than as an open door to the colonization. The Delaware River, on the other hand, became a major artery for commerce and settlement for three colonies: Pennsylvania, New Jersey, and Delaware.[7]

Two rivers exceeded all others along the Atlantic coast for the routes they provided into the interior: the St. Lawrence and the Hudson. Not surprisingly, both became vital to the ambitions of European powers and a comparison of New France and New Netherland illustrates the advantages each offered. The St. Lawrence provided French ships with a navigable corridor into the continent as far as Québec, and from there smaller watercraft, primarily the birch bark canoes made by the Indians of the region, could be used to reach Lakes Ontario and Erie. The Ottawa River, from its juncture with the St. Lawrence at Montréal, provided another water-borne route to the west via Lakes Huron, Michigan, and Superior. The French presence in northeastern America spread out along these inland arteries, creating an empire held together by canoes, trade goods, and forts positioned at strategic portages throughout the Great Lakes watershed. French farmers, known as *habitants*, lived mostly in the lower St. Lawrence Valley and the eastern province of Acadia (modern Nova Scotia), but missionaries, traders, and soldiers built alliances with Indians as far west as modern Minnesota.

Despite the remarkable geographic extent of this French influence, the colonial population of New France grew slowly. Crown-sponsored efforts to promote migration to Canada could not overcome the preference French adventurers had for colonial destinations in the Caribbean, and official restrictions on the migration of Protestants to France's colonies sent French-speaking religious refugees to Dutch and English colonies instead. By 1750, the colonial population of New France numbered only about 55,000, while the number of British subjects in North America stood near one million.[8]

Similar to the French experience in Canada, Dutch colonization in North America moved in a thin ribbon along a great river. Large watercraft aided by the tides could sail as far north as Fort Orange (modern Albany). From there, a portage road around the Cohoes Falls made it possible to connect with the Mohawk River and follow a water route all the way to Lake Ontario with only one significant portage at the Oneida Carrying Place (modern Rome, New York). Unlike their French rivals, however, the Dutch did not press westward in search of furs to buy or souls to save. They built Fort Orange and were content to let the Indians bring furs to them. Schenectady, established at the end of the portage road around the Cohoes, became the westernmost Dutch settlement. Neither it nor Beverwijck, the town that grew up around Fort Orange, ever became the seat of a missionary enterprise to rival what Jesuit priests were undertaking in Canada.[9]

When comparing New Netherland to New France, it is easy to over-state the insularity of the Dutch. They certainly were not the explorers the French were. Who was their Champlain or LaSalle? They lacked the stoic resignation and cultural adaptability of French missionaries and fur traders, who disappeared for months at a time to join Indian families on their sea-sonal migrations. French travelers recorded detailed ethnographies of Native cultures they encountered in North America. The only Dutch document that comes close to such cultural immersion is the brief journal kept by Harmen Meyndertsz van den Bogaert, a barber-surgeon at Fort Orange who ventured into Mohawk country on a diplomatic mission in 1634–1635.[10] Dutch maps of New Netherland are embarrassingly vague in their depictions of territory north and west of the Hudson River, as if they never bothered to look out their back door.[11] (See Figure 9.)

New World dominion meant little to the Dutch if it did not yield commercial profits. Adriaen van der Donck's *A Description of New Netherland* (1655) provided the most spirited defense of Dutch claims in North America.

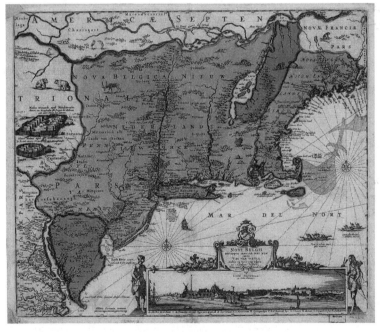

Figure 9. Nicolaes Visscher, *Novi Belgii Novaeque Angliae nec non partis Virginiae tabula multis in locis emendate* (1651–1656). This map of New Netherland captures visually the importance the Dutch attached to the Delaware, Hudson, and Connecticut Rivers and their poor sense of geography north and west of Fort Orange.

Significantly, he described the colony's borders in terms of waterways rather than land: the North [Hudson] and East Rivers on either side of Manhattan, the South [Delaware] River and the Fresh [Connecticut] River, all of which were well-suited for bringing furs and other goods extracted from the American interior to Atlantic markets.[12]

Like the French in Canada, the Dutch had a perpetual problem with recruiting settlers for New Netherland. The West India Company wished to maintain a monopoly on the fur trade but still needed a settler population to defend its colony from hostile Indians and neighboring powers. The Hudson River gave the Dutch one decided advantage over the St. Lawrence in this regard: it had a much more temperate climate, with a longer growing season and a harbor that remained ice-free during the winter. Nevertheless, patroonship grants, a system devised by the West India Company to encourage its investors to recruit settlers for the colony, failed in their purpose. Migrants who came to New Netherland preferred engaging illicitly in the fur trade to clearing land and planting crops. The only patroonship to flourish belonged to the Van Rensselaer family in the northern Hudson Valley, and its success can be attributed in part to the access it gave its tenants to the fur trade at Fort Orange. Between Kiliaen van Rensselaer's patroonship and Manhattan, the colonial population thinned and became more vulnerable to its enemies. Wiltwijck (modern Kingston) was the only village of note between Beverwijck and New Amsterdam. In his treatise on New Netherland, Van der Donck noted ominously that the Hudson Valley "is still entirely under Dutch control and has not been invaded, but were the population not to increase, continued possession would be in great danger."[13] On the eve of the English conquest in 1664, the colonial population of New Netherland was approximately 9,000, concentrated heavily in New Amsterdam and the western end of Long Island.[14] By comparison, the colonial populations of New England and Virginia were about 50,000 and 40,000, respectively.[15]

The West India Company's relations with Indians did little to help strengthen its hold on the colony. Unlike the French, the Dutch tended to keep their Indian neighbors at arm's length, defining their connection to them in commercial terms rather than the fictive kinship ties Indians cultivated in such relationships. In Canada, missionary work and the fur trade knit Native and colonial populations into a web of interdependence that provided a foundation for cultural understanding and synthesis. In New Netherland, Dutch fur traders appeared to be more fascinated by the beaver than their Indian customers. Van der Donck noted that very few Indians had converted to Christianity since the arrival of the Dutch and that no "particular official measures [have] been resorted to or applied to induce them to do so."[16]

Sexual relations between Dutch traders and Native women did occur (the seventeenth-century Mohawk chief known as the "Flemish Bastard" is proof of that). Such evidence notwithstanding, Dutch-Indian relations in New Netherland lacked the physical and social intimacy found in New France.[17] As a result, Indian relations in New Netherland were fragile, and warfare erupted between the Dutch and their Algonquian neighbors in the Hudson Valley several times during the 1640s and 1650s.

New Netherland and New France were similar in that both took their shape from the river systems that provided their entry into the continent. In both cases, the fur trade attracted investment and colonizers, but it also retarded the growth of self-perpetuating settler populations that could rival colonies in New England and the Chesapeake. Other factors of geography and culture caused the paths of these colonies to diverge. The Hudson Valley's more temperate climate and the West India Company's endorsement of religious freedom of conscience made New Netherland a more attractive destination for some emigrants than Canada. However, New France engrossed a much larger share of the northern fur trade because of its missionaries' and traders' willingness to forge spiritual and familial ties with Indians deep into the continent's interior. Neither colony ever succeeded in solving its population problem, although New Netherland did show progress on this front after the West India Company gave up its monopoly on the fur trade. In both cases, the river in question served far more effectively as an avenue for trade out of the colony than as a conveyor of people into it.

The English in New York

The English conquest of New Netherland in 1664 involved about as much bloodshed and mayhem as a modern corporate merger. At the time, no one thought to unfurl a banner proclaiming "Under New Management" outside the city wall of New Amsterdam, but it certainly would have captured the spirit of the venture. King Charles II of England gave a proprietary charter to his brother (and eventual successor) James, Duke of York, for all the territory between the Connecticut and Delaware Rivers, and James dispatched a naval squadron to convince the population of New Netherland of his title. The residents of New Amsterdam, after being assured of their security in property and person, readily capitulated. New Netherland moved overnight from being a joint-stock corporation to the personal fiefdom of a royal family grandee. On the evolutionary scale of capitalism, this was certainly a step backward, but the colony's economy did not suffer unduly from the change.

Nor did the conquest have an immediate impact on the colony's cultural geography. In a flurry of charter writing and grant making, Charles II and James gave away much of what had been New Netherland to the colonies of Connecticut and East and West Jersey, so that New York assumed the shape we recognize on a map today. The English changed some names too—Beverwijck to Albany, Wiltwijck to Kingston, and New Amsterdam to New York City—but migration to the colony remained sluggish. The demise of New Netherland formally ended the patroonship system (of the many patroonship grants made by the West India Company, only Rensselaerswijck survived), but James and his agents indulged in a similar practice, doling out enormous manorial estates in the Hudson Valley to Dutch, English, and Scottish friends who supported the new regime. Compared to the widespread distribution of land among the free white population in other British North American colonies, the land tenure system in New York remained downright medieval, elevating a small number of manor lords with special legal and economic privileges over their tenants.

Change came in earnest to the Hudson Valley during the 1690s, and ironically, a Dutchman was the catalyst. James II succeeded his brother to the English throne in 1685, but his Catholicism and absolutist politics got him into trouble with Parliament, whose opposition forced him to flee the country in 1688. Parliament offered the crown jointly to the Dutch prince William of Orange and his wife Mary, the daughter of James II. Besides his marriage, William's chief qualification for the throne was his Protestantism. His accession ended the Anglo-Dutch imperial rivalry that had divided the two powers since the 1650s and redirected England's military and naval resources against William's most powerful European enemy, Louis XIV of France. New York's long, unguarded frontier with Canada became a hot spot in Anglo-Dutch conflict with France. The War of the Grand Alliance (1688–1697) and the War of the Spanish Succession (1701–1713)—known in British North America as King William's War and Queen Anne's War, respectively—saw the first large-scale military mobilizations in the Hudson Valley, as Albany became the staging ground for attempted English invasions of Canada. What had been a commercial frontier of the seventeenth-century Dutch Empire became in the eighteenth century the most important military frontier in North America.

William and Mary's accession to the English throne also opened a new era in migration to New York. After Louis XIV revoked the Edict of Nantes in 1685, a tide of Protestant refugees left France in search of new homes, and many came to British North America. Approximately one thousand Huguenots, as these French-speaking Protestants were known, established themselves along the Hudson Valley in New York City, New Rochelle, and New Paltz.[18] Another group of migrants, the German-speaking "poor Palatines," arrived *en masse* in the colony in 1710. They had left their homelands in the Rhine River Valley to seek economic opportunity in North America, but rapacious officials and recruiting agents left them impoverished and stranded in London, where Daniel Defoe and other sympathizers depicted them in newspapers and pamphlets as Protestant victims of Louis XIV's aggression. With Queen Anne's approval, Governor Robert Hunter of New York arranged for three thousand of them to sail to New York, where he put them to work in the Hudson Valley, manufacturing pitch, tar, and other naval stores for British ships. The Palatines quickly became disenchanted and rebelled against the governor's scheme. Negotiating directly with nearby Indians, they purchased lands along the Mohawk and Schoharie Rivers and became the colony's western vanguard of colonial settlement.[19]

Scots and Scots-Irish joined this growing tide of migration into early eighteenth-century New York. The Anglo-Scottish Union of 1707 opened England's overseas empire to ambitious Scots, who found employment in the military and civilian colonial service. Robert Livingston, a Dutch-speaking Scot who had arrived in New York during the 1670s, blazed the trail for his countrymen, using his linguistic skills and political connections to acquire Livingston Manor in the mid-Hudson Valley. Other prominent Scots to leave their imprint on the colony's government and politics included the royal governors Robert Hunter and William Burnet and officeholders Archibald Kennedy and Cadwallader Colden. New York was hardly unique among British colonies for attracting so many well-educated Scottish émigrés, but the mark they left on the Hudson Valley, evident in the creation of Livingston Manor, the sponsorship of the Palatine migration, and Colden's surveying work for the colony, is undeniable. Having tied their economic and political fortunes to the British Empire, these Scottish officials aggressively pushed British expansion into the Mohawk Valley, breaking the control that Albany's Dutch magistrates had long held on land acquisition and relations with the Iroquois in that region. Scots-Irish Presbyterians, exiles from high rents and religious discrimination in Ireland, also came to New York. Wishing to avoid exploitive landlords in the New World, they settled on the west side of the Hudson and established Ulster and Orange counties. Adding to this mix from the British Isles, two Mohawk Valley landlords, Peter Warren and William Johnson, began sponsoring migration from their native Ireland to their estates during the 1740s.

These new arrivals reworked the ethnic mosaic of New York. Dutch-speaking descendants of New Netherland's original colonists were surrounded by British, German, and French neighbors by 1750.[20] Landlords and government officials promoted the Hudson and Mohawk Valleys to migrants from Europe and the Celtic regions of the British Isles as a land of economic opportunity. The biggest drag on migration remained the colony's unequal land distribution. Settlers who wished to own their land outright rather than renting it headed for New Jersey or Pennsylvania. Indentured servants and transported convicts from the British Isles typically arrived in the Chesapeake, where they served their time on the tobacco plantations of Maryland and Virginia. Most African slaves imported into British North America ended up in the southern colonies as well, although it is worth noting that the Hudson River was the most significant point of entry for slaves north of the Chesapeake. Dating back to the Dutch era, African slavery had taken firm root in New York City, and after the English conquest, it spread along the Hudson and Mohawk corridors, where Africans could be found working as field laborers and domestic servants. During the 1740s, free and enslaved Africans made up about fifteen percent of New York's population.[21]

A traveler's journal from a trip along the Hudson River in 1744 reflected these changes in the region. Dr. Alexander Hamilton was a Scottish doctor who undertook a tour of the northern colonies from his home in Annapolis, Maryland. With his keen eye and pen, he recorded many of the details that made the Hudson Valley a prosperous and distinctive place in British North America (Figure 10). The boat trip up the Hudson took several days, but it was hardly a journey into the heart of darkness. Along the way, Hamilton saw and often visited the homes of New York's leading families, including the DeLanceys, Philipses, Livingstons, Schuylers, and Van Rensselaers. Even a family living in a small log cottage showed signs of prosperity: although the couple and their seven children were "quite wild and rustic" in their appearance and manners, they were able to outfit their modest home with goods that displayed their participation in the Atlantic consumer economy—"a looking glass with a painted frame," pewter plates and spoons, and a "set of stone tea dishes, and a tea pot." Hamilton decried the "rough-sounding Dutch" he heard spoken throughout his trip, but his hosts in Albany also wined and dined him in style. He visited a Mohawk town on the Schoharie Creek, where he encountered Christian Mohawks who lived in wood and brick houses "built after the Dutch fashion." In Albany, he also met an old retired soldier named Scots Willie, an African who entertained him by playing the fiddle, and an "impudent fellow" who claimed to be Hamilton's Scottish countryman but then betrayed his Irish roots with his singing.[22] In a few days' travel through the Hudson Valley, Hamilton had come in contact with a multi-ethnic cross-section of colonial

Figure 10. Detail of the Van Bergen overmantel, circa 1729. *Image published by permission of the Fenimore Art Museum, New York State Historical Association, Cooperstown, New York.* This depiction of a prosperous Hudson Valley farm, with its European, African, and Native American figures populating the landscape, captures the human mosaic that this region had become by the mid-eighteenth century. Photograph by Richard Walker.

America. Some of the people he met were refined and others quite motley, but few places on his itinerary could have matched it in providing him with both material comforts and exotic strangeness.

Hamilton's trip up the Hudson coincided with the renewal of Anglo-French warfare on the New York-Canadian frontier. King George's War (1744–1748) and the French and Indian War (1754–1763) transformed this region, as New York became the seat of British operations against the French for control of North America. Despite the long peace between 1713 and 1744, the militarization of this borderland had continued apace as the French and British tried to pre-empt each other's claims to the Great Lakes region. The French, because of their previous explorations and expansive fur trade, enjoyed the advantage in this race, and they built a fortified trading post at the Niagara portage during the 1720s. The British responded with the construction of Oswego at the western terminus of the trade route between Albany and Lake Ontario. The fur trade's importance to New York's economy steadily declined during the eighteenth century, but as imperial tensions with France heated up, it became central to British designs for asserting possession of the continent's interior. In the long stretch of British colonies from Maine to Georgia, only the Hudson-Mohawk corridor offered a convenient route past the Appalachian Mountains. To lose it would mean conceding the entire Great Lakes, Ohio, and Mississippi watersheds to the French.

British imperialists such as Kennedy, Colden, and Johnson knew that the best way for the British to defeat the French was to imitate them. That meant extending the fur trade westward and establishing possession of key portages. During the French and Indian War, the British built Fort Stanwix at the Oneida Carrying Place to guard the route between Albany and Oswego. Likewise, they built Forts Edward and William Henry along the portage between the upper Hudson River and Lake Champlain. During the 1750s, thousands of British and provincial soldiers poured into the upper Hudson Valley, ending the isolation that had preserved Albany's distinctive Dutch character for almost a century after the English conquest. These armies left their own imprint on the cultural geography of the region. Military engineers built not only forts, but also roads and large watercraft to navigate rivers and lakes. Troops needed quarters and provisions, giving a boost to the building trades, local agricultural markets, and the distilling industry. They were also incubators for venereal diseases, smallpox, and other afflictions that spread easily to neighboring Native and colonial populations. Many soldiers never left the region. After being discharged from their service, they chose to stay (like Hamilton's Scots Willie), settling in Albany as tradesmen or on farms now made secure by the forts and roads they had helped build.[23]

After the fall of Québec in 1759, New York loomed even larger in Britain's imperial designs. Starting with Lord Loudoun in 1756 and continuing through Thomas Gage, successive commanders in chief of the British forces in North America made the Hudson Valley their base of operations, using Albany as a winter camp for their troops and relying on New York City's packet ships and post office to communicate with London and the other colonies. Not surprisingly, quartering of troops became one of the most incendiary issues in New York in the decade before the American Revolution. In the Mohawk Valley, Johnson worked as the king's Superintendent of Indian Affairs and made the Covenant Chain alliance with the Iroquois the focus of British Indian relations. Even the Anglican Church, for so long an underdeveloped branch of royal power and patronage in the colonies, made eighteenth-century New York a priority by funding missionaries to the Mohawk Indians and by trying to make King's College (modern Columbia University) its institutional and intellectual foundation in America. Thus, between 1744 and 1775, the English conquest of New Netherland finally came to fruition, as royal officials imposed a new imperial design on the old Anglo-Dutch commercial order. In military affairs, Indian relations, and matters of church and state, Britain remade New York into the cockpit of its North American dominion.[24]

New Netherland and the New Nation

It would seem then that the story of the Hudson River's colonization is best told as an epic passage from a commercial to a military frontier, from tentative origins as a corporate enterprise to great importance as a theater of war and seat of empire. That would be a fitting place to end our story if the Hudson Valley's connection to the outside world had not shifted again during the early nineteenth century.

As it had been during the Seven Years War, the Hudson-Mohawk corridor was crisscrossed by military campaigns during the American Revolution. American independence ended British rule in New York, but Canada was still within the empire and the Great Lakes remained a contested borderland in which Native Americans held the balance of power. Only after the War of 1812 did the New York frontier finally appear secure to the government of the new United States and its citizens. A few years after that conflict ended, construction began on the Erie Canal not far from where Fort Stanwix had once guarded the Oneida Carrying Place. The canal's route ran through the heart of what had once been Iroquois country, its Native inhabitants now either confined to reservations in the western part of the state or resettled in Canada.

When the full length of the canal opened for business in 1825, it connected the waters of Lake Erie and the Atlantic Ocean in a single, unbroken waterway, and sparked another dramatic transformation in the Hudson and Mohawk Valleys. Barges on the Erie Canal did not carry soldiers and artillery, and its locks were not guarded by forts and garrisons. Rather, the canal became the great commercial highway of the United States, ferrying people and goods back and forth between the Atlantic Ocean and the Great Lakes and helping to bind together the nation's Midwest and Northeast.[25]

In the plodding of mules along the Erie Canal's towpath, the ghost of New Netherland at last triumphed. In the towns that dotted the canal's route, thousands of businesses were launched and stock certificates issued. Canal traffic turned the Hudson River into the nation's main street of getting and spending, where everyone chased after what Washington Irving called the almighty dollar. The Dutch founders of New Netherland, satirized so mercilessly by Irving in his *Knickerbocker's History of New-York* (1809), had the last laugh after all.

Notes

1. See "From 'The Third Voyage of Master Henry Hudson,' by Robert Juet, 1610," in *NNN*, pp. 16–28. This excerpt from the Juet journal was recently reprinted with a new introduction by Daniel K. Richter in *Early American Studies* 7 (2009), pp. 426–441.

2. For Hudson's subsequent career and final voyage, see Peter C. Mancall, *Fatal Journey: The Final Expedition of Henry Hudson, A Tale of Mutiny and Murder in the Arctic* (New York: Basic Books, 2009).

3. Russell Shorto, *The Island at the Center of the World: The Epic Story of Dutch Manhattan and the Forgotten Colony that Shaped America* (New York: Doubleday, 2004). For a history of New Netherland from the perspective of the West India Company, see Oliver A. Rink, *Holland on the Hudson: An Economic and Social History of Dutch New York* (Ithaca, NY: Cornell University Press, 1986).

4. For more on the fabled purchase, see Peter Francis, Jr., "The Beads That Did Not Buy Manhattan Island," *New York History* 67, no. 1 (1986), pp. 5–22.

5. For an introduction to the Iroquois Confederacy and its affiliated native peoples, see Daniel K. Richter and James H. Merrell (eds.), *Beyond the Covenant Chain: The Iroquois and Their Neighbors in Indian North America, 1600–1800* (Syracuse, NY: Syracuse University Press, 1987).

6. *A Treaty, Held at the Town of Lancaster, in Pennsylvania, by the Honourable the Lieutenant-Governor of the Province, and the Honourable the Commissioners for the Provinces of Virginia and Maryland, with the Indians of the Six Nations, in June, 1744.* (Philadelphia, 1744), pp. 11–13.

7. On the river routes that shaped early American colonization, see D. W. Meinig, *The Shaping of America: A Geographical Perspective on 500 Years of History: Volume I: Atlantic America, 1492–1800* (New Haven, CT: Yale University Press, 1986), pp. 92–94, 109–131.

8. On the history of New France, see W. J. Eccles, *France in America* (New York: Harper and Row, 1972), and Allan Greer, *The People of New France* (Toronto: University of Toronto Press, 1997).

9. For a comprehensive social history of New Netherland, see Jaap Jacobs, *The Colony of New Netherland: A Dutch Settlement in Seventeenth-Century America* (Ithaca: Cornell University Press, 2009). For local studies of Albany and Schenectady, see, respectively Donna Merwick, *Possessing Albany, 1630–1710: The Dutch and English Experiences* (Cambridge: Cambridge University Press, 1990), and Thomas E. Burke, *Mohawk Frontier: The Dutch Community of Schenectady, 1661–1710* (Ithaca: Cornell University Press, 1991).

10. Harmen Meyndertsz van den Bogaert, *A Journey into Mohawk and Oneida Country, 1634–1635*, Charles T. Gehring and William A. Starna (eds. and trans.) (Syracuse: Syracuse University Press, 1988). For the French ethnographic tradition in travel writing about North America, see Gordon M. Sayre, *Les Sauvages Américains: Representations of Native Americans in French and English Colonial Literature* (Chapel Hill: University of North Carolina Press, 1997).

11. On Dutch cartographic depictions of New Netherland, see Benjamin Schmidt, "Mapping an Empire: Cartographic and Colonial Rivalry in Seventeenth-Century Dutch and English North America," *WMQ* 54 (1997), pp. 549–578.

12. Adriaen van der Donck, *A Description of New Netherland*, Charles T. Gehring and William A. Starna (eds.) (Lincoln, NE: University of Nebraska Press, 2008), pp. 5–15.

13. Van der Donck, *Description of New Netherland*, p. 11.

14. Rink, *Holland on the Hudson*, pp. 214–263.

15. See Michael Kammen, *Colonial New York: A History* (New York: Charles Scribner's Sons, 1975), p. 38.

16. Van der Donck, *Description of New Netherland*, p. 107.

17. On the "Flemish Bastard," see Timothy J. Shannon, *Iroquois Diplomacy on the Early American Frontier* (New York: Penguin Books, 2008), pp. 38–40.

18. On the Huguenot experience in New York, see Jon Butler, *The Huguenots in America: A Refugee People in New World Society* (Cambridge, MA: Harvard University Press, 1983), pp. 41–67, 144–198.

19. On the Palatine migration experience from the Rhine to the Hudson, see Philip Otterness, *Becoming German: The 1709 Palatine Migration to New York* (Ithaca: Cornell University Press, 2004).

20. For the changing ethnic composition of New York in the wake of the English conquest, see Joyce D. Goodfriend, *Before the Melting Pot: Society and Culture in Colonial New York City, 1664–1730* (Princeton, NJ: Princeton University Press, 1992).

21. On the experience of free and enslaved Africans in colonial New Netherland and New York, see Ira Berlin, *Many Thousands Gone: The First Two Centuries of Slavery in North America* (Cambridge, MA: Harvard University Press, 1998), pp. 47–63, 177–94. For white and black population statistics in eighteenth-century New York, see Milton Klein (ed.), *The Empire State: A History of New York* (Ithaca: Cornell University Press, 2001), pp. 150–151.

22. Carl Bridenbaugh (ed.), *A Gentleman's Progress: The Itinerarium of Dr. Alexander Hamilton, 1744* (Pittsburgh, PA: University of Pittsburgh Press, 1992 [1948]), pp. 54–55, 64–70.

23. For a good overview of the Anglo-French military contest in North America in the mid-eighteenth century, see Ian K. Steele, *Warpaths: Invasions of North America* (New York: Oxford University Press, 1994), pp. 175–247. For the uses of the fur trade as a tool of imperial expansion, see Thomas Elliot Norton, *The Fur Trade in Colonial New York, 1686–1776* (Madison, WI: University of Wisconsin Press, 1974). For an interesting study of the Seven Years War's impact on Albany, see

Justin DiVirgilio, "Rum Punch and Cultural Revolution: The Impact of the Seven Years War in Albany," *New York History* 86 (2005), pp. 435–449.

24. For the imperial management of military affairs, Indian relations, and the religious establishment in New York after the Seven Years' War, see, respectively, John W. Shy, *Toward Lexington: The Role of the British Army in the Coming of the American Revolution* (Princeton: Princeton University Press, 1965); Shannon, *Iroquois Diplomacy*, pp. 134–69; Patricia U. Bonomi, *Under the Cope of Heaven: Religion, Society, and Politics in Colonial America* (New York: Oxford University Press, 1986), pp. 199–209.

25. On the Erie Canal's impact on New York and the nation, see Carol Sheriff, *The Artificial River: The Erie Canal and the Paradox of Progress, 1817–1862* (New York: Hill and Wang, 1996).

5

Henry Hudson, the Munsees, and the Wampum Revolution[1]

Paul Otto

*L*ikely the first European to navigate much of the river that now bears his name, Henry Hudson initiated ongoing European-Native American contact in the Hudson River Valley in 1609.[2] As a result of his voyage, Dutch traders came to the region, followed by colonial officials, soldiers, settlers, and others. As with encounters throughout North America, European and Native American contact in the Hudson Valley meant profound changes for the Indigenous peoples. The Hudson Valley was home to Munsees, Mahicans, and Mohawks.[3] Living in the lower Hudson Valley, the Algonquian-speaking Munsees stood on the front lines of this European exploration, trade, and settlement.[4]

Those Munsees living on the coast held a unique position among the Indians of the Hudson Valley as makers of shell beads that are now commonly known as *wampum*. Like many other coastal dwellers on the mid-Atlantic shores, the Munsees manufactured shell beads, which in turn followed trade networks that brought the beads into the hands of Iroquoian speakers of the interior. But while wampum originated among Native people, its later development owes much to the intersection of European and Indian worlds. After the arrival of Europeans to North American shores between the Delaware and Narragansett Bays, Native-produced shell beads went from occasional production in small numbers to mass production in the hundreds of thousands. Wampum's nature, use, and application also evolved. These revolutionary changes to wampum accompanied changes in Munsee society that paralleled transformations experienced by Native Americans throughout coastal North America. Furthermore, these changes took place not simply as the result of intercultural contact, but also as a result of trans-Atlantic forces.

The Atlantic world comprised myriad relationships created by the intersection of peoples and economies from four continents tied together by transportation, communication, and commerce across the Atlantic Ocean, in which the wampum revolution can be understood, as historian David Armitage defines it. Indeed, Armitage's characterization of the study of "particular places as unique locations within an Atlantic world" that "seeks to define that uniqueness as the result of the interaction between local particularity and a wider web of connections (and comparisons)" ideally describes the context in which wampum evolved in the seventeenth century. Henry Hudson's voyage initiated sustained contact between the Dutch and the Munsees. It also brought together the Atlantic world exchange of goods and peoples and the Native wampum trade network, bringing profound changes to the Munsee people of the lower Hudson River Valley.[5]

The Munsees

Within a year or two of Hudson's voyage, the Dutch began exploiting trade opportunities in New York Bay, up the Hudson River, and along Long Island Sound. They soon expanded south to Delaware Bay and east to Narragansett Bay. Named "New Netherland" by the Dutch, this territory encompassed the lands of various Native Americans. These included those of the Algonquian language stock such as Unami speakers in the Delaware Bay region, the Munsee speakers of the lower Hudson River Valley including eastern New Jersey and western Long Island, and many others to the east including the Pequots and Narragansetts, to name two of the most well-known. Inland from the Unamis were the Susquehannocks of Iroquoian language stock and north of them the Mohawks, Onondagas, and other members of the Five Nations Iroquois. Neighbors to the east of the Mohawks and controlling the upper Hudson at the time of the English mariner's voyage were the Mahicans, another group of Algonquian-speaking Indians. The Hudson Valley, however, became the center of Dutch colonization, and thus to keep matters simple we can speak of three groups with whom the Dutch had primary and sustained contact—the Munsees, Mahicans, and Mohawks. Of these, the Munsees most profoundly experienced the impact of European colonization and played an important role in the wampum revolution. But the term Munsee should not be understood to mean a unified nation of Native people. Like most Native Americans, the Munsees functioned at various levels of social organization including the clan, the village, and larger groups. Grouping them as Munsees reflects only that they shared a common language and culture and, on occasion, acted in broad concert with one another. Most Munsee people would have understood their most important political organization to center on the extended family and village.

The Munsees shared many cultural characteristics with other Native people of the eastern woodlands with some local and regional variations. Their subsistence consisted of hunting, gathering, and horticulture that was typically accomplished through a pattern of seasonal migration. During the winter, villages would disperse into small hunting parties that tracked game in territories recognized by themselves and neighboring groups. In the spring, they might gather at river or ocean shores to harvest the bounty of those waterways and bodies. In their summer villages they planted crops such as corn, squash, and beans while taking advantage of the natural bounty offered through wild berries, nuts, and so forth. Being tied so closely to the land, Native people felt beholden to the spirits of the woods, animals, and elements that they sought to appease through various ceremonies and religious practices consistent with animistic beliefs. With their coastal neighbors, the Munsees also manufactured wampum.

Wampum

Highly valued among the Munsees and other Native people of New Netherland and surrounding region was wampum. Wampum is the shortened term of the Algonquian word *wampumpeague*, which means "a string of white [shell beads]."[6] Among the Dutch and the Munsees, wampum was commonly referred to as *sewant*, from the Munsee term *séewan* meaning "it is scattered" or "it's all over [the place]."[7] Native people throughout North America used a variety of shell products for diverse purposes, but a very specific form of bead—cylindrical in shape and manufactured from the coastal whelk[8]—emerged in the Northeast, particularly among Iroquoian speakers. Using stone tools, Northeastern Woodland Indians had manufactured various beads for thousands of years, but several hundred years ago there emerged cylindrical or tubular beads that became smaller in size, more uniform in shape, and more refined over time. At the time of contact, the manufacturers of wampum included the coastal Munsees and other Algonquian speakers in the region such as the Shinnecocks of eastern Long Island and the Pequots and the Narragansetts of coastal Connecticut and Rhode Island. According to Dutch and English observers at the time, these other Indian groups represented the major producers of wampum. However, the Munsee people living on western Long Island, Manhattan Island, Staten Island, and on the nearby mainland shores also made wampum.[9] Long Island became such a prominent place for wampum production that it was known as *Sewanhacky*, the land of *sewan*.[10]

Networks of exchange and trade existed throughout North America in the centuries prior to the encounter,[11] but the wampum exchange was especially noteworthy. For centuries, shell product and shell bead precursors to wampum had made their way to the land occupied by the Five Nations Iroquois.[12] Along the coasts of what would become New Jersey, New York, Connecticut, and Rhode Island, Algonquian peoples labored over the shells of Channeled Whelk and Knobbed Whelk—breaking, grinding, cutting, drilling, and polishing—crafting the beads that they traded to the Indians of the interior.

These beads held great spiritual and ceremonial significance for the Native peoples of New Netherland. The Munsees adorned themselves with wampum, employed it in marriage proposals, used it as an indication of social rank, and buried their dead with it.[13] But while coastal peoples manufactured and used wampum, it was much more highly valued by inland peoples, especially the Iroquois who received the shell beads in trade from its coastal producers. Wampum figures prominently in the Iroquois legends of the origins of their League in which Hiawatha discovered wampum and used it to soothe the angry spirit of the Onondaga sachem Tadadaho. Indeed, Hiawatha taught the Five Nations how to employ wampum in rituals created to unify the League.[14] European observers noted the importance of wampum in Iroquois ceremonies and inter-tribal diplomacy. One early observation of this was provided by Harmen Meyndertsz van den Bogaert. Journeying among the Oneidas in the winter of 1634–1635, he observed inter-tribal diplomacy first hand:

> In the evening the Indians hung up a belt of [wampum] and some other strung [wampum] that the chief had brought back from the French Indians as a token of peace that the French Indians were free to come among them.[15]

Finally, wampum's white color was key to Native appreciation of this sacred substance. As anthropologist George Hamell has described, wampum's white color reinforced positive social states of being since, for Indian people, "light, white and bright things are good to think."[16]

Dutch Discovery of Wampum

The earliest recorded observation of wampum in the Hudson River Valley comes from Henry Hudson's voyage. On 21 September 1609 and anchored in the vicinity of present-day Albany, Hudson and his crew received on board a group of Mahicans who were returning to the ship to care for their countryman who, heavily intoxicated by the crew's *aqua vitae*, had passed out there. They "came again, and brought stropes of Beades: some had sixe, seven, eight, nine, ten; and gave him," intending to heal or restore him. The ill Mahican spent the night aboard the vessel and his comrades came the next day, this time apparently seeking to ransom or somehow recover him. This time they "brought Tabacco, and more Beades, and gave them to our Master, and made an Oration, and shewed him all the Countrey round about." After this the man returned to his village, and Hudson and his crew continued downstream until a few days later when this man and another caught up with the *Halve Maen*, again came aboard, and "brought more stropes of Beades, and gave them to" Hudson.[17]

There is no evidence, however, that Hudson or his crew drew any lasting significance regarding wampum from this encounter or that the Dutch traders who sailed in his wake immediately sought to exploit the value Indians placed upon wampum. But by the end of the following decade it is clear that the Dutch had come to appreciate wampum's significance and may have learned of its value to the Indians several years earlier. Dutch traders followed Hudson's path a year or two later in their pursuit of North American furs. By the middle of the 1610s, European traders had explored the waters of Long Island Sound and the southern New England coast including Narragansett Bay—the heart of the wampum producing region.[18] In this era, Captain Adriaen Block produced his Carte Figurative, a map detailing coastal features, the location of principle Indian groups, and the broader geographic context of these geographic and ethnological discoveries, implying that Block and his fellow traders were well familiar with this important Native product.[19]

If the Dutch had not learned the importance of wampum in these earliest years, it is certainly clear that they had by 1620. In this year, the ship of Captain Willem Jorisz Hontom with supercargo Jacob Eelkens was nearly taken over by a group of Munsees on the Hudson River,[20] until they regained control running most of the Natives off and capturing "four of the most principal." They interrogated these to determine "the cause as to why they had such intentions against them" and then released them after the Indians paid a ransom with "a few *coraelen*," likely wampum beads.[21] Two years later Jacob Eelkens put to use his appreciation of wampum's value when he kidnapped a leader of the wampum-producing Sequins and held him in exchange for 140 fathoms of the shell beads.[22]

The other activities of Jacob Eelkens also indicate a growing appreciation by the Dutch for wampum's importance to Native people. Eelkens emerged at this time as a trader of some importance and had been among the first to establish contact with the Mohawks.[23] It appears that Eelkens learned of wampum production in the greater Long Island Sound region, discovered wampum's especial importance to the Mohawks and other Iroquois, and began to exploit this knowledge by initiating a two-stage trade process whereby the Dutch traded manufactured goods to coastal peoples for wampum and then exchanged the wampum to the Mahicans and Iroquois of the upper Hudson in exchange for furs.[24] This pattern was apparently repeated by Pieter Barentsz. Like Eelkens, he was active both on the upper Hudson and among the Pequots and other wampum producers. Employed by the West India Company, he served for a time overseeing trade at Fort Orange.[25] About the same time he negotiated an exclusive trade agreement with the "chief" of the "Sickenannes," apparently Tattobam of the Pequots, from whom he acquired wampum to trade to the Indians of the upper Hudson River.[26]

Thus when the West India Company established a permanent presence in North America in the mid-1620s, they stepped into a middle-man status in the wampum trade already established by earlier Dutch traders—wampum produced on the coastal regions was acquired with European goods and then traded to the interior for peltries. As one source described it, wampum was "the currency of the country, with which the produce of the interior is paid for."[27] Indeed, in correspondence from the late 1620s, colonial secretary Isaac de Rasière repeatedly pointed out the importance of wampum in the trade at Fort Orange. With the proper goods, he wrote, "I shall know how to get wampum and to stock Fort Orange." Wampum attracted not just the Native people in the vicinity of the outpost, but those from Canada as well, who, according to the secretary, "come to us for no other reason than to get wampum."[28]

Contact and Changes

Dutch intrusion into the land of the Munsees, Mahicans, and Mohawks, and insertion into their trade networks was not a simple matter of adding a middleman to an existing trade network. Instead, Dutch commercial activities in New Netherland led to a revolution in wampum production and to profound changes among the Munsees and other wampum producers.

For centuries, shell product and shell bead precursors of wampum had made their way into Iroquoia. By the mid-seventeenth century, however, there was an explosion of wampum production. Two sites inhabited by the Seneca (Iroquois) and dated to 1640–1675 have yielded a huge number of beads—at one site 100,000 beads and fifteen wampum belts have been found and at the other 250,000 beads and eight belts. If these are representative of what was happening throughout Iroquoia at the time, then wampum beads were being produced in the millions. Indeed, anthropologist Lynn Ceci has estimated that at least seven million beads were produced in eastern Long Island and the mainland opposite between 1634 and 1663.[29]

Native producers using traditional methods could not have wrought such massive bead output; important changes had been taking place in wampum production to make such results possible. In the first place, wampum producers quickly adopted new methods for manufacturing wampum. Documentary evidence tells us little about how Indians originally produced wampum, but it is clear that lithic tools formed the main component of their wampum production tool kits. Roger Williams, the founder of Rhode Island, wrote that the Indians in his neighborhood "made shift to bore this their shell money with stone."[30] The Dutch and other Europeans offered nails, awls, and other metal tools as well as whet stones that greatly facilitated the fabrication of wampum.[31] Even if stone tools could accomplish the same drilling as metal tools, as at least one archaeologist has suggested, the latter could be applied in more effective ways such as bow drilling or drilling, as one European observed, by sticking a "Nail . . . in a Cane or Reed" which "they roll . . . continually on their Thighs, with their Right-hand, holding the Bit of Shell with their Left."[32]

Not only did such tools change how wampum was produced and how much was produced, but the nature of wampum also changed to include dark as well as white shells. In popular conceptions, wampum is comprised of both white and dark (actually purple) beads.[33] But at the time of contact, dark cylindrical shell beads were virtually nonexistent—hence the meaning of the term *wampumpeague*. Documentary sources, some of which offer very specific commentary upon wampum, say nothing about cylindrical dark-colored beads before the 1630s.[34] Dark beads are also absent from the pictorial record before this time. For example, both the seal and coat of arms, adopted around 1630 by the West India Company for New Netherland include wampum strings and belts, but not dark beads. And while dark-colored discoidal beads can be found in archaeological settings before the 1630s, cylindrical dark beads can only be found in archaeological sites dated after this period.[35] Metal tools made possible the manufacture of dark beads because Native people could now craft cylindrical shell beads from the purple portions of the quahog clam shell,[36] which were harder and denser than the white whelk.[37]

Those familiar with wampum belts and popular images of wampum appreciate how significant this change was. Dark beads would now be employed to produce first geometric and then pictographic designs on belts and other wampum products. Picture, for instance, famous wampum belts such as the William Penn Great Treaty Belt that apparently depicts a colonist and Native American holding hands in friendship, the Great League Belt depicting the five Iroquois nations as white squares and a white tree on the a background of black beads, or the Washington Treaty Belt depicting thirteen men (the thirteen first states) holding hands with one another and with the Longhouse. Or, consider this description of a belt worn by Metacom, King Philip of the Wampanoags in the 1670s: it was "curiously wrought with wompom, being nine inches broad, wrought with black and white wompom in various figures and flowers, and pictures of many birds and beasts."[38] What is popularly assumed to be a unique Native product instead turns out to have resulted from the interaction of Native and Atlantic world economies.

As wampum evolved, so too did its use among Native Americans and Europeans. The Iroquois had traditionally used it in ceremonial giving and social exchange. The Dutch and other Europeans who sought to do business with the Five Nations learned the role of wampum in Native gift-giving exercises. Eventually, wampum became more prominent in negotiations with Native people while European envoys became more accommodating to Native ways. Thus, by the beginning of the eighteenth century, mutually accepted patterns of intercultural diplomacy emerged. In these, wampum functioned in several ways. First, it served ceremonial functions such as the Edge of the Woods rite. Second, it accompanied messengers and envoys as individual strings and beads were thought to carry specific messages. Third, and closely related to the previous reasons, wampum was used to "punctuate" the speeches each side made in their meetings. Finally, Europeans and Indians produced elaborate wampum belts employing alternating white and dark beads to create designs or pictographs memorializing the results of their agreements with each other.

Increased use of wampum in intercultural diplomacy and elsewhere depended not only upon the introduction of metal tools. The wampum producing labor force also increased. In particular, Native people became full-time producers of wampum, representing a major shift from traditional lifeways. Traditionally, wampum production had been a seasonal pastime, undertaken by coastal peoples during the winter months. But as the seventeenth century wore on it appears that wampum producers dedicated greater amounts of time to its manufacture. In the 1670s, for example, one Munsee man begged off from a request to guide a Dutch traveler explaining, "I will lose so much time in making *zeewant* [wampum]."[39]

This development was part of a larger shift in Munsee society that paralleled similar transformations among other Native Americans. These included the transition from subsistence-based economies and social exchange to market-based economies. Along with this economic transformation came a shrinking land base and economic dependency upon the Dutch. Where many small Munsee settlements had once existed, soon there would be fewer, more densely populated villages. In these communities, social stratification increased as evidenced by the more elaborate array of goods accompanying some Munsees (presumably leaders) in their graves. Such leaders may also have attained greater and more centralized authority over their people.[40]

One case serves to demonstrate the important shifts taking place—the experience of Long Island Munsee leader, Tackapousha.[41] Hemmed in by the English and the Dutch, experiencing defeats during the First Dutch-Munsee War, suffering losses from European-borne diseases, and possibly falling into some tributary status to the Indians of eastern Long Island and the Narragansetts, Tackapousha and his people drew increasingly close to the Dutch in the 1650s and 1660s. Among the Dutch they sought both economic and military security. Believing the best hope for survival lay in building alliances with Europeans, Tackapousha pledged to support the Dutch in the Second Dutch-Munsee War and committed Native auxiliaries to aid the Dutch in the Third Dutch-Munsee War.

Significantly, in 1656, Tackapousha accepted Dutch Director-General Petrus Stuyvesant's offer to "build a house or fort upon such place as they shall show." This structure would not just provide for the Long Island Indians' military defense, but would also be "furnished with Indian trade goods or commodities." Although not identified with absolute certainty, this structure was likely Fort Massapeag whose remains are buried in a park in the town of Massapequa in southern Long Island, which archaeological evidence has demonstrated to have been a center for wampum manufacture and exchange to the Dutch for European goods. Diminished in numbers, alienated from much of their original lands, and largely dependent upon European goods, Tackapousha's people clung to traditional activities such as wampum production, but these were increasingly structured and shaped by the economic forces that accompanied Dutch colonization of their lands. Tackapousha and his people became full-time wampum producers, supplying not just the local economy, but becoming integrated into the larger Atlantic world.

Ongoing demand created by these forces led to increased production in other ways as well. Not only did many Native people turn to year-round production, they also increased their number of producers. Archaeological evidence from Narragansett Bay, for example, indicates that while wampum production had once been restricted to men, women had joined the craft by the mid-seventeenth century.[42]

The demand for wampum that drove the coastal Algonquians and others to increase their production did not come just from Iroquoian interest. Wampum had soon become the currency of New Netherland and New England. Both colonies were cash poor and naturally sought some means to complete financial transactions as they would in Europe. Both beaver skins and wampum emerged in New Netherland as currency. While both had been commodities in inter-Indian trade before European contact, they were now transformed into currency—items of universal exchange value. "No gold or silver circulates here," wrote Dutch resident Nicasius de Sille, "but beads, which the Indians make and call seawant. . . . We can buy everything with it and gladly take it in payment."[43] Throughout the records we see evidence of wampum being paid to purchase goods and services, to satisfy fines, and to fulfill debt obligations.[44] From the 1620s until the 1670s, the English and Dutch relied heavily upon wampum as their colonial currency.

With the European discovery of wampum and its growing importance in the fur trade and as a local currency already in the 1630s, Europeans began to vie for control of the rich resource. Although wampum was produced throughout coastal New Netherland, the wampum mother lode, as it were, could be found on the mainland between the Connecticut Valley and Narragansett Bay and on eastern Long Island. This was territory in which the Dutch had originally explored and trafficked for wampum and furs. However, within a few short years of Plymouth's discovery of wampum (after being introduced to it by the Dutch) and after the founding of Massachusetts Bay, the English went to war against the Pequots, the Native tribe at the center of power in this wampum-rich region. Whatever else may have been the cause of the war, control of the wampum trade doubtless played a role.[45] By the war's end, the Pequots were vanquished and the English became the masters of the central source of wampum. This had important implications for the Dutch and their wampum-producing neighbors, the Munsees. These implications have not been fully explored, but at the very least it seems that the loss of richer wampum resources increased Dutch demand for wampum output among the Munsees.[46] This in turn led to an expansion of the Dutch into coastal Munsee territories seeking greater access to wampum through trade or control of its production.[47]

As those colonies and their economies matured, and as specie began to flow more freely through European hands, wampum's importance to Europeans as currency in the late-seventeenth century diminished. Nevertheless, it continued to play an important role in the fur trade and in frontier diplomacy, continuing a demand that would be satisfied, in part, through the Atlantic world market. In the first place, European men and women took up the craft. For example, court records in New Amsterdam from the 1660s reveal that Dutch women were actively involved in the making and stringing of wampum beads.[48] Furthermore, after the Pequot War, when the English dominated the main source of domestic shells on eastern Long Island, the Dutch were forced to look elsewhere for raw materials, and they began to import shell from the West Indies.[49] By the eighteenth century, virtually all wampum production was undertaken by Europeans, using both local clam and imported conch shells. Some of this manufacture took place in the shops of artisans, some by orphans and widows, but eventually most of it would be produced in small-scale factories such as the Campbell operations in New Jersey.[50]

Atlantic World

In several ways, the history of Dutch-Munsee interaction and the evolution of wampum, while unique to the American geographic context, also owes something to the broader Atlantic world context in which these developments took place. The most obvious is the extension of European trade that brought demand for American furs and European-manufactured goods to pay for them. Of course, in the case of wampum, the fur trade stimulated wampum production that was in turn facilitated by the European goods that paid for and made the wampum. In other ways, too, the wampum revolution was a product of its Atlantic context. It has been argued, for example, that the Dutch, who learned so quickly to exploit the trade in wampum were primed to do so by their experience with the trade in cowry shells in west Africa. It is even suggested that the Dutch proactively turned wampum into a local currency.[51] Whether or not the Dutch intentionally transformed wampum into currency, its economic transformation was necessarily a result of the Atlantic connection of European and Native American worlds. Furthermore, as demand for wampum continued and after the Dutch lost access to the major source of wampum in New England and eastern Long Island, they turned to other sources of shells—the West Indies. Wampum production, then, came to depend in various ways on Atlantic exchanges—first the metal tools and whet stones that facilitated its manufacture, then the introduction of Dutch and other European labor, and finally the importation of raw materials from elsewhere in the Atlantic world.

The Atlantic world context of many colonial developments is often taken for granted, but connections across the sea and between the lands on the Atlantic's multiple shores significantly shaped events in New Netherland. Had a handful of Europeans come to the lands of the Munsees simply to establish themselves in permanent agricultural communities without any economic and commercial connections to Europe, Africa, and the Caribbean, it is hardly conceivable that wampum would have evolved in the explosive way it did. But instead, Dutch and other Europeans came as traders, adventurers, entrepreneurs, and settlers—many with connections beyond the limits of the Hudson Valley and across the waters of the Atlantic. Their connections—commercial, religious, social, political, cultural—to the Dutch Fatherland, to the West Indies, and to Africa helped connect North America with peoples, structures, and lands across the Atlantic. Not all of these contributed to the evolution of wampum in the seventeenth century, but it was in the context of these connections that wampum did evolve. Adjusting our perspective as we consider intercultural relations in North America in light of the Atlantic world helps us see qualities of the encounter made unique by these Atlantic connections and which would not have existed apart from them.

This Atlantic context meant a change in perspective for the Munsees themselves. While wampum continued to flow from the coast to the interior, the Munsees, who were once oriented toward the interior, had become re-oriented to the Atlantic from whence came the goods that they valued so highly and needed so much to continue their production of wampum.[52] Whether or not they fully appreciated this change, it nonetheless took place. Wampum, once a product of Native North America, became a product of intercultural, Atlantic-world forces, and the traditional wampum producers—including the Munsees—became participants of this broader Atlantic world.

Notes

1. Part of the research for this essay was conducted at the Henry E. Huntington Library in San Marino, California, with the support of an Andrew Mellon fellowship. My thanks to the Pacific Northwest Early Americanist Workshop, hosted by Richard Johnson, for their constructive feedback on my wampum research. Finally, anthropologist George Hamell continues to provide me with gracious encouragement and support for which I am very grateful.

2. Paul Otto, *The Dutch-Munsee Encounter in America: The Struggle for Sovereignty in the Hudson Valley* (New York: Berghahn Books, 2006), pp. 34–46, 49n.

3. The Munsees were not a tribe in the traditional sense of the word. The term refers linguistically to the people of the lower Hudson Valley who also shared much culturally and, at times, acted with a degree of political cohesion. The latest work on the Munsees is Robert Grumet, *The Munsee Indians: A History* (Norman, OK: University of Oklahoma Press, 2009).

4. In *The Dutch-Munsee Encounter in America*, I survey the history of Dutch-Munsee interaction in three frontier stages—first contact, trade, settlement.

5. Armitage, "Three Concepts of Atlantic History," in idem and Michael J. Braddick (eds.), *The Briish Atlantic World, 1500–1800*, pp. 15, 21–25 (London: Palgrave, 2002). Or, as he puts it elsewhere, it is "the history of any particular place—a nation, a state, a region, even a specific institution—in relation to the wider Atlantic world."

6. For this survey of wampum I generally draw on many secondary sources including George Hamell, "Wampum: Light, White, and Bright Things Are Good to Think," in Alexandra van Dongen (ed.), *One Man's Trash is Another Man's Treasure* (Rotterdam, Neth.: Museum Boymans-van Beuningen, 1995), pp. 41–51; and Lynn Ceci, "Native Wampum as a Peripheral Resource in the Seventeenth-Century World-System," in Laurence M. Hauptman and James D. Wherry (eds.), *The Pequots in Southern New England: The Fall and Rise of an American Indian Nation* (Norman, OK: University of Oklahoma Press, 1990), pp. 48–64.

7. Ives Goddard, e-mail correspondence with author, 18 May 2010.

8. Busycon c. (Channeled Whelk) and other species.

9. Isaac de Rasière to Samuel Blommaert, in *NNN*, p. 103; Alanson Skinner, "Exploration of Aboriginal Sites at Throgs Neck and Classon's Point, New York City," *Contributions from the Museum of the American Indian*, Heye Foundation 5, no. 4 (1919), pp. 65–66; Jerome Jacobson, *Burial Ridge: Archaeology at New York City's Largest Prehistoric Cemetery* (St. George, NY: Staten Island Institute of Arts and Sciences, 1980), p. 64; John H. Morice, "Long Island's Indian Deeds," *Long Island Forum* 12, no. 7 (1949), p. 123. Native people in the mid-Hudson valley also manufactured wampum, see Joseph E. Diamond, "Terminal late Woodland/early Contact period in the Mid-Hudson Valley" (PhD diss., State University of New York at Albany, 1999), pp. 169–173. Lynn Ceci argues that wampum was originally made by the Senecas using shell or semi-processed shells imported from the coastal regions, "Tracing Wampum's Origins: Shell Bead Evidence from Archaeological Sites in Western and Coastal New York," in Charles F. Hayes III and Lynn Ceci (eds.), *Proceedings of the 1986 Shell Bead Conference, Selected Papers*, pp. 63–80 (Rochester, NY: Rochester Museum and Science Center, 1989).

10. Robert S. Grumet, *Native American Place Names in New York City* (New York: Museum of the City of New York, 1981), p. 55.

11. William A. Turnbaugh, "Wide-Area Connections in Native North America," *American Indian Culture and Research Journal* 1, no. 4 (1976), pp. 22–28.

12. Ceci, "Tracing Wampum's Origins," pp. 63–80. That wampum or something similar that preceded it had a long history among Iroquoian speakers is attested to by Gunther Michelson in "Iroquoian Terms for Wampum," *International Journal of American Linguistics* 57, no. 1 (1991), pp. 108–131.

13. This claim is based on documentary evidence, De Rasière to Blommaert, in *NNN*, pp. 106, 109; David de Vries, "Korte Historiael," in *NNN*, p. 224. It may be that archaeological evidence does not support extensive use among the Munsees, but this needs to be looked into further.

14. Daniel K. Richter, *The Ordeal of the Longhouse: The Peoples of the Iroquois League in the Era of European Colonization* (Chapel Hill, NC: University of North Carolina Press, 1992), pp. 38–48.

15. Harmen Meyndertsz van den Bogaert, *A Journey into Mohawk and Oneida Country, 1634–1635: The Journal of Harmen Meyndertsz van den Bogaert*, Charles Gehring and William Starna (eds. and trans.) (Syracuse, NY: Syracuse University Press, 1988), p. 14.

16. Hamell, "Wampum," pp. 41, 47, 51. Similar color symbolism was important among the Munsees, Lynn Marie Pietak, "Body Symbolism and Cultural Aesthetics: The Use of Shell Beads and Ornaments by Delaware and Munsee Groups," *North American Archaeologist* 19, no. 2 (1998), pp. 135–161, and "Bead Color Symbolism among Post-Contact Delaware and Munsee Groups," *Journal of Middle Atlantic Archaeology* 15 (1999), pp. 3–20.

17. Robert Juet, "The Third Voyage of Master Henry Hudson," in *NNN*, pp. 23–24.

18. Reports by these merchant seafarers became the basis for the earliest extant descriptions of New Netherland and its inhabitants. While not specifically mentioning wampum, these descriptions provided detailed information about the geography and inhabitants of the territories that we now know were rich wampum production regions.

19. Johannes de Laet, "New World," in *NNN*, pp. 41–44; Nicolaes van Wassenaer, "Historisch Verhael," February 1624, in *NNN*, pp. 61–96; Adriaen Block, Carte Figurative, 1614, Nationaal Archief, Den Haag, Verzameling Buitenlandse Kaarten Leupe, number 4, VEL, inventory number 520.

20. Or so the crew reported.

21. We know of this account because the crew, having risked their lives in this voyage, made a claim against the ship owners for the value of the *coraelen*. While this term was used by the Dutch to refer to various kinds of beads, the context here invites the interpretation that these were wampum beads and that the Dutch sailors recognized their value to the Indians. Stadsarchief Amsterdam, Notarial Archives 200, 14 August 1620, fol. 625–626v.

22. Van Wassenaer, "Historisch Verhael," November 1626, p. 86. Later scholars have identified this kidnapped sachem as Tattobam, leader of the Pequots, Kevin A. McBride, "The Source and Mother of the Fur Trade: Native-Dutch Relations in Eastern New Netherland," in Laurie Weinstein (ed.), *Enduring Traditions: The Native*

Peoples of New England (Westport, CT: Bergin and Garvey, 1994), p. 36; Alfred A. Cave, *The Pequot War* (Amherst, MA: University of Massachusetts Press, 1996), p. 50.

23. Daniel K. Richter, "Rediscovered Links in the Covenant Chain: Previously Unpublished Transcripts of New York Indian Treaty Minutes, 1677–1691," *Proceedings of the American Antiquarian Society* 92 (1982), pp. 49–55, idem, *The Ordeal of the Longhouse*, pp. 87–89, William A. Starna, "Retrospecting the Origins of the League of the Iroquois," *American Philosophical Society* 152, no. 3 (Sept 2008), pp. 279–321 at 301–305, 307–308. Starna goes so far as to suggest that Eelkens was somehow tied to the formation of the Iroquois League of the Longhouse.

24. Although no documentary evidence is yet known that supports this claim, it is a reasonable hypothesis.

25. After Daniel van Krieckenbeeck's death and before Bastiaen Jansz Krol became superintendent.

26. Van Wassenaer, pp. 85–86; McBride, "Source and Mother," p. 38. While the sources do not say what goods the Pequots offered, corollary evidence would indicate that the Pequots were becoming a major source of wampum to the Dutch.

27. "Patroon's Claim, 1634," in John B. Linn and William H. Egle (eds.), *Papers Relating to the Colonies on the Delaware, 1614–1682* (Harrisburg, PA, 1890), p. 42.

28. Isaac de Rasière to the Directors of the Amsterdam chamber, 23 September 1626, in A. J. F. van Laer (ed. and trans.), *Documents Relating to New Netherland, 1624–1626, in the Henry E. Huntington Library* (San Marino, CA, 1924), pp. 223–228.

29. Ceci, "Wampum as a Peripheral Resource," pp. 50, 61.

30. Roger Williams, *A Key into the Language of America*, John J. Teunissen and Evelyn J. Hinz (eds.) (Detroit. MI: Wayne State University Press, 1973), p. 213.

31. Evidence for the first or earliest arrival of awls is unfortunately hard to come by. A survey of the earliest records noting trade goods do not identify awls among the products exchanged for native products. This is based upon research in the Notarial Archives of the Stadsarchief Amsterdam. These records are one of the few sources covering the 1610s, but do not provide comprehensive coverage of the events of the period since they were produced in the context of lawsuits, business agreements, etc. Margriet de Roever used these sources (but perhaps not exhaustively) for her essay "Merchandises for New Netherland: A Look at Dutch Articles for Barter with the Native American Population," in idem, *One Man's Trash*. She itemizes the "goods destined for North America and listed in the records prior to the found of the WIC" in 1621. These included "linen, broadcloth and yarn, leather and velvet, axes, buttons, beads, bread and cheese, kettles, adzes and knives." She does not identify awls. I have looked at several of these sources myself but my own notes, taken when I was not particularly focusing on the manufacture of wampum, do not include any references to wampum. A thorough examination of the notarial records is necessary to gain a clearer picture of when tools for wampum production were first exported to New Netherland. However, even such research will not lead to firm conclusions since the records themselves do not provide a complete picture of the trade goods exported at the time. Awls are eventually recorded in the documentary sources such as

records of land transactions: Charles T. Gehring (trans. and ed.), *New York Historical Manuscripts: Dutch, Volumes GG, HH, & II. Land Papers* (Baltimore. MD: Genealogical Publishing Co., 1980), pp. 8, 63; Morice, "Long Island's Indian Deeds," pp. 124, 136; Morice, "Indian Deeds of Oyster Bay Town," *Long Island Forum* 13, no. 1 (1950), p. 4; Morice, "Some Old Indian Deeds," *Long Island Forum* 10, no. 11 (1947), p. 215; John Cox, Jr., *Oyster Bay Town Records, vol. 1—1653–1690* (New York, 1916), p. 334, and *Oyster Bay Town Records, vol. 2—1691–1704* (New York, 1924), p. 354. Archaeological evidence also records the appearance of European tools in some manufacturing sites, at least in Narragansett territory, William S. Simmons, *Cautantowit's House: An Indian Burial Ground on the Island of Conanicut in Narragansett Bay* (Providence, RI; Brown University Press, 1970), pp. 44–46, 138; Paul A. Robinson, "The Struggle Within: The Indian Debate in Seventeenth Century Narragansett Country" (Ph.D. diss., State University of New York at Binghamton, 1990), pp. 281–290.

32. Personal Communication, Kevin McBride to author, 12 August 2009; John Lawson, *A New Voyage to Carolina*, Hugh Talmage Lefler (ed.) (Chapel Hill: University of North Carolina Press, 1973), p. 204.

33. For example, a graphic representation of Van den Bogaert's journal cited above portrays the wampum belt brought by the "French Indians" as uncommonly large—it appears to be at least two feet by eight feet—it including connected black diamonds as wide as the belt. Such large belts never existed and the black beads, which made such belts possible, were only just coming into use in the 1630s, George O'Connor, *Journey into Mohawk Country* (New York: First Second, 2006), p. 92.

34. The solid documentary reference to dark beads comes from 1633 when John Winthrop noted the return of a Puritan vessel from Long Island where "they had store of the best wamponp[ea]k bothe white & blewe," Richard S. Dunn, James Savage, and Laetitia Yeandle (eds.), *Journal of John Winthrop* (Cambridge: Belknap Press of Harvard University Press, 1996), p. 98.

35. As James W. Bradley points out, however, non-white cylindrical beads could be created from whelk shells depending upon the conditions in which the sea snails lived. "Re-Visiting Wampum and Other Seventeenth-Century Shell Games," *Archaeology of Eastern North America* 39 (2011), pp. 25–26.

36. *Mercenaria mercenaria*.

37. George Hamell, e-mail correspondence, 5 November 2008, 12 July 2009. The quahog clam is also known as the hard clam or hard-shell clam, among many other names.

38. Mary Simpson (ed.), *Benjamin Church, Diary of King Philip's War 1675–1676* (Chester, CT: Pequot, 1975), p. 170.

39. Bartlett Burleigh James and J. Franklin Jameson (eds.), *Journal of Jasper Danckaerts, 1679–1680* (New York: Barnes and Noble, 1969 [1913]), p. 57.

40. Lynn Ceci, "The Effect of European Contact and Trade on the Settlement Patterns of the Coastal Indians of New York, 1524–1665: The Archaeological and Documentary Evidence" (PhD diss., Queens College, City University of New York: 1977), pp. 226–276, Otto, *The Dutch-Munsee Encounter in America*, passim.

41. Information for this and the following paragraph comes from Ralph S. Solecki and Robert S. Grumet, "The Fort Massapeag Archaeological Site National Historic Landmark," *The Bulletin, Journal of the New York Archaeological Association* 108 (1994), pp. 18–28; Solecki, "Recent Field Inspections of Two Seventeenth-Century Indian Forts on Long Island, Forts Massapeag and Corchaug," *Bulletin and Journal of Archaeology for New York State* 91 (1985), pp. 26–31; Solecki, "The Rescue of Fort Massapeag," *Cultural Resource Management* 18, no. 7 (1995), pp. 30–34.

42. Simmons, *Cautantowit's House*, p. 46; Michael S. Nassaney, "Native American Gender Politics and Material Culture in Seventeenth-Century Southeastern New England," *Journal of Social Archaeology* 4 (2004), pp. 334–367 at 349; Robinson, "The Struggle Within," pp. 281–286. There is some ambiguity in the sources regarding women's role. For example, in seeming contrast to this interpretation, Roger Williams reported the reluctance of "old & poore women" to use European tools for wampum production since they were "fearfull to leave the old tradition," possibly suggesting that women had always been involved in its manufacture. It is not clear, however, whether his comments indicate that women had always made wampum beads or if, having begun to put their hand to its manufacture, they were afraid of also adopting new techniques, Williams, *A Key*, p. 213.

43. A. J. F. van Laer (ed.), "Letters of Nicasius de Sille, 1654," *Quarterly Journal of the New York State Historical Association* 1, no. 3 (1920), pp. 98–108 at 102.

44. Otto, *Dutch-Munsee Encounter*, pp. 91–92, 110, 139–140, 169.

45. Ceci, "Wampum as a Peripheral Resource," pp. 60–61.

46. It is easy to imagine, although not readily supportable, that the Dutch initiated the First Dutch-Munsee War (Kieft's War) as a means to acquire greater control over local wampum resources by turning the Munsees into wampum-paying tributaries as the English had to the Pequots, Narragansetts, and others.

47. Ceci, "Effect of European Contact," pp. 226–234.

48. *RNA*, 5:176.

49. Ibid.; Charles T. Gehring (trans. and ed.), *Curaçao Papers, 1640–1665* (Interlaken. MI: Heart of the Lakes Publishing, 1987), pp. 138, 139, 169, 201, 214, 218.

50. Elizabeth S. Peña, "The Role of Wampum Production at the Albany Alms-house," *International Journal of Historical Archaeology* 5 (2001), pp. 155–174; Adolph B. Benson (ed.), *Peter Kalm, Travels in North America*, 2 vols. (New York: Dover Publications, 1966 [1937]), 1:129; Charles E. Hanson, Jr., "Campbell Wampum," *Museum of the Fur Trade Quarterly* 21, no. 4 (1985), pp. 2–6. German immigrants worked in the Campbell factory in the nineteenth century; Johann Georg Kohl, *Kitchi-Gami: Life among the Lake Superior Ojibway*, Lascelle Wraxall (trans.), with introduction by Robert E. Bieder and additional translation Ralf Neufang and Urike Bocker (St. Paul. MN: Minnesota Historical Society Press, 1985 [London, 1860]), p. 135.

51. Elizabeth Shapiro Peña, "Wampum Production in New Netherland and Colonial New York: The Historical and Archaeological Context" (PhD diss., Boston University, 1990), p. 50; Peña, "Role of Wampum Production," p. 159.

52. In fact, throughout New Netherland's history, several Munsee people were forcibly transported into various quarters of the Atlantic world. An Indian named Jacques, for example, was transported to Amsterdam during the First Dutch-Munsee War while Indian captives taken during the Third Dutch-Munsee War were exiled to Curaçao, Otto, *Dutch-Munsee Encounter*, pp. 119, 152; Alden T. Vaughan, *Transatlantic Encounters: American Indians in Britain, 1500–1776* (New York: Cambridge University Press, 2006), pp. 102–104.

6

Separate Vessels

Iroquois Engagements with the Dutch of New Netherland, c. 1613–1664

Jon Parmenter

Abstract

*P*ersistent Anglocentric biases in North American historiography have obscured the unique texture of Iroquois engagements with Dutch traders and settlers in New Netherland. Taking as a point of departure the terms of a controversial circa 1613 agreement negotiated between visiting Dutch traders and Mohawk leaders, this paper analyzes documentary and archaeological evidence and sheds new light on the ways in which the idea of *kaswentha*, an Iroquois-conceived model of mutually beneficial intergroup relations represented by a Two Row wampum belt, shaped Dutch exchanges with their Iroquois neighbors from the era of initial direct contact to the English conquest of 1664.

Introduction: The Tricentennial

Native Americans occupied a curious position in the 28 September 1909 Hudson-Fulton parade in Manhattan that commemorated both Henry Hudson's voyage of 1609 and the one-hundredth anniversary of Robert Fulton's invention of the commercial paddle steamer. Categorized as neither "old families of New York," nor "members of the leading patriotic and hereditary societies," or one of the multiple "nationalities composing the cosmopolitan population of the state," Native Americans were defined ambiguously as "other nations," and marched behind the members of various ethnic societies in the order of procession, marking, it would seem, their ineligibility for hyphenated-American status.[1] Nevertheless, it is clear that the organizers of the parade paid significant attention to how they wished to see Native peoples portrayed:

> The aboriginal possessors of New York State were represented by 70 real Iroquois Indians—men, women, and children—who were secured for the Commission by Mr. F. E. Moore, and who took the characters on the floats representing the Indian period. These Indians, dressed in their picturesque Native costumes, and still speaking the language of their ancestors, were the objects of intense interest alike to the American spectators and to the official representatives of foreign nations at the [parade's] Court of Honor, before whom they executed a ceremonial dance.[2]

The Hudson-Fulton Commemoration parade featured 54 floats that aimed to provide "by moving tableaux memorable scenes in the history of the City and State for public education and entertainment." Divided into five historical periods (Indian, Dutch, English, American, and Modern), the Indian period consisted of just ten floats (the fewest allotted to any era), but the Iroquois contingent involved in the parade used the opportunity to emphasize representations of the traditional founding of the Iroquois League and of their agricultural heritage and hunting techniques. These scenes stressed Iroquois peoples' connectedness to, and capacity for freedom of movement on, their homelands—assertions of nationhood that seem clear in retrospect (if perhaps not to the 1909 audience) and that stood in stark contrast to the carceral status they then endured on the state's reservations.[3]

Once the parade ended, the Iroquois performers remained in New York for another week offering ceremonial dances at the dedications of various parks and historical monuments. Edward Hagaman Hall, chair of the Hudson-Fulton Commemoration Commission, was at pains to assure the crowds that the performers were "real Indians," not "white people painted up for this occasion," and he defended his selection of exclusively Iroquois performers on the grounds that their ancestors were "the controllers of the Indians who lived on these [i.e., Manhattan, Long, and Staten] Islands," a longstanding historical myth deployed for its power to impress contemporary audiences.[4] The pinnacle moment for the Iroquois in the Hudson Tricentennial came at

Figure 11. Hudson-Fulton Tricentennial Parade Float, "The Indian Period" from Edward Hagaman Hall, *The Hudson-Fulton Celebration 1909: The Fourth Annual Report of the Hudson-Fulton Celebration Commission to the Legislature of the State of New York, Transmitted to the Legislature May twentieth, nineteen ten* (2 vols., Albany, 1910), 2:629.

the "Naval Fete" held at Columbia University on 2 October 1909; here, their agent, one Frank E. Moore of Middletown, Ohio (an amateur photographer and promoter of historical reenactments involving Native people):

> appeared, dressed in the style of Henry Hudson's time and imper-
> sonating the Navigator, and, walking toward the Indians, extend-
> ed to them a friendly greeting. Sitting down in their midst, he
> solemnly accepted the pipe of peace, and offered as gifts strings
> of bright colored beads, which were received with manifestations
> of delight and which were passed from hand to hand. For a
> moment, those who could forget their very modern surroundings
> were transported back to the far away past.[5]

While the official report of the commission offers no hint of the degree of agency the Iroquois performers exercised over the content of their appearances, we ought to allow for at least the strong possibility that those Iroquois

Figure 12. Iroquois Performers at the Columbia Lawn Fete from Hall, *The Hudson–Fulton Celebration 1909*, 2:711.

performers in 1909 sought to make manifest another very "far away" moment, one that articulated their memory of their relationship with the Dutch, and that would later serve as a diplomatic blueprint for their foreign relations with other European colonizers.[6] The scene may seem patronizing at first glance (Indians "delighted by trinkets") and historically challenged to boot (no Iroquois are known to have met Hudson, whose famous 1609 voyage did not penetrate as far north as the eastern limits of their ancestral homelands in the Mohawk River Valley, west of modern Albany).[7] Yet everything else about the Iroquois presence in the 1909 commemoration suggests a consciousness on their part of the legacy of *kaswentha*, a Mohawk term denoting the ideal character of Iroquois relations with other nations, and rooted in their memory of early interactions with the Dutch. Indeed, the representation of separate Iroquois nationhood in the parade, the selection of content in the floats, and the reenactment of the scene with Moore in the role of Hudson, all combine to reveal that consciousness, even if it was effectively hidden in plain sight.

This essay reverses the usual trajectory of "colonial" history, in which settlers arrive and act, and Native people subsequently react.[8] It seeks instead to reconstruct the entangled state of cross-cultural relations that prevailed in Hudson's wake in what is now New York. The essay also contends that our understanding of the character of early Dutch relations with the Iroquois is greatly enriched by an integration of Iroquois oral tradition with the bodies of evidence more commonly employed by historians (such as documents and archaeological data). Such an approach facilitates an appreciation of history-as-lived for all parties concerned, and that appreciation is the first step toward an escape from the persistent colonial mindset that emphasizes the effects of colonization on Native peoples to the exclusion of any consideration of the ways in which Native polities shaped the experience of settler colonies in early North America.[9]

The Idea of *Kaswentha*

Kaswentha, for the purposes of this essay, may best be understood as an Iroquois symbol for the ongoing negotiation of their relationship to European colonizers and their descendants; depicted in material form as a long beaded belt of white wampum with two parallel lines of purple wampum along its length—the lines symbolize the distinct identity of the two peoples and a mutual engagement to coexist in peace without interference in the affairs of the other. Thus, *kaswentha* signifies a separate-but-equal relationship between two entities based on mutual benefit and mutual respect for freedom of movement—the spatial metaphor bound up in *kaswentha* asserts that neither side may attempt to "steer" the vessel of the other as it travels along its own, self-determined path.[10] A nineteenth-century French dictionary of the Mohawk language defines the very word for wampum belt (*kahionni*) as a human-made symbol emulating a river, due in part to its linear form and in part to the way in which its constituent shell beads resemble ripples and waves. Just as a navigable water course facilitates mutual relations between nations, thus does *kahionni*, "the river formed by the hand of man," serve as a sign of "alliance, concord, and friendship" that links "divergent spirits" and provides a "bond between hearts."[11]

Present-day Haudenosaunee oral tradition associates the original elaboration of *kaswentha* relations between Iroquois nations and Europeans with a circa 1613 agreement negotiated between Mohawks and a Dutch trader named Jacob (a.k.a., Jacques) Eelckens at Tawagonshi (near modern-day Norman's Kill, south of modern-day Albany, prior to the formal establishment of Dutch Fort Nassau nearby) and associated with a Two Row wampum belt.[12] Iroquois activists and scholars have consistently asserted the historical veracity of the Two Row relationship in colonial-era cross-cultural negotiations and during the past two decades they have increasingly pointed to the utility of the concept of *kaswentha* as a renewable model for repairing indigenous-settler relations in contemporary North America.[13]

Non-Native scholars of the Iroquois, however, have been at considerable pains of late to dismiss the idea of *kaswentha* and/or the Two Row agreement as a legitimate historical phenomenon. Francis Jennings' edited volume, *The History and Culture of Iroquois Diplomacy*, widely regarded as the standard scholarly reference on Iroquois diplomacy, contains no mention of *kaswentha*, only a statement questioning the authenticity of a document purporting to represent the 1613 "treaty of friendship" often identified as the original agreement underlying all subsequent "Two Row" diplomacy.[14] In 1987, three prominent Iroquoianist scholars authored an article that established a "parchment" document purporting to represent the 1613 Tawagonshi Treaty as a twentieth-century forgery.[15] A 2007 article in the *American Indian Quarterly* not only dismissed the idea of the Two Row (as manifested in a repatriated wampum belt) as a nineteenth-century "verbalization" of "an ancient assumption of autonomy" by Haudenosaunee people residing in Canada for contemporary political purposes, but also went so far as to warn contemporary Haudenosaunee people against employing the concepts associated with the Two Row wampum belt in support of any "political claim" in court given its supposedly "perplexing origins" and "ambiguous" status.[16] Finally, the most recent book-length study of early Native American diplomacy with European settlers in the Hudson River Valley eschews any mention of Eelckens or the Two Row agreement, arguing instead that political negotiations between the Dutch and neighboring indigenous nations did not begin until circa 1640.[17]

While the inauthenticity of the particular "parchment" document has been established persuasively in the 1987 study mentioned above, substantial written evidence in support of Iroquois oral tradition concerning *kaswentha* does indeed exist. Iroquois speakers recited the *kaswentha* tradition for Anglo-American and French colonial audiences on at least fourteen different occasions between 1656 and 1748.[18] One of the richest examples of these recitations corroborating the early seventeenth-century origins of a *kaswentha* relationship between Iroquois nations and the Dutch may be found in a 27 June 1689 speech by a delegation of Seneca, Cayuga, Onondaga, and Oneida headmen in Albany. These Iroquois leaders reminded the magistrates of Albany that in former times the Mohawks, Oneidas, and Onondagas "did carry the Ankor of the ship that Jaques [Eelckens] came in to onnondage, that being the meeting place of the Five Nations." The speaker for the four-nation delegation announced that they had come in 1689 "to renew the old Covenant made with Jaques many years ago who came with a ship into their waters and rec[eive]d them as Bretheren, & then the maquase [Mohawks], oneydes, and onnondages desired him to establish himself in this country and the Sinnekes & Cayouges they drew into that General Covenant, & that they had with one accord Planted the Tree of Good Understanding."[19]

While we cannot say with certainty that the 1613 agreement between the Mohawks and Jacob Eelckens involved the exchange of a Two Row wampum belt, recent archaeological studies indicate the strong possibility of such an association between the Mohawk-Dutch alliance and the oral memory of the concept of *kaswentha*. The technological needs for the production of a patterned belt with geometrical designs or representational imagery would include: (1) short tubular white shell beads (a.k.a. "wampum"), (2) a method of weaving that permitted side-to-side stringing of tubular beads, and (3) dark-colored tubular beads (either purple wampum made from the shell of the quahog clam (*Mercenaria mercenaria*), dark-colored tubular glass beads obtained in trade with Europeans, or the use of a pigment to color appropriate sections of a monochrome [white] belt) for the production of patterned belts with geometrical designs or other representational imagery. The presence of white shell wampum, as described above, is well-documented at Iroquois sites after the mid-sixteenth century.[20] Side-to-side stringing of tubular beads cut from European sheet brass is noted at the Seneca Culbertson site, occupied circa 1575–1590, and early evidence of wampum woven into small objects dates from the turn of the seventeenth century.[21] The availability of tubular purple wampum in 1613 is a matter of debate among scholars owing to the perceived need for iron drills in the manufacturing process, but examples have been found at the Seneca Fugle site (occupied circa 1605–1625).[22] Flat discoidal beads rendered in purple and white shell appear at the Mohawk Klock site (occupied circa 1560–1580), which may signal the origins of two-color mnemonics in bead usage (albeit in strung rather than woven format).[23] Purple discoidal beads likely represented the conceptual precursor to the tubular purple wampum beads known to exist in significant quantity after 1630.[24]

Establishing the possibility of a Two Row belt's existence in 1613 is not the same as direct evidence of association, but given that archaeological recovery does not necessarily represent an expression of the earliest use of a particular cultural form (valued items may have been reused, kept in circulation, and neither lost nor buried with the dead, or simply remain undiscovered in the archaeological record), and given the increasing significance of wampum as a material form to facilitate communication across cultural boundaries at this precise moment in time, serious consideration of the oral tradition associating the Mohawk-Dutch alliance with principles of *kaswentha*, or the Two Row wampum belt, is warranted.[25]

If *kaswentha* was indeed part of the conceptual vocabulary operative among historical actors during the early seventeenth century, a review of the history of early Iroquois relations with the Dutch from 1613 to 1664, should yield evidence of those principles in Iroquois actions and words (such as assertions of mutual aid, mutual non-interference and freedom of movement) captured in the documentary record. The following sections of this essay undertake that exercise, and shed new light on the enormous difficulties that Iroquois people experienced in their attempts to communicate their vision of the *kaswentha* relationship to the Dutch, who only gradually came to grasp its import.

Forging the Relationship: Early Struggles, 1609–1640

In September 1609, Henry Hudson's voyage on behalf of the Dutch East India Company took him as far as Norman's Kill and just fifty miles from the easternmost extant Mohawk villages. Although Hudson recorded no direct contact with the Mohawks (no Iroquois contact with any Dutch national is documented in written sources until five years later), archaeological evidence suggests extensive Mohawk involvement in the Hudson River Valley trade by 1611, and the rapid movement thereafter of what one archaeologist has described as a "tidal wave" of Dutch trade goods as far west as the Genesee River Valley (contemporary Seneca country).[26] The establishment of a regular Dutch presence in the Hudson River Valley after 1613 afforded the Iroquois a crucial opportunity to reorient their patterns of trade and alliance-building and thereby to articulate a coherent new geography of internal solidarity in which the sentient branches of a metaphorical "Tree of Peace" at once encompassed the Five Nations that would later constitute the Iroquois League and provided a means of engaging the multiple European colonies on the periphery of their homelands on explicitly Iroquois terms.[27]

Relationships patterned on the principles articulated in post-contact *kaswentha* ideology doubtless existed between Iroquois and other Indigenous nations prior to the intrusion of Europeans as a means of facilitating long-distance economic and social exchange.[28] What is interesting for our purposes are the ways in which the nations of the emerging Iroquois League endeavored during the early decades of the seventeenth century to establish ties of mutual assistance and noninterference with the Dutch as an extension of similar processes they had undertaken with neighboring Indigenous populations prior to Hudson's visit.

The founding moment of the *kaswentha* agreement likely took place at some point prior to the formal establishment of Dutch Fort Nassau on Castle Island (now mostly occupied by the port of Albany) in 1614.[29] Jacques Eelckens's negotiations, often described as a "treaty," might better be understood as a trading agreement that facilitated secure movement for both parties to and from a defined center of exchange. In an early test of their *kaswentha* relationship with the Dutch, the Mohawks persuaded three sailors left at Fort Nassau over the winter of 1614–1615 to accompany them on a military expedition against the Susquehannocks, likely seeking an advantage provided by Dutch firearms. The fate of the expedition is unknown, but the Dutch were abandoned by their Mohawk escorts and captured by the Susquehannocks at some time during April or May 1615. The hapless sailors were recovered later in 1615 near Delaware Bay by another Dutch trader, Cornelis Hendricksen, who ransomed them from the Susquehannocks for "kettles, beads, and merchandise."[30]

Following the destruction of Fort Nassau in a 1618 flood, the Dutch presence on the Hudson assumed a more intermittent and unreliable character, and relations with the Iroquois suffered proportionately. In 1622, a Dutch trader named Hans Jorisz Hontom, a longtime associate of Eelckens, appeared at Fort Nassau and for unknown reasons took an unnamed Mohawk "sachem" hostage and demanded a ransom. After the Mohawks paid the ransom, Hontom reportedly "cut out the male organs of the aforesaid chief, and [hung] them on the mast stay with rope, and thus killed the sachem." This act, as brutal and overt a rejection of *kaswentha* principles as exists in the documentary record, cast a pall over Iroquois relations with the Dutch for more than a decade.[31]

By the time the Dutch reestablished themselves at Fort Orange in 1624, the Iroquois had embarked on a campaign to displace their Mahican rivals and thereby to gain direct access to Dutch traders. This was no petty squabble—significant, collective Iroquois objectives, such as obtaining a crucial alternative to French markets in the St. Lawrence River Valley, securing the power to broker other Native nations' access to Dutch trade goods, and testing the promises of mutual defense made by all Iroquois nations during the latter stages of the formation of the Iroquois League, all operated in what scholars have usually referred to in parochial terms as the "Mohawk-Mahican War."[32]

Iroquois observers, noting the invitations issued by the Mahicans to northern Algonquin and Montagnais trading partners to bring their peltries to Fort Orange in 1624, quickly surmised that the Mahicans, if successful,

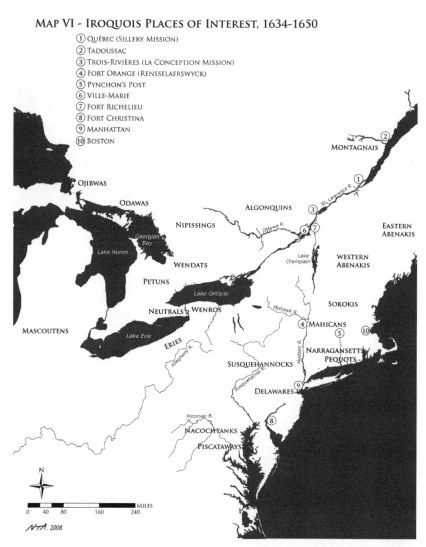

MAP VI - IROQUOIS PLACES OF INTEREST, 1634-1650

① QUÉBEC (SILLERY MISSION)
② TADOUSSAC
③ TROIS-RIVIÈRES (LA CONCEPTION MISSION)
④ FORT ORANGE (RENSSELAERSWYCK)
⑤ PYNCHON'S POST
⑥ VILLE-MARIE
⑦ FORT RICHELIEU
⑧ FORT CHRISTINA
⑨ MANHATTAN
⑩ BOSTON

Figure 13. Map of Iroquoia reprinted with permission from Jon Parmenter, *The Edge of the Woods: Iroquoia, 1534–1701* (East Lansing, MI: Michigan State University Press, 2010), p. 42.

might link rich subarctic furs (that might otherwise have been traded to the French in the St. Lawrence Valley) with mid-Atlantic based trade goods (notably the highly desired shell wampum that was chronically scarce in

New France). Given the crucial role that east-west exchange routes linking Iroquois nations with the Atlantic world (via Dutch traders on the Hudson) had played in completing the process of League formation after roughly 1614, we can better appreciate the collective interest of the Five Nations in challenging the Mahicans' innovative effort to reorient regional trade patterns in their favor.[33]

After an initial Mohawk offensive, the Mahicans destroyed the easternmost Mohawk village in either 1625 or 1626. The Mohawks rebuilt their villages on the south side of the Mohawk River, moving even closer to Fort Orange, which prompted the Mahicans to enlist the aid of Dutch soldiers against the Mohawks. Early in July 1626, less than three miles' distance from the fort, Daniël van Krieckenbeeck's anti-Mohawk expeditionary party ran into a Mohawk ambush that killed 24 Mahicans and four Dutch soldiers (including Van Krieckenbeeck). Angered over this latest violation of *kaswentha* and perhaps recalling Hontom's horrific murder of their leader four years earlier, the Mohawks "devoured" one of the Dutch soldiers, and "carried a leg an arm home" from the other victims "to be divided among their families, as a sign that they had conquered their enemies." Several days later, in a conversation with a trusted Dutch trader, unnamed Mohawks "asked the reason why [the Dutch] had meddled" in their conflict with the Mahicans.[34]

Dutch "meddling," notwithstanding explicit official West India Company recommendations to the contrary, continued in the Mohawk-Mahican War until the Mohawks defeated and dispersed the Mahicans in 1628. Iroquois-Dutch relations appear to have stabilized thereafter, as the latter acclimated themselves to a profitable economic relationship with the Mohawks at Fort Orange. A Mohawk warrior captured by the Montagnais in 1632 and subjected to public torture prior to execution taunted his tormentors by describing his extensive network of personal allies and trading partners, one of whom was a "Flemish [i.e., Dutch] Captain."[35] Despite such hints of growing Mohawk affinity, the Dutch were held to acceptable standards of behavior. When Saggodryochta, then the "head chief" of the Mohawks, discovered that the hated Hontom had been appointed to the position of commissary at Fort Orange in 1633, 900 Iroquois warriors appeared before the fort and demanded his surrender. Hontom refused to leave, and the assembled Iroquois army retaliated by burning a West India Company sloop, slaughtering all the livestock they could find in Kiliaen van Rensselaer's patroonship of Rensselaerswijck, and finally by diverting most of their traffic away from Fort Orange to rival French and English traders.[36]

Sent in the dead of winter 1634–1635 to inquire about declining Iroquois business at Fort Orange, Dutch surgeon Harmen Meyndertsz van den Bogaert and two of his associates received an important refresher on *kaswentha* principles from their Oneida hosts at the town of Oneyuttehage on 3 January 1635. While taking care to advertise their new contacts with French and English traders, the Oneidas nevertheless assured Van den Bogaert that if they received "four hands of sewant [wampum] and four hands of long cloth for each large beaver" pelt (a potentially significant increase in their buying power at Fort Orange) they would conduct their business "with no one else." They cemented their offer with a present of five beaver pelts to Van den Bogaert and assured him that he (and by extension, all Dutch traders and emissaries) would enjoy free movement among and generous hospitality at all the "castles" of the League nations. The Dutch emissaries declined to respond formally to the offer, claiming to lack the authority to arrange the prices of trade goods, but promised to report the request to their superiors and to return in the spring with an official answer.[37]

Relations between the Iroquois and Dutch remained chilly for the remainder of the 1630s. Van den Bogaert never returned with an answer to the Oneidas' request. In October 1636, patroon Kiliaen van Rensselaer described persistent Mohawk antagonism toward Fort Orange and the settlers of Rensselaerswijck near modern-day Albany, but he failed to draw any connection between Mohawk sentiments and his own dogged efforts to collect an indemnity from that nation for the property they had destroyed in 1633.[38] Yet three crucial elements of the Dutch colonial enterprise in New Netherland kept connections to the Mohawks alive. The first was the comparatively weak missionary impulse on the part of Calvinist ministers in New Netherland, which eliminated one potentially explosive source of intercultural antagonism.[39] The second was the official stance of the West India Company on recognizing Indigenous land rights and insistence on purchasing land.[40] Third, and perhaps most significant, was the comparatively liberal attitude of the Dutch toward making firearms and ammunition available as trade goods in exchanges with Native Americans. While neighboring settler colonies attached serious restrictions to this trade (most notably the French, who made conversion to Christianity a prerequisite for any would-be purchaser of guns), the Dutch refused to deny themselves the economic and political benefits of a de facto free trade in firearms with their Native business partners. By 1641, the Mohawks could field "four hundred armed men," and guns, like shell wampum and brass kettles before them, soon spread rapidly throughout Iroquois homelands.[41]

Refining the Relationship: Dutch Responses, 1640–1664

The flourishing firearms trade provided a basis for Dutch efforts to mend fences with the Iroquois; in the hypercompetitive economic atmosphere in New Netherland following the West India Company's termination of its monopoly on the fur trade in 1639, Dutch officials realized that the Mohawks, who could now drive increasingly hard bargains, required some diplomatic attention. Van Rensselaer abandoned his effort to collect an indemnity payment from the Mohawks and instead sent his *commies* (commissary) Arent van Curler to Mohawk country in July 1640 with "three very fine blankets" for Mohawk leaders, a gift that was to signify the "great friendship" prevailing between the two nations.[42]

Three years later, Van Curler returned to Mohawk country on an official errand to attempt the ransom of the French Jesuit Isaac Jogues and two of his associates then in captivity among the Mohawks. Van Curler's opening speech proposed that "we [the Dutch] should keep on good terms as neighbors and that they [the Mohawks] should do no injury either to the colonists or to their cattle." Leaders from all three Mohawk towns "thankfully accepted" Van Curler's articulation and renewal of the *kaswentha* relationship, and they listened politely to Van Curler's offer of Dutch brokerage of Jogues's ransom as a means of repairing the Mohawks' strained relations with New France. Ultimately, they declined Van Curler's offer of "about 600 guilders in goods" for the ransom of Jogues, preferring to manage his repatriation on their own terms.[43] In reality, the Mohawks planned to use their prominent Jesuit captive as a prop in their efforts to convey their military might (and thereby secure tribute payments ensuring their non-involvement in Kieft's War) from the Native nations of the lower Hudson River Valley. Jogues later escaped to Fort Orange, and, with the aid of Dutch officials there and in Manhattan, sailed to France. Outraged Mohawks threatened to destroy Rensselaerswijck entirely in the aftermath of Jogues's Dutch-facilitated escape, but "presents to the value of three hundred [French] livres" eventually persuaded them to return home peacefully.[44] The incident apparently spurred a change in strategy in Mohawk captive-taking. After 1643 Mohawk warriors would routinely bring French prisoners (such as the Jesuit François-Joseph Bressani) into Fort Orange for the purpose of obtaining "quite dear" ransom payments from the increasingly beleaguered Dutch, who then had to chase down French authorities for reimbursements.[45]

Mohawk leaders provided crucial diplomatic assistance to the Dutch in 1645, helping to negotiate an end to Kieft's War, the latter's conflict with the

Munsees and Mahicans of the Hudson River Valley.[46] These efforts inaugurated a pattern in which the Mohawks exchanged their diplomatic acumen and military power for continued Dutch subsidization of that military power through a thriving arms trade that increasingly witnessed Dutch traders carrying large cargoes of arms and ammunition directly into Mohawk country to exchange for Iroquois-procured beaver pelts. By 1647, the Mohawks were requisitioning teams of horses and Dutch laborers to assist in hauling timber for their reinforcement of their towns' palisades, claiming this was their due in exchange for permitting the Dutch to reside at Rensselaerswijck. From 1648 to 1650, Mohawk parties regularly commandeered the patroon's house to collect gifts of Dutch military stores as well as tribute payments from "subsidiary" nations of the lower Hudson Valley.[47]

In addition to the military aid and diplomatic recognition that the Mohawks elicited from the Dutch, by mid-century a number of persons of mixed Mohawk and Dutch ancestry began to appear, most notably the Mohawk leader named Canaqueese, a.k.a. Smits Jan, John Smith, and "the Flemish Bastard," whom French Jesuits described in colorful terms as "an execrable issue of sin, the monstrous offspring of a Dutch Heretic Father and a Pagan [Mohawk] Mother." While a recent archaeological study has argued that the Dutch manifested only limited sexual interest in Mohawk women (and vice versa), the documentary record reveals abundant evidence to the contrary. Matrilineal descent reckoning among the Iroquois meant that individuals like Canaqueese could be raised by their mothers as Mohawks without the stigma of illegitimacy; such practices were normative among Indigenous peoples prior to the intrusion of Europeans for the purpose of establishing mutual ties between different communities. At a minimum, Mohawk-Dutch intermarriages increased the likelihood that the *kaswentha* relationships would endure, and, from the perspective of the Mohawks, the offspring of these unions also contributed to the making of "one people" with their Dutch allies.[48]

Deepening interpersonal ties notwithstanding, the Mohawks continually had to remind the Dutch of their obligations as allies in a *kaswentha* relationship. When a large party of 300 Mohawks arrived at Fort Orange on 19 November 1655, they asked for "a renewal of harmony and peace" with New Netherland officials but stated their unhappiness about the "not altogether brotherly" demands of Dutch blacksmiths for payment for the repair of Mohawk firearms. The Dutch authorities responded with a paltry gift of 15 bars of lead and 25 pounds of gunpowder. Evidently dissatisfied with this insubstantial gesture, the Mohawks plundered a number of Dutch traders near Fort Orange, "taking away by force guns, powder, shot, [and] coats."[49]

Mohawk efforts to assert, secure, and build the *kaswentha* relationship rarely involved such levels of physical violence. On 19 April 1658, Mohawk delegates escorted French Jesuit Simon Le Moyne to Fort Orange, where, in the presence of New Netherland authorities, they expressed their desire for brotherly relations with New France (independent Mohawk efforts to integrate the French into a broader *kaswentha*-style alliance had been attempted previously in 1641 and 1645). Restating the principles of their *kaswentha* alliance with the Dutch, the Mohawks outlined their plan to have Le Moyne ask officials in New France to "do like the Dutchman, who interferes not in the wars of" allied Native nations. In an unprecedented move, several "Manhattan Dutch" accompanied an embassy consisting of Le Moyne and headmen from each of the Mohawks' three constituent Turtle, Wolf, and Bear clans to Québec in May 1658, where they floated the idea of a Mohawk-forged "iron chain" binding the Iroquois League, New France, and New Netherland. French authorities rejected the proposal, but their resistance does not diminish the clear willingness of the Dutch to assist in this innovative Mohawk diplomatic initiative.[50] A few weeks after this embassy departed, fifteen of the Mohawks' "eldest sachems" visited Fort Orange, where they reminded Dutch officials of their assistance in brokering an end to hostilities in the Peach War (1655–1656). In return, they argued that it was the "duty" of the Dutch "to do the same in such circumstances for them," and soon they had secured the services of a Dutch soldier fluent in French to accompany another Mohawk peace embassy to New France, as well as a written cover letter (in the French language) attesting to the sincerity of the Mohawks' intentions.[51]

Despite the Mohawks success in capitalizing on the solicitous attitude of Dutch officials at Fort Orange, Mohawk leaders were back in early September 1659, complaining that "the Dutch say we are brothers and that we are joined together by chains, but that lasts only as long as we have beavers. After that, we are no longer thought of." The Mohawks, then engaged in multiple conflicts with a number of Indigenous nations, communicated a lengthy list of grievances that suggested many reasons for the recent decline in the volume of Iroquois-procured peltries arriving in New Netherland. To resolve these problems, the Mohawks requested free repair of their firearms by Dutch smiths, thirty men with horses to haul logs for the repair of their towns' palisades, as well as a commitment on the part of Dutch authorities to provide fifty to sixty men to assist the Mohawks in homeland security. Finally, the Mohawks pointed out to Dutch authorities that Dutch spouses of deceased Mohawks were obligated to supply their mourning in-laws with "one or two suits of cloth," a subtle but significant indicator of the Mohawks' continuing hopes for positive outcomes from the numerous interpersonal relationships between members of their nation and the settler population of New Netherland.[52]

Alarmed by this speech, Dutch officials at Fort Orange assembled a seventeen-man delegation (including such notable persons as Jeremias van Rensselaer, Arent van Curler, and Philip Pietersen Schuyler) to make a direct reply in Mohawk country (the third of just three such embassies known to have occurred during the Dutch regime). On 24 September 1659, in the Mohawks' easternmost "Castle called Kaghnuwage," the Dutch emissaries announced their intention to "renew our old friendship and brotherhood." Referring to Van Curler's 1643 embassy, the Dutch brightened the "iron chain" that had linked them with the Mohawks "sixteen years ago," and stated that "henceforth you will have no reason to doubt that we shall be and remain brothers." While the Dutch failed to answer the Mohawks' specific grievances, they punctuated their speech with a significant present, consisting of 75 pounds of powder, 100 pounds of lead, 15 axes, and "two beavers'" worth of knives.[53]

Within a year of what proved to be the last Dutch embassy to Iroquoia, Mohawk leaders were back once more at Fort Orange, warning that ongoing physical assaults and verbal insults perpetrated by Dutch traders threatened an end to the "old friendship" that they had "enjoyed for more than thirty years." In late July 1660, Onondaga leaders echoed these Mohawk complaints of abuses committed by Dutch traders outside the boundaries of Fort Orange and Beverwijck, and noted the inconsistency of having to rely on the Dutch at Fort Orange for gunpowder to fight Susquehannock enemies armed by Dutch traders on the Delaware River. These complaints appear to have motivated the significant uptick in New Netherland officials' attention to the abuses by traders of their Mohawk allies for the remainder of the Dutch regime.[54]

Although friction within the Iroquois-Dutch relationship lingered, the Mohawks demonstrated continuing desire and capacity to renew and amplify the ties of *kaswentha* down to the final years of New Netherland's existence. On 27 July 1661, three Mohawk headmen representing each of the nation's clans signed a deed at Fort Orange granting their longtime negotiating partner Arent van Curler a tract of land in the vicinity of modern-day Schenectady, New York. In doing so, the Mohawks alienated then-unoccupied territory they claimed after their 1628 dispersal of the Mahicans in hopes of leveraging their gift of cleared land to Van Curler into a new Dutch trading post 24 miles closer to their easternmost settlement. Mohawk-brokered trade and diplomacy at this new locale would spare Iroquois traders the tedious overland passage from the Mohawk River to the increasingly rough-and-tumble trading scene at Fort Orange and Beverwijck. The Mohawks had grounded their plans on growing ties of kinship with members of the Dutch settler population, personified by Van Curler, who then had a nine-year-old daughter living with her mother's family in Mohawk country. Additionally, Van Curler was a known quantity in the eyes of the Mohawks, boasting a long track record of selling firearms to Iroquois customers. Despite delays in surveying that deferred settlement of the Schenectady Patent until 1664, and official bans on trading at Schenectady by Dutch (and later, English) authorities, the innovative "sale" of Schenectady lands by the Mohawks demonstrated the ongoing interest of the Natives in deepening ties of mutual interest with Dutch settlers, as well as the capacity of Iroquois people more generally to think creatively about the potential uses of their abundant territorial holdings in engaging settler colonialism.[55]

The Iroquois, preoccupied with their own wars on multiple fronts, including a renewed conflict with the Mahicans that hindered their access to Fort Orange, offered no assistance to the Dutch when English forces compelled the surrender of New Netherland in September 1664. Less than three weeks following the formal surrender in Manhattan, a delegation of Iroquois headmen from all of the League's constituent nations arrived at the former site of Fort Orange (now "Fort Albany"), to confer with newly arrived English officials. George Cartwright and Richard Nicolls, treating on behalf of the Duke of York, offered the Iroquois favorable terms of peace and alliance: they would have "wares and commodityes" from the English in quantities and at prices equivalent to those of the former Dutch regime; additionally, English officials pledged to punish any offense committed by the settler population of New York against "Indyan princes or their subjects" throughout "all other English Plantations" in North America, provided that Iroquois "sachems" agreed to undertake investigation, punishment, and arrangements for compensation for any crimes committed by their people. In their reply, the Iroquois delegates (one of whom was Canaqueese, the "Flemish Bastard"), accepted these terms and added *kaswentha*-style provisions asserting the right of the Iroquois to free trade with other nations of their choosing, and committing the English to non-interference in Iroquois wars with other Native nations.[56]

Conclusion: Persistent Reminders

If Native Americans occupied a curious position in the 1909 commemoration of Hudson's voyage, one might argue that they have been marginalized to an even greater degree from the highly academically oriented Quadricentennial celebrations on both sides of the Atlantic.[57] At the conclusion of a 4 April 2009 Hudson Commemoration conference at the Westerkerk in Amsterdam, a Mohawk individual in the audience named Jerry Thundercloud McDonald arose and delivered an impromptu speech highlighting the history of the *kaswentha* relationship between the Iroquois and the Dutch. McDonald's action resulted in a hastily arranged press conference the following day, during which he presented (while wearing full ceremonial regalia) a replica Two Row wampum belt to Deputy Mayor Carolien Gehrels of Amsterdam.[58] Iroquois leaders from the seventeenth century, could they have witnessed this sequence of events, would likely have exchanged knowing smiles.

Careful study of Iroquois-Dutch relations from 1609 to 1664, informed by Iroquois oral tradition of the *kaswentha* relationship, helps us to more fully appreciate the degree to which the principles of *kaswentha* operated in the daily lives of settlers and Native people alike in New Netherland. By extending principles of intergroup relations from the precontact era to new Dutch arrivals after 1613, the Iroquois sought to incorporate these potentially valuable neighbors as allies while maintaining their own freedom of movement, in both the literal and figurative senses. The Dutch, after an initial learning curve of some duration, appear to have recognized the degree to which their interests would also be served by a relationship of peers in separate vessels. In 1699 local authorities of Dutch descent in Albany reflected positively on the alliance between the colony of New York and the Iroquois League, describing it as so old "that there is none now living that can remember the beginning of it."[59]

Kaswentha relations were not static—they evolved over time as ties between the Iroquois and the Dutch (and the latter's English successors) deepened and sociopolitical circumstances grew more complex—but they did exist. Indeed, this case study suggests strongly that it is incumbent upon all scholars, when considering the historicity of particular Iroquois oral traditions (especially regarding something as fundamentally significant as *kaswentha*), to do more than simply identify a single document as a fake, or to set the bar for evidentiary proof of a concept's existence to practically impossible standards (such as requiring a surviving "physical" Two Row belt from the colonial era that can be explicitly associated with a documentary source, an especially difficult task given the extensive loss and/or disassembly of Iroquois wampum belts conveyed to non-Native recipients, and ethnographic evidence indicating that belts were occasionally disassembled and the beads reused among the Iroquois themselves),[60] or to dismiss the tradition entirely as a mere invention.[61] Given the obvious circumstances of the settler majority population's control of the archives and the structural disinterest of set-tler nation-states in documenting the distinct and divergent visions of law informing traditions of resistance and opposition among colonized peoples, why is it so difficult to accept the possibility that "Iroquois traditionalists who speak confidently of agreements that their forebears entered into may be better custodians of the spirit of history than we later Americans who remain preoccupied with the written record"?[62]

One of the oldest tricks in the colonizer's playbook has been to deny the authenticity and/or the antiquity of Indigenous traditions. Eurocentric scholarship, in adopting these approaches, works to conflate contemporane-ous cultural and political differences between Indigenous and settler nations into temporal sequence—shorn of a "true" or "authentic" past, the Indigenous nation is placed in an inferior position, "behind" in terms of its cultural development and thus susceptible to the demands of the colonizing mission. Mohawk legal scholar Joyce Tekahnawiiaks King adds a further salient point regarding the difficulties Iroquois nations face in contending with voting democracies in the United States and Canada, as each new settler regime leaves behind the policies of its predecessor, it tends to forget the agreements and lessons of the past, thereby placing the burden of education regarding those agreements on Iroquois leaders.[63]

Non-Native scholars are only beginning to recognize the value of Indigenous knowledge and ways of knowing to their research.[64] It is worth noting in this context that the very concept of *kaswentha* facilitates a fuller recognition of the reality of historical coevalness, of the simultaneous coex-istence of others with their own historical trajectories, their own political priorities, and their own stories to tell. Analyzing the historicity of *kas-wentha* raises our awareness of an Iroquois understanding of cross-cultural relationships that works toward unity—not uniformity—by demonstrating how differences between individuals, communities, and nations have to be acknowledged and integrated, rather than annihilated or absorbed. Iroquois people extended this invitation to the Dutch upon their first arrival in what is now New York, they did so in highly constrained circumstances in 1909, and they continue to do so today, if only we were willing to listen.

Notes

1. Edward Hagaman Hall, *The Hudson-Fulton Celebration 1909: The Fourth Annual Report of the Hudson-Fulton Celebration Commission to the Legislature of the State of New York, Transmitted to the Legislature May twentieth, nineteen ten*, 2 vols.

(Albany, 1910), vol. 1, p. 287 (quotes), 289–290. For a recent analysis of this event, albeit one that pays minimal attention to Native American aspects, see Roger Panetta, "The Hudson-Fulton Celebration of 1909," in idem (ed.), *Dutch New York: The Roots of Hudson Valley Culture* (Yonkers, NY: Hudson River Museum, 2009), pp. 301–338.

2. Hall, *Hudson-Fulton Celebration*, vol. 1, p. 287.

3. Ibid., (quote), pp. 293–295. Fordham University's interactive Hudson-Fulton Celebration website enables users to virtually witness the parade in a sequence of panned still photographs: <http://www.fordham.edu/academics/colleges__graduate_s/undergraduate_colleg/fordham_college_at_l/special_programs/honors_program/honors_history/homepage/index.asp> (accessed 7 December 2012).

4. After 1640, the Mohawks endeavored to force the Algonquian-speaking peoples of the lower Hudson Valley into a tributary relationship with occasional, though far from complete, success, see Ted J. Brasser, "Mahican," in Bruce G. Trigger (ed.), *Northeast*, vol. 15 in William C. Sturtevant (ed.), *Handbook of North American Indians* (Washington, DC: Smithsonian Institution, 1978), pp. 202–204; John A. Strong, "Mohawk Sovereignty over the Long Island Indians: Fact or Fiction? A Re-examination of the Primary and Secondary Sources," *Long Island Historical Journal* 14 (1–2) (2002), pp. 15–26. Cf. Paul Otto, *The Dutch-Munsee Encounter in America: The Struggle for Sovereignty in the Hudson Valley* (New York: Berghahn Books, 2006), p. 124; Shirley W. Dunn, *The Mohicans and Their Land, 1609–1730* (Fleischmanns, NY: Purple Mountain Press, 1994), pp. 107–108; Robert Steven Grumet, "Children of Muhheahkkunnuck: A Lower River Indian History," in Catherine Coleman Brawer (ed.), *Many Trails: Indians of the Lower Hudson Valley* (Katonah, NY: The Katonah Gallery, 1983), p. 19; Allen W. Trelease, *Indian Affairs in Colonial New York: The Seventeenth Century* (Lincoln, NE: University of Nebraska Press, 1997 [1960]), pp. 23–24.

5. Hall, *Hudson-Fulton Celebration*, vol. 1, pp. 412, 439 ("real Indians," "white people painted . . ."), p. 440 ("controllers of the . . ."), pp. 446; vol. 2, pp. 852, 856–857 ("appeared, dressed in the . . .").

6. Philip J. Deloria, *Indians in Unexpected Places* (Lawrence. KS: University Press of Kansas, 2004), pp. 52–108.

7. Peter C. Mancall, *Fatal Journey: The Final Expedition of Henry Hudson: A Tale of Mutiny and Murder in the Arctic* (New York: Basic Books, 2009), p. 70. It is worth noting the proximity of the Iroquois to three famous explorers in eastern North America. Hudson reversed course on the river bearing his name on 3 October 1609 (23 September 1609 on the Old Style, or Julian calendar), at a point less than fifty miles from the Mohawks' easternmost settlement. Samuel de Champlain fought his famous battle with Mohawk warriors near present-day Ticonderoga, New York on 30 July 1609 (see Henry P. Biggar (ed.), *The Works of Samuel de Champlain*, 6 vols. (Toronto, 1922–1936), 2:97–100), and Captain John Smith had previously encountered "Seaven boats" full of warriors from western Iroquois nations (whom he identified as "Massawomekes"), near the head of Chesapeake Bay early in the month of July 1608 (see Philip L. Barbour (ed.), *The Complete Works of Captain John Smith*, 3 vols. (Chapel Hill, NC: University of North Carolina Press, 1986), 1:166).

8. For a recent book-length example of this scholarly trope in the context of New Netherland history, see Donna Merwick, *The Shame and the Sorrow: Dutch-Amerindian Encounters in New Netherland* (Philadelphia, PA: University of Pennsylvania Press, 2006), an indictment of Dutch settler colonialism that casts Native people in the role of victims. William A. Starna, though critical of Merwick (see his "Encounters in New Netherland," *New York History* 88 (2007), pp. 322–326), falls into a similar interpretive trap by asserting the rapid descent of Indigenous people into complete material dependency on the Dutch in "The Native-Dutch Experience in the Mohawk Valley," in Martha Dickinson Shattuck (ed.), *Explorers, Fortunes, and Love Letters: A Window on New Netherland* (Albany, NY: Mount Ida Press, 2009), pp. 27–38.

9. See important comments to this effect in James D. Rice, *Nature and History in the Potomac Country: From Hunter-Gatherers to the Age of Jefferson* (Baltimore, MD: Johns Hopkins University Press, 2009), pp. 9–10; Pekka Hämäläinen, *The Comanche Empire* (New Haven, CT: Yale University Press, 2008), pp. 1–17.

10. Michael Mitchell, "An Unbroken Assertion of Sovereignty," in Boyce Richardson (ed.), *Drumbeat: Anger and Renewal in Indian Country* (Toronto, Ont.: Summerhill Press, 1989), pp. 107–138 at 109–110; Richard Hill, Sr., "Oral Memory of the Haudenosaunee: Views of the Two Row Wampum," *Northeast Indian Quarterly* 7 (Spring 1990), pp. 21–30; Oren Lyons, "The American Indian in the Past," in idem and John C. Mohawk (eds.), *Exiled in the Land of the Free: Democracy, Indian Nations, and the U.S. Constitution* (Santa Fe, NM: Clear Light Publishers, 1992), pp. 13–42 at 40–42; see also Francis Boots Ateronhiakaton, "Iroquoian Use of Wampum," in Joseph Bruchac (ed.), *New Voices from the Longhouse: An Anthology of Contemporary Iroquois Writing* (Greenfield Center, NY: Greenfield Review Press, 1989), pp. 32–39 at 37–38; Howard R. Berman, "Perspectives on American Indian Sovereignty and International Law, 1600 to 1776," in Lyons and Mohawk, *Exiled in the Land of the Free*, pp. 125–188 at 135; Doug George-Kanentiio, *Iroquois Culture and Commentary* (Santa Fe: Clear Light Publishers, 2000), pp. 118–121; James W. Ransom and Kreg T. Ettenger, "Polishing the Kaswentha: A Haudenosaunee View of Environmental Cooperation," *Environmental Science and Policy* 4 (2001), pp. 219–228 at 222; Irving Powless, Jr., "Treaty Making," in G. Peter Jemison and Anna M. Schein (eds.), *Treaty of Canandaigua 1794: 200 Years of Treaty Relations between the Iroquois Confederacy and the United States* (Santa Fe: Clear Light Publishers, 2002), pp. 15–23 at 23; Alfred Taiaiake, *Wasasé: Indigenous Pathways of Action and Freedom* (Peterborough, Ont.: Broadview Press, 2005), p. 266; Joyce Tekahnawiiaks King, "The Value of Water and the Meaning of Water Law for the Native Americans Known as the Haudenosaunee," *Cornell Journal of Law and Public Policy* 16 (2007), pp. 459–465; Salli M. Kawennotakie Benedict, "Made in Akwesasne," in James V. Wright and Jean-Luc Pilon (eds.), *A Passion for the Past: Papers in Honour of James F. Pendergast*, Canadian Museum of Civilization Mercury Series 164 (Gatineau, Qué., 2004), pp. 435–453 at 441–442; <http://www.onondaganation.org/culture/wpm_tworow.html> (accessed 7 December 2012). For visual representations of "Two Row" belts, see William M.

Beauchamp, "Wampum and Shell Articles Used by the New York Indians," *New York State Museum Bulletin* 41.8 (February 1901), p. 406, plate 3 (item 32a); George G. Heye, "Wampum Collection," *Heye Foundation Indian Notes* 7 (1930), pp. 320–321; Tehanetorens, *Wampum Belts* (Ohsweken, Ont.: Iroqrafts, 1983), pp. 10–11.

11. An image of the Two Row belt may be found in Jon Parmenter, *The Edge of the Woods: Iroquoise, 1534–1701* (East Lansing, MI: Michigan State University Press, 2010), p. 24. J.-A. Cuoq, *Lexique de la Langue Iroquois avec Notes et Appendices* (Montréal, 1882), pp. 160–161. Thanks to Darren Bonaparte for drawing this reference to my attention. See also J. N. B. Hewitt, "Wampum," in Frederick Webb Hodge (ed.), *Handbook of American Indians North of Mexico*, Bureau of American Ethnology Bulletin 30, 2 vols. (Washington, DC: Smithsonian Institution, 1907–1910), 2:908; Michael K. Foster, "Another Look at the Function of Wampum in Iroquois-White Councils," in Francis Jennings et al. (eds.), *The History and Culture of Iroquois Diplomacy: An Interdisciplinary Guide to the Treaties of the Six Nations and Their League* (Syracuse, NY: Syracuse University Press, 1985), pp. 99–114 at 109; David Graeber, *Toward an Anthropological Theory of Value: The False Coin of Our Own Dreams* (New York: Palgrave, 2001), p. 131.

12. *DRCHNY*, 1:79–80; *NNN*, pp. 47–48; Peter Wraxall, *An Abridgment of the Indian Affairs Contained in Four Folio Volumes, Transacted in the Colony of New York, from the Year 1678 to the Year 1751*, C. H. McIlwain (ed.) (Cambridge, MA, 1915) (hereinafter "*WA*"), p. 95; Jan Kupp, "Dutch Influences in Canada, 1589–1624," *de Halve Maen* 56, no. 2 (1981), pp. 14–16 at 15; Charles T. Gehring and William A. Starna, "Dutch and Indians in the Hudson Valley: The Early Period," *Hudson Valley Regional Review* 9, no. 2 (1992), pp. 1–25 at 13; Cornelius Jaenen, "Champlain and the Dutch," in Raymonde Litalien and Denis Vaugeois (eds.), *Champlain: The Birth of French America* (Montréal, Qué. and Kingston, Ont.: McGill-Queen's University Press, 2004), p. 241; Otto, *Dutch-Munsee Encounter in America*, pp. 54–55, 61–62, 70; Starna, "Retrospecting the Origins of the League of the Iroquois," *American Philosophical Society Proceedings* 152, no. 3 (2008), pp. 279–321 at 305–308.

13. Foster, "Another Look at the Function of Wampum," p. 112n; James Tully, *Strange Multiplicity: Constitutionalism in an Age of Diversity* (New York: Cambridge University Press, 1995), pp. 135–136; Robert Vachon, "Guswenta, Or, The Intercultural Imperative: Towards a Re-Enacted Peace Accord between the Mohawk Nation and the North American Nation-States and Their Peoples," *Interculture* 28, no. 2 (Spring 1995), pp. 1–73; 28, no. 3 (Summer 1995), pp. 2–41; 28, no. 4 (1995), pp. 2–46; Paul Williams and Curtis Nelson, "Kaswentha," in *For Seven Generations: An Information Legacy of the Royal Commission on Aboriginal Peoples, Research Reports: Treaties* (Project Area 1, "Early Treaty Making in Canada") (CD-ROM, Ottawa: Libraxus, 1997), Records 53283-56744; Robert A. Williams, Jr., *Linking Arms Together: American Indian Treaty Visions of Law and Peace, 1600–1800* (New York: Oxford University Press, 1997), pp. 4–5; Deborah Doxtator, "Inclusive and Exclusive Perceptions of Difference: Native and Euro-Based Concepts of Time, History, and Change," in Germaine Warkentin and Carolyn Podruchny (eds.), *Decentering the Renaissance:*

Canada and Europe in Multidisciplinary Perspective, 1500–1700 (Toronto: University of Toronto Press, 2001), pp. 33–47 at 46–47; Jeff Lambe, "Relational Boundaries: Kaswentha and Inter-Group Relations," in Jill Oakes (ed.), *Aboriginal Cultural Landscapes* (Winnipeg. Man.: Aboriginal Issues Press, 2004), pp. 22–34; Dale Turner, *This Is Not a Peace Pipe: Towards a Critical Indigenous Philosophy* (Toronto: University of Toronto Press, 2006), pp. 47–52; Paula Sherman, "Picking Up the Wampum Belt as an Act of Protest," in Lynne Davis (ed.), *Alliances: Re/Envisioning Indigenous/Non-Indigenous Relationships* (Toronto: University of Toronto Press, 2010), pp. 114–130; T'hohahoken Michael Doxtater, "Tutelo Heights Short-Term 'Two Row' Lessons Central to Long-Term Mediation in the Grand River Valley," *Wicazo Sa Review* 26 (Spring 2011), pp. 43–65.

14. Jennings et al., *History and Culture of Iroquois Diplomacy*, pp. 158 (quote), 226. This book was reissued in paperback by the same publisher in 1995. See also Trelease, *Indian Affairs*, p. 34.

15. Charles T. Gehring, William A. Starna, and William N. Fenton, "The Tawagonshi Treaty of 1613: The Final Chapter," *New York History* 60 (1987), pp. 373–393. Cf. Vernon Benjamin's critique, "The Tawagonshi Agreement of 1613: A Chain of Friendship in the Dutch Hudson Valley," *Hudson Valley Regional Review* 16, no. 2 (1999), pp. 1–20.

16. Kathryn V. Muller, "The Two 'Mystery' Belts of Grand River: A Biography of the Two Row Wampum and the Friendship Belt," *American Indian Quarterly* 31 (2007), pp. 129–164, quotations at 131, 152, 153.

17. Tom Arne Midtrød, *The Memory of All Ancient Customs: Native American Diplomacy in the Colonial Hudson Valley* (Ithaca: Cornell University Press, 2012), pp. 15–18.

18. Fourteen documented instances of recitations of the *kaswentha* tradition exist from 1656 to 1748, see *JR*, 43:107–109 (26 April 1656), 44:207 (4 February 1658); *WA*, p. 9; Daniel K. Richter, "Rediscovered Links in the Covenant Chain: Previously Unpublished Transcripts of New York Indian Treaty Minutes, 1677–1691," *American Antiquarian Society Proceedings* 92 (1982), pp. 45–85 at 76 (3 October 1678); ibid., at 81 (7 July 1689); *DRCHNY*, 3:775 (12 June 1691); *WA* 24 (15 May 1694); *An Account of the Treaty Between his Excellency Benjamin Fletcher, Captain-General and Governour in Chief of the Province of New-York &c. and the Indians of the Five Nations, viz., the Mohaques, Oneydes, Onnondages, Cajonges, and Sennekes, at Albany* (New York, 1694), 7 (25 August 1694); *Propositions Made by the Five Nations of Indians, viz., The Mohaques, Oneydes, Onnondages, Cayouges, and Sinnekes, to his Excellency Richard, Earl of Bellomont, Capt. General and Governour in Chief of his Majesties Province of New-York, &c. in Albany, the 20th of July, Anno. Dom. 1698* (New York, 1698), pp. 4–5 [1 August 1698; reported at Montréal 21 August 1698 (see *DRCHNY*, 9:685–686)]; *DRCHNY*, 4:773 (8 September 1700); ibid., 909 (30 July 1701); ibid., 5:667 [14 September 1722]; Richter, *The Ordeal of the Longhouse: The People of the Iroquois League during the Era of European Colonization* (Chapel Hill: University of North Carolina Press, 1992), pp. 278–279 (2 September 1723); *DRCHNY*, 6:446;

Susan Kalter (ed.), *Benjamin Franklin, Pennsylvania, and the First Nations: The Treaties of 1736–1762* (Urbana, IL: University of Illinois Press, 2006), pp. 94–5 (26 June 1744); John Heckewelder, *History, Manners, and Customs of the Indian Nations Who Once Inhabited Pennsylvania and the Neighboring States* (New York: Arno Press, 1971 [1876]), pp. xxvii–xxix (circa 1742–1748).

19. Richter, "Rediscovered Links," p. 81 (quote).

20. James W. Bradley, "Re-visiting Wampum and Other Seventeenth-Century Shell Games," *Archaeology of Eastern North America* 39 (2011), pp. 25–51 at 31. Mohawk linguistic evidence establishes the association of the noun root for wampum with a device to fulfill certain societal functions to the pre-contact era, see Gunther Michelson, "Iroquoian Terms for Wampum," *International Journal of American Linguistics* 57 (1991), pp. 108–116 at 115.

21. Charles F. Wray et al., *The Adams and Culbertson Sites*, Rochester Museum and Science Center Research Records, no. 19 (Rochester, NY, 1987), p. 52, Figure 3–19; Lynn M. Ceci, "Native Wampum as a Peripheral Resource in the Seventeenth-Century World System," in Laurence M. Hauptman and James D. Wherry (eds.), *The Pequots in Southern New England: The Fall and Rise of an American Indian Nation* (Norman, OK: University of Oklahoma Press, 1990), pp. 48–63 at 53; Marshall Becker, "A Wampum Belt Chronology: Origins to Modern Times," *Northeast Anthropology* 63 (2002), pp. 49–70 at 50.

22. Martha L. Sempowski and Lorraine Saunders, *Dutch Hollow and Factory Hollow: The Advent of Dutch Trade Among the Seneca*, Rochester Museum and Science Center Research Records no. 24 (Rochester, NY, 2001), p. 722. On wampum manufacture, see Elizabeth S. Peña, "Wampum Production in New Netherland and Colonial New England: The Historical and Archaeological Context" (PhD diss., Boston University, 1990), pp. 23–29; William N. Fenton, *The Great Law and the Longhouse: A Political History of the Iroquois Confederacy* (Norman: University of Oklahoma Press, 1998), pp. 225–226; Matthew Lesniak, "New Evidence of Wampum Use and Production From Albany, New York," in Charles L. Fisher (ed.), *People, Places, and Material Things: Historical Archaeology of Albany*, New York State Museum Bulletin 499 (Albany, NY: The University of the State of New York, State Education Department, 2003), pp. 129–134 at 129.

23. Robert E. Funk and Robert D. Kuhn, *Three Sixteenth-Century Mohawk Iroquois Village Sites*, New York State Museum Bulletin 503 (Albany: University of the State of New York, State Education Department, 2003), p. 44. See also Wayne Lenig to Kurt Jordan, personal electronic mail correspondence dated 17 October 2012 (copy in author's possession). My thanks to Kurt Jordan and Wayne Lenig for sharing this information.

24. William J. Engelbrecht, *Iroquoia: The Development of a Native World* (Syracuse: Syracuse University Press, 2003), p. 156; Ceci, "Native Wampum as a Peripheral Resource," p. 50. Cf. George Hamell, "The Iroquois and the World's Rim: Speculations on Color, Culture, and Contact," *American Indian Quarterly* 16 (1992), pp. 451–470 at 460, who suggests that dark blue glass trade beads available in increasing quantities

after the turn of the seventeenth century inspired Iroquois interest in purple tubular shell wampum.

25. Angela M. Haas, "Wampum as Hypertext: An American Indian Intellectual Tradition of Multimedia Theory and Practice," *Studies in American Indian Literatures* 19, no. 4 (2007), pp. 77–100; Elizabeth Hill Boone, "Presidential Lecture: Discourse and Authority in Histories Painted, Knotted, and Threaded," *Ethnohistory* 59 (2012), pp. 225–230. See also the related discussion in Mark Meuwese, *Brothers in Arms, Partners in Trade: Dutch-Indigenous Alliances in the Atlantic World, 1595–1674* (Leiden: Brill, 2012), pp. 257–275.

26. *NNN*, pp. 7, 22–23; Charles F. Wray, "The Volume of Dutch Trade Goods Received by the Seneca Iroquois, 1600–1687 A.D.," *Bulletin KNOB: Tijdschrift van de Koninklijke Nederlandse Oudheidkundige Bond* 84 (2–3) (June 1985), pp. 100–112 at 103 (quote); Ian Kenyon and William Fitzgerald, "Dutch Glass Beads in the Northeast: An Ontario Perspective," *Man in the Northeast* 32 (1986), pp. 1–35 at 26; Wayne Lenig, "Patterns of Material Culture during the Early Years of the New Netherland Trade," *Northeast Anthropology* 58 (1999), pp. 50–53.

27. *DRCHNY*, 4:353; Victor Enthoven, "Early Dutch Expansion in the Atlantic Region," in Johannes Postma and idem (eds.), *Riches from Atlantic Commerce: Dutch Transatlantic Trade and Shipping, 1585–1817* (Leiden: Brill, 2003), pp. 17–47 at 36–38; Evan Haefeli, "On First Contact and Apotheosis: Manitou and Men in North America," *Ethnohistory* 54 (2007), pp. 407–43 at 415–419.

28. Mary A. Druke, "Linking Arms: The Structure of Iroquois Intertribal Diplomacy," in Daniel K. Richter and James H. Merrell (eds.), *Beyond the Covenant Chain: The Iroquois and Their Neighbors in Indian North America, 1600–1800* (Syracuse: Syracuse University Press, 1987), pp. 29–39; William J. Engelbrecht, "Iroquoian Ethnicity and Archaeological Taxa," in Ronald F. Williamson and Christopher M. Watts (eds.), *Taming the Taxonomy: Toward a New Understanding of Great Lakes Archaeology* (Toronto, Ont.: Eastend Books, 1999), pp. 51–60 at 53; Richard W. Hill, Sr., "Making a Final Resting Place Final: A History of the Repatriation Experience of the Haudenosaunee," in Jordan E. Kerber (ed.), *Cross-Cultural Collaboration: Native Peoples and Archaeology in the Northeastern United States* (Lincoln, NE: University of Nebraska Press, 2006), pp. 3–17 at 10–11; Leanne Simpson, "Looking After Gdoonaaginaa: Precolonial Nishnabeg Diplomatic and Treaty Relationships," *Wicazo Sa Review* 23 (2008), pp. 29–42.

29. Charles T. Gehring, "New Netherland: The Formative Years, 1609–1632," in Hans Krabbendam, Cornelis A. van Minnen, and Giles Scott-Smith (eds.), *Four Centuries of Dutch-American Relations, 1609–2009* (Albany: State University of New York Press, 2009), pp. 75–76.

30. Charles T. Gehring (ed. and trans.), *Delaware Papers (Dutch Period): A Collection of Documents Pertaining to the Regulation of Affairs on the South River of New Netherland, 1648–1664* (Baltimore: Genealogical Publishing Co., 1981), p. 29; Jaap Jacobs, "Truffle Hunting with an Iron Hog: The First Dutch Voyage up the Delaware River" (unpublished paper presented to the McNeil Center for Early American

Studies Seminar, 20 April 2007), manuscript copy in author's possession. Thanks to Dr. Jacobs for permission to cite this essay.

31. Gehring and Starna, "Dutch and Indians in the Hudson Valley," p. 16 (quote); *VRBM*, pp. 302–304; A. J. F. van Laer (ed.), "Early Dutch Manuscripts," *New York History* 3 (1922), pp. 221–233 at 231.

32. E. B. O'Callaghan (ed.), *Documentary History of the State of New York*, 4 vols. (Albany, 1849–51), 3:50–51; *DRCHNY*, 3:473; Bruce G. Trigger, "The Mohawk-Mahican War: The Establishment of a Pattern," *Canadian Historical Review* 52 (1971), pp. 276–286; William A. Starna and José A. Brandão, "From the Mohawk-Mahican War to the Beaver Wars: Questioning the Pattern," *Ethnohistory* 51 (2004), pp. 725–750; Otto, *Dutch-Munsee Encounter*, p. 78.

33. *JR*, 7:217; 9:175; 10:75; 14:101; 28:113–115; Biggar, *Works of Champlain*, 5:214–115; Paul R. Huey, "Dutch Sites of the 17th Century in Rensselaerswyck," in David G. Orr and Daniel G. Crozier (eds.), *The Scope of Historical Archaeology: Essays in Honor of John L. Cotter* (Philadelphia: Temple University Department of Anthropology, 1984), pp. 63–85 at 71; Lynne Ceci, "The Value of Wampum among the New York Iroquois: A Case Study in Artifact Analysis," *Journal of Anthropological Research* 38 (1982), pp. 97–107; George Hamell, "Wampum: Light, White, and Bright Things are Good to Think," in Alexandra van Dongen et al. (eds.), *One Man's Trash is Another Man's Treasure: The Metamorphosis of the European Utensil in the New World* (Rotterdam: Museum Boymans van Beunigen, 1996), pp. 41–51.

34. *NNN*, pp. 84–85 (quotes); *VRBM*, p. 306.

35. *JR*, 5:55 (quote).

36. *VRBM*, pp. 243, 303–304 (quote at 303), 330; *NNN*, p. 78; Jaap Jacobs, *New Netherland: A Dutch Colony in Seventeenth Century America* (Leiden: Brill, 2005), pp. 198–199. On Rensselaerswijck, see Jacobs, "Dutch Proprietary Manors in America: The Patroonships in New Netherland," in L. H. Roper and Bertrand Van Ruymbeke (eds.), *Constructing Early Modern Empires: Proprietary Ventures in the Atlantic World, 1500–1750* (Leiden: Brill, 2007), pp. 301–327 at 311–321.

37. Charles T. Gehring and William A. Starna (trans. and ed.), *A Journey into Mohawk and Oneida Country, 1634–1635: The Journal of Harmen Meyndertsz van den Bogaert* (Syracuse, NY: Syracuse University Press, 1988), pp. 7–14 (quotes).

38. Ibid., p. 16; *VRBM*, p. 330.

39. Willem Frijhoff, "Jesuits, Calvinists, and Natives: Attitudes, Agency, and Encounters in the Early Christian Missions in the North," *de Halve Maen* 81 (Fall 2008), pp. 47–54.

40. Meuwese, *Brothers in Arms, Partners in Trade*, pp. 233–235.

41. *NNN*, p. 274 (quote); *VRBM*, pp. 426, 565–566, 626; Biggar, *Works of Champlain*, 5:313–318; Brian J. Given, *A Most Pernicious Thing: Gun Trading and Native Warfare in the Early Contact Period* (Ottawa, Ont.: Carleton University Press, 1994), pp. 57–68; Peter Lowensteyn, "The Role of the Dutch in the Iroquois Wars," *de Halve Maen* 58, no. 3 (1984), pp. 3–4; Jan Piet Puype, "Dutch and other Flint-locks from Seventeenth Century Iroquois Sites," in Charles F. Hayes III (ed.), *Pro-*

ceedings of the 1984 Trade Gun Conference, Rochester Museum and Science Center Research Records 18 (Rochester, NY, 1985), pp. 69–91; James Bradley, *Before Albany: An Archaeology of Native-Dutch Relations in the Capital Region, 1600–1664*, New York State Museum Bulletin 509 (Albany: The University of the State of New York, State Education Department, 2007), pp. 124–125.

42. *VRBM*, pp. 416, 483–484, 508–509 (quotes); A. J. F. van Laer (ed.), "Arent van Curler and his Historic Letter to the Patroon [16 June 1643]," *Dutch Settlers' Society of Albany Yearbook* 3 (1927–8), p. 24; James W. Bradley, "Visualizing Arent van Curler: A Biographical and Archaeological View," *de Halve Maen* 78, no. 1 (2005), pp. 3–5; Jan M. Baart, "Cloth Seals at Iroquois Sites," *Northeast Historical Archaeology* 34 (2005), pp. 77–80.

43. Van Laer, "Arent van Curler," pp. 27–28 (quotes).

44. François Du Creux, *The History of Canada, or New France*, 2 vols., Percy J. Robinson, trans. (Toronto: The Champlain Society, 1951–2 [1664]),1:382–385 (quotes), 396n; *ERNY*,1:166, 436. While calculating early modern currency exchange is an imprecise exercise at best, the value of the compensation paid to the Mohawks (300 livres) may have represented less than one-third of the value of the original ransom offered (600 guilders), see Jan de Vries, *The Economy of Europe in an Age of Crisis, 1600–1750* (Cambridge: Cambridge University Press, 1976), p. x.

45. Dean Snow, Charles T. Gehring, and William A. Starna (eds.), *In Mohawk Country: Early Narratives about a Native People* (Syracuse: Syracuse University Press, 1996) (hereinafter *IMC*), pp. 43, 48–55 (quote at 54); *ERNY*, 1:168; Charles T. Gehring (ed. and trans.), *Correspondence, 1647–1653* (Syracuse: Syracuse University Press, 2000), pp. 87–91, 110.

46. Meuwese, *Brothers in Arms, Partners in Trade*, pp. 241–249.

47. *NNN*, pp. 273–274, 303; Janny Venema, "The Court Case of Brant Aertz van Slichtenhorst against Jan van Rensselaer," *de Halve Maen* 74 (2001), pp. 3–8 at 6; Charles T. Gehring (ed.), *Council Minutes, 1652–1654* (Syracuse: Syracuse University Press, 1983), p. 43; Gehring (ed.), *Correspondence, 1647–1653*, p. 33; Kevin Moody, "Traders or Traitors: Illicit Trade at Fort Orange in the Seventeenth Century," in Charles L. Fisher (ed.), *Peoples, Places, and Material Things: Historical Archaeology of Albany, New York*, New York State Museum Bulletin 199 (Albany: The University of the State of New York, State Education Department, 2003), pp. 25–38; Janny Venema, *Beverwijck: A Dutch Village on the American Frontier, 1652–1664* (Albany: State University of New York Press, 2003), pp. 44, 182, 254, 275–77, 448; Jacobs, *New Netherland*, pp. 205, 208–209.

48. *JR*, 19:211–213, quote at 213); 41:37; Du Creux, *History of Canada*, 2:679–680; Meuwese, "From Intercolonial Messenger to 'Christian Indian': The Flemish Bastard and the Mohawk Struggle for Independence from New France and Colonial New York in the Eastern Great Lakes Borderland, 1647–1687," in Karl Hele (ed.), *Lines Drawn Upon the Water: First Nations and the Great Lakes Borders and Borderlands* (Waterloo, Ont.: Wilfrid Laurier University Press, 2008), pp. 43–63. Nan Rothschild's assertion, based exclusively on archaeological evidence, of the ostensibly

limited sexual interest of Dutch men in Mohawk women (and vice versa), appears in *Colonial Encounters in a Native American Landscape: The Spanish and Dutch in North America* (Washington, DC: Smithsonian Institution, 2003), pp. 217–220. For documentary evidence of Mohawk-Dutch sexual relations, intermarriage, and individuals of Dutch-Mohawk ancestry in seventeenth-century New Netherland and New York, see *JR*, 50:183; *IMC*, pp. 43, 196–197; Charles T. Gehring (ed.), *Fort Orange Court Minutes, 1652–1660* (Syracuse: Syracuse University Press, 1990), p. 454; William H. Browne et al. (eds.), *Archives of Maryland* (72 vols. to date, Baltimore, 1883–), vol. 17, p. 201; A. J. F. van Laer (ed.), *Minutes of the Court of Albany, Rensselaerswyck, and Schenectady, 1668–1685*, 3 vols. (Albany, 1926–32), 3:264; *DRCHNY*, 3:323, 325, 328, 431; Lawrence H. Leder (ed.), *The Livingston Indian Records, 1666–1723* (Gettysburg, Pa.: Pennsylvania Historical Association, 1956), pp. 29, 31, 45, 80, 111–113, 120, 127, 131–133, 139–140, 146, 156–157; Victor Hugo Paltsits (ed.), *Minutes of the Executive Council of the Province of New York: Administration of Francis Lovelace, 1668–1673*, 2 vols. (Albany, 1910), 2:668; Bartlett B. James and J. Franklin Jameson (eds.), *Journal of Jasper Danckaerts, 1679–1680* (New York, 1913), pp. 201–211; Jonathan Pearson, *A History of the Schenectady Patent in Dutch and English Times, Being Contributions Toward a History of the Lower Mohawk Valley* (Albany, 1883), pp. 17, 169, 188–89; Barbara Sivertsen, *Turtles, Wolves, and Bears: A Mohawk Family History* (Bowie, Md.: Heritage Books, 1997), pp. 1–10; Nancy L. Hagedorn, "Brokers of Understanding: Interpreters as Agents of Cultural Exchange in Colonial New York," *New York History* 76 (1995), pp. 379–408 at 381–382; Bradley, "Visualizing Arent van Curler," p. 7; Susan J. Staffa, *Schenectady Genesis: How a Dutch Colonial Village Became an American City, ca.1661–1800, vol. 1, The Colonial Crucible, 1661–1774* (Fleischmanns: Purple Mountain Press, 2004), pp. 33–34, 38, 49–50, 72; John P. Ferguson, *The Schoharie Mohawks* (Howes Cave, NY: Iroquois Indian Museum, 2009), pp. 16–19; Marcus P. Meuwese, "'For the Peace and Well-Being of the Country': Intercultural Mediators and Dutch-Indian Relations in New Netherland and Dutch Brazil, 1600–1664" (PhD diss., University of Notre Dame, 2003), pp. 351–353.

49. Massachusetts Historical Society *Collections*, 4th ser., vol. 6 (1863), p. 477 ("taking away by . . ."); Jonathan Pearson (ed.), *Early Records of the City and County of Albany, and Colony of Rensselaerswyck* (Albany, 1869), p. 237 (all other quotes); cf. Starna, "Native-Dutch Experience," p. 33.

50. *JR*, 44:95–101 (quotes), 223–235; *Le Journal des Jesuits, Publié d'après le Manuscrit Original Conservé aux Archives du Seminaire du Québec* (Montréal: Éditions François Xavier, 1973 [1871]) (hereafter "*JJ*"), pp. 235–236.

51. *JR*, 44:101–107, 111, 225–231; *JJ*, pp. 237–238; Gehring, *Fort Orange Court Minutes*, pp. 400–402 (quotes); *DRCHNY*, 12:99; 13:13, 122.

52. Gehring, *Fort Orange Court Minutes*, pp. 453–454 (quotes). On declining peltry volumes in *New Netherland* after 1657, see A. J. F. van Laer (ed.), *Correspondence of Jeremias van Rensselaer, 1651–1674* (Albany, 1932) (hereinafter "*CJVR*"), pp. 104, 106–107; Burke, *Mohawk Frontier*, pp. 7–11; Venema, *Beverwijck*, pp. 159, 178, 203, 206; Jacobs, *New Netherland*, pp. 212–213. For a colorful account of the frenzied com-

petition at Beverwijck during *handelstijd* (the annual trading season spanning from May to November, but peaking between June and August), see Merwick, *Possessing Albany: The Dutch and English Experiences* (Cambridge: Cambridge University Press, 1990), pp. 77–103; Jaap Jacobs and Martha Dickinson Shattuck, "Beavers for Drink, Land for Arms," in Van Dongen et al. (eds.), *One Man's Trash*, pp. 95–113 at 101–104.

53. Gehring, *Fort Orange Court Minutes*, pp. 454–459 (quotes); *CJVR*, p. 186; *DRCHNY*, 13:123, 164, 179–184. "Kaghnuwage" was the Mohawk Turtle clan village located on the south side of the Mohawk River, known to archaeologists as the Freeman site.

54. Gehring, *Fort Orange Court Minutes*, pp. 463–464, 503 (quote), 515–518; E. B. O'Callaghan (ed.), *Laws and Ordinances of New Netherland, 1638–1674* (Albany, 1868), pp. 383, 425–427, 463–464; Dennis Sullivan, *The Punishment of Crime in Colonial New York: The Dutch Experience in Albany during the Seventeenth Century* (New York: Peter Lang, 1997), p. 160.

55. *CJVR*, p. 225; *DRCHNY*, 13:203, 219, 244; 14:296; A. J. F. van Laer (ed.), "Albany Notarial Papers, 1666–1693," *Dutch Settlers' Society of Albany Yearbook* 13 (1937–38), p. 2; Arthur C. Parker, *The Archeological History of New York*, New York State Museum Bulletin 235–236 (Albany, 1920), p. 692; Pearson, *History of the Schenectady Patent*, pp. 11–17; Burke, *Mohawk Frontier*, pp. 19, 31, 68–73; Bradley, "Visualizing Arent van Curler," pp. 7–13; Ferguson, *Schoharie Mohawks*, pp. 17–20.

56. Peter R. Christoph and Florence A. Christoph (eds.), *Books of General Entries of the Colony of New York, vol. 1, Orders, Warrants, Letters, Commissions, Passes and Licenses Issued by Governors Richard Nicolls and Francis Lovelace, 1664–1673* (Baltimore: Genealogical Publishing Co., 1982), pp. 47–49; compare *DRCHNY*, 3:67–68. A significant thread of Mohawk oral tradition locates the origins of the Two Row wampum belt symbolizing the *kaswentha* to the 1664 Cartwright Treaty, see Paul Williams, "The Chain" (LL.M. thesis, York University, 1992), pp. 96–98 at 97); idem, "Wampum of the Six Nations Confederacy at the Grand River Territory: 1784–1986," in Charles F. Hayes III and Lynn M. Ceci (eds.), *Proceedings of the 1986 Shell Bead Conference: Selected Papers*, Rochester Museum and Science Center Research Records, no. 20 (Rochester, NY, 1989), pp. 200–202; Patricia Monture-Angus, *Journeying Forward: Dreaming First Nations Independence* (Halifax, N.S.: Fernwood Publishing, 1999), p. 39; Jim Miller, "Compact, Contract, Covenant: The Evolution of Indian Treaty-Making," in Ted Binnema and Susan Neylan (eds.), *New Histories for Old: Changing Perspectives on Canada's Native Pasts* (Vancouver, BC: University of British Columbia Press, 2007), pp. 66–91 at 74.

57. For a listing of Hudson Quadricentennial Commemoration events, see "Celebrating Four Hundred Years of Dutch-American Relations: NY 400," *de Halve Maen* 82, no. 2 (Summer 2009), pp. 33–36. One exception to the trend of Native marginalization was the 27 November 2009 "ceremony of apology" held at the National Museum of the American Indian in Manhattan, during which the Reverend Robert Chase, pastor of Collegiate Church in New York City, apologized to an audience of Lenape delegates for "massacring and displacing Native Americans 400 years ago,"

see Verena Dobnik, "Christian Church, Native American Tribe Reconcile," *Buffalo News*, 27 November 2009 (quote); Paul Grondahl, "After 400 Years, Peace: Apology Ceremony Lauded by Native Americans, Descendants of the Dutch," *Albany Times-Union*, 5 December 2009.

58. Sam Roberts, "Proud Amsterdam Celebrates New York, and Itself," *New York Times*, 6 April 2009. See also the photographs and descriptions of this event in the entries for 5 April 2009 and 9 April 2009 on the "Amsterdam-New York-Art-Station" weblog, <http://newyork.amsterdamart.net/blog.html> (accessed 10 December 2009).

59. *DRCHNY*,4:568 (quote). See also Ian K. Steele, *Warpaths: Invasions of North America* (New York: Oxford University Press, 1994), pp. 110–117; José A. Brandão, "Competing Ambitions: Native-Native and Native-Dutch Relations in the Era of Beverwyck," *de Halve Maen* 76, no. 3 (2003), pp. 52–56 at 55.

60. James Folts, "Before the Dispersal: Records of New York's Official Records with the Oneidas and Other Indian Nations," in Laurence M. Hauptman and L. Gordon McLester III (eds.), *The Oneida Indian Journey: From New York to Wisconsin* (Madison, WI: University of Wisconsin Press, 1999), pp. 151–170 at 153; Graeber, *Toward an Anthropological Theory of Value*, p. 132; Fenton, Great Law and the Longhouse, pp. 235–236, 576; Jonathan C. Lainey, *La "Monnaie" des Sauvages: Les Colliers de Wampum d'hier à aujourd'hui* (Sillery, Qué.: Les Éditions du Septentrion, 2004), pp. 79–86; Marshall Becker, "Wampum Held by the Oneida Indian Nation, Inc. of New York: Research Relating to Wampum Cuffs and Belts," *Bulletin: Journal of the New York State Archaeological Association* 123 (2007), pp. 1–18 at 4, 13; idem, "Small Wampum Bands Used by Native Americans in the Northeast: Functions and Recycling," *Material Culture* 40 (2008), pp. 1–17 at 8; cf. Paul Williams, "Reading Wampum Belts as Living Symbols," *Northeast Indian Quarterly* 7 (1990), pp. 31–35 at 34–35, who acknowledges the disassembly of certain belts but asserts that "permanent commitments" such as the "Two Row Wampum" were likely preserved. One possible candidate for a preserved Two Row belt is the so-called "Path Belt" (woven in an unmistakable Two Row pattern and referred to in those terms by Fenton, Great Law and the Longhouse, p. 234) that was acquired under vague circumstances by Beauchamp at an unspecified date between 1898 and 1901, purchased by the New York State Museum in 1949, and eventually repatriated to the Onondaga Nation in October 1989, see Beauchamp, "Wampum and Shell Articles," p. 406; Charles H. Gillette, "Wampum Beads and Belts," *Indian Historian* 3 (1970), pp. 33–38 at 36; Fenton, "The New York State Wampum Collection: The Case for the Integrity of Cultural Treasures," *American Philosophical Society Proceedings* 115, no. 6 (1971), pp. 437–461 at 458; [Anonymous] "Wampum Belts Returned to the Onondaga Nation," *Man in the Northeast* 38 (1989), pp. 109–117 (esp. fig.12, at 117); Jose Barreiro, "Return of the Wampum," *Northeast Indian Quarterly* 7 (Spring 1990), pp. 8–20 at 12; Martin Sullivan, "Return of the Sacred Wampum Belts of the Iroquois," *History Teacher* 26 (November 1992), pp. 7–14; Christopher N. Matthews and Kurt A. Jordan, "Secularism as Ideology: Exploring Assumptions of Cultural Equivalence in

Museum Repatriation," in Reinhard Berbeck and Randall H. McGuire (eds.), *Ideologies in Archaeology* (Tucson, AZ: University of Arizona Press, 2011), pp. 214–229. For an example of a study of a surviving Iroquois wampum belt linked to a documentary source, see "Historic Wampum," *Buffalo Historical Society Publications* 25 (1921), pp. 208–213.

61. Starna has recently claimed that the fraudulent nature of the document purporting to represent the 1613 treaty renders the whole "idea of any formal agreement made in 1613" equally false, see Glenn Coin, "400 Years Later, A Legendary Iroquois Treaty Comes Under Attack," *Syracuse Post-Standard*, 9 August 2012; cf. Benjamin, "Historic Dispute: Review of Article on 1613 Treaty Revealed Errors," *Syracuse Post-Standard*, 12 August 2012, who notes that Starna's statement directly contradicts the argument advanced in the latter's 2008 article "Retrospecting the League of the Iroquois" (see Note 12 above).

62. Fenton, *Great Law and the Longhouse*, pp. 623–624 (quote); Williams, *Linking Arms Together*, pp. 12–13.

63. King, "Value of Water," p. 461.

64. Peter Nabokov, *A Forest of Time: American Indian Ways of History* (New York: Cambridge University Press, 2002): Claudio Saunt, "Telling Stories: The Political Uses of Myth and History in the Cherokee and Creek Nations," *Journal of American History* 93 (2006), pp. 673–697; Keith Thor Carlson, "Reflections on Indigenous History and Memory: Reconstructing and Reconsidering Contact," in John Sutton Lutz (ed.), *Myth and Memory: Stories of Indigenous-European Contact* (Vancouver: University of British Columbia Press, 2007), pp. 46–68 at 47–48.

III

THE ESTABLISHMENT
OF COLONIAL WORLDS

7

The Other 400th Anniversary

Samuel de Champlain and the French Atlantic Empire

Leslie Choquette

The year 2009 marked the four hundredth anniversary, not only of Hudson's voyage, but of another crucial event in the history of the future Empire State: In July of 1609, two months before Henry Hudson began his exploration of the Hudson River, Samuel de Champlain arrived at the lake that today bears his name. Champlain's trip that year, unlike Hudson's, was not simply a voyage of exploration, nor was Champlain its leader. He was participating, with two other Frenchmen, in a Huron and Algonquian war party directed against the Haudenosaunee, the powerful Iroquois League. According to Champlain, the sixty or so allied warriors made short work of a larger force of some 200 Iroquois owing to the use of French firearms.[1] Champlain's musket earned him the status of war chief along with an enemy scalp; it also embroiled the new French settlement at Québec in nearly a century of warfare that would have profound consequences for the fledgling colony of New France.

To understand fully that fateful encounter on the shores of Lake Champlain in the summer of 1609, we need to take a step backward and consider what the French were doing in North America in the first place. Like the English and Dutch, they were acquiring an Atlantic empire in the seventeenth century, not only on the North American mainland but also in the Caribbean. The goal of this essay is to provide an overview of that empire, from its tentative beginnings to the middle of the seventeenth century.

The French, like the English and Dutch, came later to the scramble for empire than the Spanish and Portuguese. There were several failed attempts at colonization in the sixteenth century, leading to lost colonies in Québec (1541–1543), Brazil (1555–1560), Florida (1562–1565), and Sable Island near Nova Scotia (1598–1603).[2] The first permanent settlements were both the work of Samuel de Champlain, a middle-class mariner from the port of Brouage in central western France. Like King Henry IV, in whose army he had served during France's Wars of Religion, Champlain was probably a convert from Protestantism to Catholicism. His enthusiasm for colonization had been kindled by a two-year voyage to the Spanish American colonies, after the Edict of Nantes restored religious peace to France in 1598.[3]

Champlain's first voyage to Canada took place in 1603, when he embarked as a cartographer for a French fur trading expedition. At the end of May, the French ship came ashore at Tadoussac, a summer encampment of Algonquian Indians where the Saguenay River empties into the St. Lawrence. The following day the French and Indian trading partners shared a feast of moose, bear, seal, and beaver, smoked the peace pipe, and listened to speeches. For French historians Gilles Havard and Cécile Vidal, the significance of this feast cannot be overestimated. For it set the stage for something that would distinguish the French empire in North America not only from the English and Dutch empires, but from France's own colonies in the Caribbean: "a type of colonization marked by alliance with indigenous peoples."[4]

Champlain returned to North America the following summer, this time with the intention of establishing a permanent French presence. His men (there were no women or children) overwintered on Saint Croix Island, which is shared by Maine and New Brunswick today. But after 35 of 79 pioneers died of scurvy, Champlain moved the habitation across the Bay of Fundy to Port Royal, now Annapolis Royal in Nova Scotia. Although he evacuated Port Royal in 1607, prior to establishing a new habitation in Québec in 1608, it was reoccupied by the French in 1610 and thus qualifies as France's first permanent outpost in North America.[5]

It should be noted that Champlain was not working directly for the French crown when he founded Port Royal and Québec. In New France as in New England and New Netherland, colonial settlement initially took place through the mechanism of individual or corporate proprietorship. The initiative for both habitations therefore came from Pierre De Monts, the Protestant officer whom Henry IV had named exclusive proprietor of New France. De Monts's royal charter granted him a commercial monopoly and seigneurial rights over eastern North America from present-day Philadelphia to Newfoundland, in return for which he agreed to transport sixty settlers across the Atlantic. Seigneurial rights gave De Monts the ability to hand out large estates called seigneuries, which entitled their holders—the seigneurs—to collect dues from the farmers who would settle on them. This arrangement foreshadows the New Netherland system of patroonships, in which the Dutch West India Company after 1628 granted land in fief to patroons in return for settling fifty colonists within three years time.[6]

While Champlain focused his energies on Québec, De Monts granted the seigneurie of Acadia (the French term for the maritime region from Maine to Nova Scotia) to Jean de Poutrincourt, a Catholic nobleman who had helped found Port Royal. In theory, French colonization now entered a new phase. Instead of being the sole responsibility of the proprietor—De Monts—it would become the shared responsibility of the proprietor and his seigneur, Poutrincourt. The return on Poutrincourt's investment would come not from trade, since De Monts had the trade monopoly, but from his seigneurie. To succeed he would have to recruit dues-paying farmers. Unfortunately for the colony, neither Poutrincourt nor his son Biencourt, who inherited the seigneurie after his father's death, had the means to do so. Biencourt died a pauper in 1623.

Meanwhile De Monts lost his trading monopoly due to complaints from rival merchants, and it passed to a succession of politically connected members of the upper nobility. All but one of the new proprietors (now known as viceroys) worked in association with a merchant company, and all agreed to send immigrants to Québec as a condition of their exclusive privilege. Starting in 1624, they began to grant seigneuries along the banks of the St. Lawrence.

Colonization proceeded slowly nevertheless. Three years later, New France in its entirety had about 100 French inhabitants, 75 in Québec and 25 in Acadia. To make matters worse, there were no French women at all in Acadia and fewer than a dozen in Québec. By that time, the Virginia colony, despite a rocky start in 1607, had an English population of 2,000, plus there were 300 English living in Massachusetts (Plymouth and Salem) and another 100 in Newfoundland. Even New Netherland, with 200 people, was twice the size of New France, and since more than half of its settlers were French-speaking Walloon families, it had a faster growing French population.[7]

This situation was unacceptable to Cardinal Richelieu, chief minister of King Louis XIII (r. 1610–1643). Richelieu's main goal was to increase French power, whether on the European continent or in the Atlantic. In 1627, therefore, he decided to reorganize New France with a view to creating an important settlement colony. Still, the resulting Company of New France, more commonly known as the Company of the Hundred Associates, differed from earlier companies only in scope. While it brought together moneyed interests from a broad geographical and social spectrum, it remained a private proprietary venture. The company received a perpetual monopoly on the fur trade and a fifteen-year monopoly on all other trade except the fisheries. In return, it agreed to transport 4,000 French Catholics of both sexes to New France within fifteen years.[8]

The Company of the Hundred Associates got off to a dismal start when the English captured their first ship for Québec, then seized the colony itself in 1629. Although the English occupation ended after treaty negotiations in 1632, the company's capital had dwindled dangerously, and it never recovered its initial vigor. By 1650, when the English population of New England and the Chesapeake surpassed 50,000, there were fewer than 1,500 French settlers in Québec and only a few hundred in Acadia. By 1663, when King Louis XIV (r. 1643–1715) dissolved the company for failing to fulfill its obligations, bringing New France under direct royal authority for the first time, Québec's French population barely topped 3,000, and Acadia had fallen to the English. In comparison, the European population of New Netherland had grown from around 1,000 to nearly 10,000 between 1650 and 1663.[9]

It might be tempting to attribute France's relative failure in Canada to some deficiency in the national character—if not outright military ineptitude then lack of an entrepreneurial attitude perhaps, a lesser appetite for risk. But a quick look at the development of the French West Indies shows that the French were indeed capable of colonizing. Like Canada, France's Caribbean colonies were created under the auspices of chartered companies, first the Company of St. Christopher (today's St. Kitts) in 1626, then the Company of the American Islands in 1635, which extended French settlement to Guadeloupe and Martinique. In spite of this late start, by 1660, the French islands were already home to between 13,000 and 15,000 French inhabitants, who in turn owned between 10,000 and 16,000 African slaves.[10] What then explains the slow growth of French Canada? I see it primarily as a matter of economics, the demand for labor in particular.

The French Caribbean colonies, like Virginia, produced one staple crop in the early seventeenth century: tobacco. Since growing tobacco was extremely labor intensive, planters needed a large labor force; demand for labor pulled French immigrants to the islands. As in the Chesapeake, immigrants were usually indentured servants, who contracted to work for a fixed term in return for their upkeep and passage. French indentured servants typically served for three years, a much shorter term than their English counterparts. From the beginning, the French islands also relied heavily on African slaves, most of them purchased from Dutch merchants in the Caribbean.[11] Meanwhile the dense Native population was seen as an obstacle to French expansion, to be removed as soon as possible. Although the Native Caribs resisted fiercely, they also succumbed in large numbers to European disease. The French largely succeeded in confining them to the reservation islands of Dominica and Saint Vincent by 1660.[12]

In contrast, the Canadian economy revolved around a very different staple—beaver fur, in great demand in Europe for the manufacture of men's hats. Pelts, of course, were obtained from Native hunters, not European servants and African slaves. The slow pace of French settlement in Canada therefore resulted primarily from dependence on a Native rather than a French and African labor force.

In Acadia and the St. Lawrence Valley, the fur supply was controlled by local Algonquian peoples. Further west, the French had to contend as well with the powerful Huron, who hunted few beaver themselves but amassed furs through longstanding and extensive trade relations. In order to stay on the good side of their fur suppliers, the French had to enter alliances on Native terms. From the day that Champlain and his companions joined the raid on the Iroquois at Lake Champlain, the fur trade enmeshed them in a complex web of diplomatic and military ties with peoples whose cultures they barely understood.[13]

Champlain's attitude toward his aboriginal allies can best be described as ambivalent. While he clearly respected their geographical and environmental knowledge, he took European cultural superiority for granted. His initial failure to grasp the subtleties of Native diplomacy, particularly the linkages between alliance and war, drew him into an escalating struggle with the Iroquois that would carry a high price for New France. Exaggerating his own prestige as a war leader, he made hopeless attempts to influence the internal politics of allied tribes. His ethnocentrism, however, coexisted with what historian John Reid has termed "a certain practical humility," a recognition that cooperation with Natives was essential to French survival, never mind expansion, in Canada.[14]

Native-French cooperation remained a hallmark of France's empire in North America until its conquest by Great Britain in 1763; however, the balance of power between the partners began to shift after 1649. In that year, France's aboriginal allies, ravaged by two decades of epidemics, fell victim to the more numerous and better armed Iroquois, wielding Dutch guns. Historians John Dickinson and Brian Young write,

> This destruction completely disrupted the French trading system and was a crucial turning point in Canadian history. The native

population in areas of French settlement along the St. Lawrence declined so dramatically that the Europeans were in a majority by 1650. Without native allies to collect and transport furs to the warehouses at . . . Quebec, the French were forced to take over these tasks themselves. This marked the end of a commercial system that had been entirely dependent on native labour and trading networks, and it marked the beginning of French territorial expansion to reach the old Huron suppliers in the western Great Lakes.[15]

Not only would French workers have to collect and transport the furs, but they would also have to farm in order to feed the fur traders. From now on, demand for French labor in both the fur trade and agriculture would provide a modest incentive for immigration, hence the doubling of Québec's French population between 1650 and 1660.

Nevertheless, Québec's powers of attraction were never as great as neighboring New England's or even New Netherland's, although those colonies had similar economies based on family farms and trade. For Québec lacked the additional "pull" factor that was critical to the growth of New England, especially in the 1630s: religious freedom for dissenters. New Netherland also respected freedom of conscience, even welcoming dissenters from New England such as Anne Hutchinson in the 1640s, as well as Jews and Quakers in the 1650s.[16]

Beginning in 1627, when Cardinal Richelieu created the Company of the Hundred Associates, Protestants were explicitly forbidden to settle in New France. In banning Protestants from the colony, Richelieu probably hoped to avoid the problems encountered by Champlain, whose first colonizing expedition in Acadia had included both Catholics and Protestants. Champlain wrote of that experiment,

> I have seen the minister and our priest get into fist fights over the difference in religion. I do not know who was the most valiant, and who threw the best punch, but I know very well that the minister complained sometimes to Sieur de Mons [the proprietor] of having been beaten, and resolved the points of controversy in this fashion. I leave to you to think whether that was fair to see; the Savages were sometimes on one side, sometimes the other, and the French, mingled according to their diverse belief, said abominable things of both religions, although Sieur de Mons made peace as best he could.[17]

These disputes continued into the following year, when both clergymen were stricken with scurvy. They died within days of one another, and, according to Marc Lescarbot, the first chronicler of Port Royal, the sailors "put them both into the same grave, to see whether dead they would live in peace, since living they had never been able to agree."[18]

Cardinal Richelieu, of course, wanted the French Empire to be Catholic for ideological as well as pragmatic reasons. The Company of the Hundred Associates granted huge seigneuries to the Jesuits, making them the largest landowners in New France. The first Catholic nuns, the Ursulines and Hospitaliers, arrived in Québec in 1639, and the Notre Dame Society, a missionary association, founded Montréal as a utopian religious community called Ville-Marie—Mary Town—in 1642.[19]

Under these circumstances, the many French Protestants fleeing religious persecution in the seventeenth century could not find refuge in New France. The French Caribbean islands proved somewhat more welcoming, in fact if not in theory; Protestants there made up about seven percent of colonists, but they were not free to practice their religion.[20] Huguenots seeking asylum were thus more likely to end up in the rival colonies of New England or New Netherland than in the French Atlantic. Prominent eighteenth-century Americans Paul Revere, Peter Faneuil, and John Jay, to name only a few, were the children or grandchildren of French Protestants.[21]

In conclusion, if the English were latecomers to the colonial game, they quickly made up for lost time. In contrast, the French colonies did not grow as rapidly as the English ones, at least on the North American mainland. In the Caribbean, as historian Philip Boucher informs us, the French islands actually looked a lot like the English ones in the middle of the seventeenth century. He writes,

Comparison with English settlement of Barbados, and especially with the Leeward Islands (St. Christopher, Antigua, Nevis, and Montserrat), yields far greater similarities than differences. Neither French chartered colonial companies nor English proprietary lordships were able to exert much control over the lives of the 'adventurers' who were risking life and limb to settle in the tropics. In both cases, the island colonies searched for a viable staple, which they found, first, in tobacco, then [after tobacco prices collapsed on the world market in the late 1630s] in alternatives like indigo, cotton, and, finally, sugar. Both tried desperately to secure adequate coerced labor in the form of white indentured servants and enslaved Africans.[22]

I would add that both fought, as well, to displace the Island Caribs to make room for their plantations.

New France, though, developed very differently from the English colonies to the south in New England and the Chesapeake. Because its economy revolved around beaver fur, a staple commodity supplied by Native American labor and trade networks, the French needed to ally with the Indians, and there was little incentive for French people to immigrate. After 1649, the defeat of France's Aboriginal allies by the Iroquois meant that French labor would indeed be required, in agriculture as well as the fur trade. Nevertheless, growth was limited both by Iroquois hostilities, which would continue until the Great Peace of 1701, and the colony's rigid Catholic orthodoxy, which made it impossible for France's many discontented Protestants to settle there. By 1650, the meager French population in the St. Lawrence Valley outnumbered the collapsing Native population for the first time, reinforcing French sovereignty.

New Netherland, meanwhile, occupied a middle ground between New France and New England, figuratively as well as literally. The important fur trade centered at Fort Orange (today Albany) required the Dutch to establish Indian alliances, which in turn embroiled them in Native warfare. Like Champlain, they learned about Native diplomacy the hard way, when the Mohawks drove the Mahicans away from Fort Orange, leaving the Iroquois as their principal trading partners. The privileged trading relationship between the Dutch and Iroquois at Fort Orange continued even after the conquest of New Netherland by the English in 1664 (attracting contraband furs from Montréal, to the dismay of authorities in New France), but relations between the Dutch and Indians grew increasingly hostile. In the 1640s and 1650s, the burgeoning colonial population sparked land disputes reminiscent of New England, and the ensuing hostilities played a part in the eventual conquest of the colony.

Beyond the narrow bands of European settlement, in "most territory outside of the colonial pales," Native nations remained in control.[23] Despite our investment in the familiar drama of colonial habitations carved from forbidding wilderness and hardened in the crucible of imperial rivalries, we need to recognize, in the words of historian John Reid, not only that "aboriginal history is *central* to any realistic understanding of seventeenth-century North America," but that seventeenth-century North American history "is *primarily* aboriginal history."[24] It is important to keep this fact in mind having commemorated the 400th anniversaries of Hudson's and Champlain's travels by telling the fascinating stories of their transatlantic worlds.

Notes

1. For Champlain's account, see W. L. Grant (ed.), *Voyages of Samuel de Champlain, 1604–1618* (New York: Barnes & Noble, 1967 [1907]), pp. 157–166.

2. For accounts of these failed colonies, see Marcel Trudel, *Histoire de la Nouvelle-France: Les vaines tentatives, 1524–1603* (Montreal: Fides, 1963).

3. See Marcel Trudel's authoritative article on Champlain in *Dictionary of Canadian Biography, vol. 1, 1000–1700* (Toronto, Ont.: University of Toronto Press, 1965). The most recent full biography is David Hackett Fischer, *Champlain's Dream* (New York: Simon and Schuster, 2008).

4. Gilles Havard and Cécile Vidal, *Histoire de l'Amérique française* (Paris: Flammarion, 2003), p. 48. All translations by author. For Champlain's account, see Edward Gaylord Bourne and Annie Thompson Bourne (eds. and trans.), *The Voyages and Explorations of Samuel de Champlain*, 2 vols. (New York, 1906), 2:156–162.

5. On the beginnings of French settlement in New France, see Marcel Trudel, *Histoire de la Nouvelle-France: Le comptoir, 1604–1627* (Montréal: Fides, 1966).

6. Wim Klooster, "Other Netherlands Beyond the Sea: Dutch America between Metropolitan Control and Divergence, 1600–1795," in Christine Daniels and Michael V. Kennedy (eds.), *Negotiated Empires: Centers and Peripheries in the Americas, 1500–1820* (New York: Routledge, 2002), pp. 171–191.

7. Trudel, *Histoire de la Nouvelle-France: Le comptoir*, pp. 406–429.

8. On the Company of the Hundred Associates, see Marcel Trudel, *Histoire de la Nouvelle-France: La Seigneurie des Cent-Associés, Les Événements* (Montréal: Fides, 1979). On French migration to New France, see Gervais Carpin, *Le Réseau du Canada: Étude du mode migratoire de la France vers la Nouvelle-France (1628–1662)* (Sillery, Qué.: Septentrion and Paris: Presses de l'Université de Paris–Sorbonne, 2001), and Leslie Choquette, *Frenchmen into Peasants: Modernity and Traditions in the Peopling of French Canada* (Cambridge, MA: Harvard University Press, 1997).

9. Marcel Trudel, *Histoire de la Nouvelle-France: La Seigneurie des Cent-Associés, Les Événements*, p. 399. See also Jaap Jacobs, *New Netherland: A Dutch Colony in Seventeenth-Century America* (Leiden: Brill, 2005).

10. See Philip P. Boucher, *France and the American Tropics to 1700: Tropics of Discontent?* (Baltimore. MD: Johns Hopkins University Press, 2008), pp. 89, 157.

11. In contrast to the French Islands, the Dutch Antilles (Curaçao in particular) developed as commercial emporia rather than as centers of crop production; Klooster, "Other Netherlands Beyond the Sea," p. 174.

12. Boucher, *France and the American Tropics*, p. 115.

13. John Dickinson and Brian Young, *A Short History of Quebec*, 4th ed. (Montréal, Qué and Kingston, Ont.: McGill-Queen's University Press, 2008), pp. 17–22.

14. John G. Reid, *Essays on Northeastern North America, Seventeenth and Eighteenth Centuries, with contributions by Emerson W. Baker* (Toronto: University of Toronto Press, 2008), p. 219.

15. Dickinson and Young, *A Short History of Quebec*, p. 20.

16. For a nuanced study of religion in New Netherland see Evan Haefeli, *New Netherland and the Dutch Origins of American Religious Liberty* (Philadelphia, PA: University of Pennsylvania Press, 2012).

17. Cited in Trudel, *Histoire de la Nouvelle-France: Le comptoir*, p. 25.

18. Cited in ibid., p. 51.

19. See Dickinson and Young, A Short History of Quebec, pp. 40–44.

20. Boucher, *France and the American Tropics*, p. 132.

21. Pieter Minuit, the director of New Netherland famously responsible for the purchase of Manhattan Island in 1626, was of Walloon rather than Huguenot descent. His French-speaking Protestant family came not from France but from Tournai in the Spanish Netherlands (today Belgium).

22. Boucher, *France and the American Tropics*, p. 111.

23. Reid, *Essays on Northeastern North America*, p. 129.

24. Ibid., pp. 224, 231.

_____

8

"In Such a Far Distant Land, Separated from All the Friends"

Why Were the Dutch in New Netherland?

Jaap Jacobs

*A*t first glance, Jeremias van Rensselaer does not appear to have been a happy colonist. In a letter of 11 May 1663 to his brother in Amsterdam he complained about being "in such a far distant land, separated from all the friends," friends meaning family members here.[1] It evokes two immediate questions: why was he in New Netherland in the first place, and how he did manage without the comfort of family ties, as all his relatives were back in the Dutch Republic? Jeremias is of course only an example, a single colonist out of the entire population of New Netherland, but his case calls to mind the larger question: why were the Dutch in New Netherland anyway?

To seek answers, we need to start at the level of the "push" and "pull" factors of transatlantic migration: why would anyone want to leave the Dutch Republic? If he or she did, why would he or she choose to go to New Netherland? And once there, what induced him or her to stay? Obviously the answers to these questions differ per individual and over time, even within such a limited period as the forty years of New Netherland's existence. Thus, when dealing with questions like these, we need to make generalizations, while being aware of their pitfalls. It is easy to state that, "the Dutch came to New York City and established a trading post there to make a buck or to make a guilder,"[2] and, thus, proclaim this as the main cause of New York City's financial primacy in the world nowadays; this line of reasoning emanates from a very common human desire to explain and justify contested values in the present by stressing their venerable lineage. Unfortunately, history is rarely so straightforward and professional historians should be reluctant to provide facile answers. Even so, initially the Dutch were certainly drawn to North America by the prospect of a lucrative fur trade.

Bucks and Beavers, 1609–1640

Henry Hudson's famous voyage of 1609 paved the way for Dutch merchants in North America. Hired by the Dutch East India Company, Hudson failed to find the elusive northern passage to Asia but he discovered that Native groups along the Hudson River could supply peltries, especially beaver skins. This prospect induced merchant companies in Amsterdam and Hoorn to send ships to the newly reconnoitered area, although fierce competition between these companies resulted in conflicts between the skippers on the Hudson and in litigation back in Amsterdam. As competition adversely affected profits, these merchants in 1614 united into the New Netherland Company, which subsequently was granted exclusive trading rights to the North American coastline from Virginia to Cape Cod by the States General.

From 1614 to 1618 several trading and exploring voyages were made, and, as they were continued, we may presume that they were on the whole profitable. Yet the States General, in 1618, turned down a request for renewal of the charter of the New Netherland Company, a decision that was in part motivated by the anticipated founding of the West India Company. Two years after its chartering in 1621, this new company launched its first activities and took over control of the Dutch fur trading interests in North America.[3]

For the West India Company, New Netherland held tertiary importance, as the Company focused on the fight against the Iberian powers in the southern Atlantic. Privateering in the Caribbean was more attractive and the conquest of parts of the Portuguese sugar colony of Brazil promised a sweet prize. New Netherland was not entirely neglected, but in order to continue the fur trade the earlier practice of seasonal trading through temporary trading posts needed to be changed. In addition, the West India Company thought that permanent Dutch settlement in the region would rebut English claim to this part of North America, based on the charters granted to the Virginia Company of London and the Virginia Company of Plymouth by

James I in 1606, although these claims had not given rise to a substantial English presence between Jamestown and New Plymouth. Thus, in either late 1623 or January 1624, the WIC sent a scouting party with a small number of colonists. A couple of months later, a second ship arrived in the fledgling colony. Together, the ships carried a number of Walloon colonists, mostly French-speaking religious refugees originating from the southern Netherlands. In an effort to claim a large area for the West India Company, the settlers were spread over four locations: Fort Orange [now Albany] on the Hudson River; Fort Good Hope, in what is now Hartford, Connecticut, on the Connecticut River; Fort Wilhelmus [now Burlington Island, New Jersey] on the upper Delaware River; and *Nooten Eylandt* [Governor's Island] just off of the southern tip of Manhattan Island. Quickly, however, all of the colonists were resettled on the southern tip of Manhattan in 1625 or 1626. This reconcentration was probably inspired by the desire to limit expense and strengthen defense, as several small outposts might be more vulnerable to Indian attacks, such as the one that took the life of Daniël van Krieckenbeeck at Fort Orange. Soon afterward, Manhattan Island was purchased from the *wilden*.[4]

It is one of the quirks of history that an event such as the purchase of Manhattan, now considered to be of the utmost importance, is only revealed to us in a simple letter, commonly called the "Schagen letter" after its author: There is no bill of sale, no indication whatsoever that the purchase was perceived as a momentous event at the time and it very likely was not. The letter was written by an Alkmaar delegate to the States General, Pieter Jansz Schagen, who was in Amsterdam as representative to the annual meeting of the Board of the West India Company, the Lords Nineteen, when the ship *Wapen van Amsterdam* arrived in the port. Schagen simply reported to his colleagues in The Hague that the news was good: to the effect that our people are doing well, a good harvest is expected, some female colonists have given birth, and, oh yes, we bought Manhattan Island for sixty guilders.

The citation of that sum, though, should not lead us to think that any coins changed hands as it is far more likely that payment consisted of trade goods. As a significant aside, in the 1840s, when the Schagen letter was discovered, the contemporary exchange rate was used to convert sixty guilders into $24, a figure which found its way into the many New Netherland myths that are so hard to eradicate. Far more important than the purchase of Manhattan to Schagen's mind were the numbers of peltries: 7,246 beaver skins, 753½ otters, 81 minx, 36 wild cat, and 34 rat skins, as well as many oak beams and timber from nut trees. Judging from this cargo, the Dutch were doing better than just making the proverbial buck. The total value of this cargo of peltries was about 45,000 guilders, which makes paying sixty guilders for the temporary right to start a trading a trading post on a hilly island with not very fertile soil, sound like a sensible business investment, even without indulging in anachronistic comparisons.[5]

On Manhattan, the Dutch started building Fort Amsterdam, which was intended to be the headquarters of the Company's operations in New Netherland. It was supported by smaller fortifications such as Fort Orange, where most of the fur trade took place. The administration of New Netherland was organized similar to that of Dutch trading posts around the globe as central authority rested with the director and council. Since New Netherland was a small colony, its chief executive initially was a *directeur*, director. Not until the appointment of Petrus Stuyvesant was the higher rank of director-general introduced, as the Dutch islands in the Caribbean, such as Curaçao, Aruba, and Bonaire were also under his governance. Traditionally, Stuyvesant has not had a good reputation: Maud Wilder Goodwin, writing in the early twentieth century, called him "a brutal tyrant,"[6] a view echoed in modern popular historiography. The administrative structure, though, did not allow autocracy, as major decisions were always taken by director (or director-general) *and* council. This was no hollow phrase: for instance, Stuyvesant's proposals in the council meetings were on occasion voted down.

As the highest institution of government in New Netherland, director-general and council held all administrative, judicial, and commercial power locally. Any ordinance drawn up in the colony was subject to approval by the superiors in the fatherland, who wanted to be kept informed about everything. Even so, the authorities in New Netherland encountered many situations in which they had to act first and ask permission later. In administering justice director-general and council had to stay within the bounds of Dutch criminal and civil law. Special regulations, laid down in so-called *artikelbrieven* (letters of articles), applied to soldiers and to Company servants; in the 1620s that comprised everyone in New Netherland, as the early Walloon colonists had signed contracts for a number of years with the Company. By 1628, the number of colonists, between 200 and 300, warranted the appointment of a minister of the Dutch Reformed Church, the offices of which had earlier been served by a comforter of the sick. Almost all colonists were concentrated at Fort Amsterdam, which by now had grown into a medium-sized trading post.[7]

The West India Company's hold on the colony was further strengthened by its monopoly over the fur trade. The export of peltries doubled from 5,000 pelts in 1624 to about 10,000 in 1632. Some WIC shareholders and *bewindhebbers* [directors], however, were disappointed by the progress made in the colonization of New Netherland, and in the mid-1620s a conflict arose within the Amsterdam chamber, the largest of the five chambers that made up the decentralized WIC. The Amsterdam chamber, which supervised New Netherland's affairs, had its headquarters in what is still called the West India House in Amsterdam, which was originally built as a meat market in 1617, but the West India Company rented it from the city of Amsterdam from 1623 to 1652. The building now houses the John Adams Institute and serves as a lecture location for visiting American writers and politicians. In the seventeenth century, though, the discussion in its halls focused on colonial policies. One faction, the "trade faction," within the Amsterdam chamber wanted the colony restricted to a few company-run trading posts that could be maintained with minimum expense and manpower; the profits from the fur trade would therefore belong solely to the WIC. Although the colony would be vulnerable to attacks from European competitors, in particular England, the financial loss in the case of a takeover would be low.[8]

The opposing "colonization faction" argued, on the other hand, that opening the colony to private investment in agricultural settlements would increase immigration, and thus strengthen New Netherland against English attacks. The conflict was temporarily resolved through the patroonship plan of 1629, which allowed private merchants to set up their own colonies, called patroonships, within New Netherland. The conditions for patroons were made public through the publication of a pamphlet that clearly shows the main aims of the West India Company. Although the publication relates to North America, the two lines of poetry refer to the Dutch privateering activities against Spanish shipping in the Caribbean:

West India can become the Netherlands' great source of gain
Diminishing the enemy's power, and brings in silver plate.[9]

The introduction of patroonships caused a small increase in immigration into New Netherland, but its population remained small in comparison to the neighboring English colonies. The West India Company found it impossible to counter the intrusion of others. In the 1630s, the English began to encroach on the Connecticut River, usurping the local fur trade. An English attempt in 1635 to settle in the southern part of New Netherland on the Delaware River was thwarted by director Wouter van Twiller. And then there were the Swedes. In early 1638 a Swedish expedition under the command of Pieter Minuit, who was well-acquainted with the area as he had been director of New Netherland in the 1620s, settled on the Delaware River, at the present site of Wilmington, Delaware. The Swedish Fort Christina effectively cut off the Dutch Fort Nassau, which was located higher up on the east side of the river, opposite present-day Philadelphia. The Swedes, by establishing several trading posts, managed to dominate the fur trade with the Native Americans along the Delaware. Thus, the new director of New Netherland, Willem Kieft, who arrived in March 1638, issued a strong protest against Swedish intrusions that summer, but he was without military means to enforce Dutch hegemony adequately. He did, though, join forces with the Swedes in 1642 to prevent a second English attempt on the Delaware. These problems on New Netherland's southern and northeastern borders made it clear to the authorities in the Dutch Republic that immigration needed to be encouraged even more in order to boost their claim to New Netherland.[10]

Company and Colonists, 1640–1654

During the late 1630s, the States General discussed this problem with the West India Company. The result was the introduction of a new set of Freedoms and Exemptions in 1640, which revived the system of patroonships. More important was the decision of the West India Company to relinquish its monopoly on the fur trade and to allow colonists to participate in the trade with the Indians as well; private shipping to New Netherland was now permitted under a system of permits, called recognition. By taking these measures, the West India Company initiated the process of transforming itself from a commercial company into an institution solely concerned with colonial government, at least as far as New Netherland was concerned.[11]

Unfortunately the intended aim, a further increase in population, was hampered by conflicts with Indigenous groups. In an attempt to supplement the company's revenue in New Netherland, it was decided in 1639 to require the Native Americans in the vicinity of Manhattan to exchange skins, maize, and wampum for the protection they were supposedly receiving from the company. The implementation of this ill-fated decision triggered a vicious and bloody war with the Native Americans. The blame for this conflict is usually laid upon director Willem Kieft, who possibly initiated the conflict, but at the very least acted indecisively in preventing it from escalating. Thus, Kieft's War, as it has therefore been called, lasted from 1640 to 1645 and involved many of the Munsee-speaking groups in the lower Hudson River area and an estimated 1,000 Native Americans were killed by the time peace was restored.

Although only some fifty colonists lost their lives, many more fled New Netherland, leaving the colony with a severely diminished population and an eroded economy. The war also diminished any attraction that New Netherland may have had for prospective emigrants in the Dutch Republic and exacerbated discontent among the colonists; a substantial part of the population, spurred on by minister Everardus Bogardus, turned against Kieft, blaming him for the war, and, not coincidentally, exonerating themselves, when they tried to persuade first the West India Company and subsequently the States General to have the director recalled. Despite Amsterdam resistance, the States General in late 1644 forced the WIC to order Kieft to return to the Dutch Republic, although he did not depart from New Netherland until August 1647, when his successor, Petrus Stuyvesant, arrived.[12]

Stuyvesant had been appointed to the position of director-general of New Netherland, Curaçao, Bonaire, Aruba, and other dependencies in the Caribbean, but his main charge was New Netherland. He attempted to establish good relations with colonists who viewed the authority of the West India Company with suspicion. Stuyvesant initially succeeded, but positions began to harden in 1649, when the settlers, against the wishes of director-general and council, decided to send a delegation of three men, headed by former Rensselaerswijck *schout* Adriaen van der Donck, to the Dutch Republic. Their main aim was to persuade the States General to provide far more assistance to the colony, as the West India Company seemed to be unwilling or unable to do so. The first step, in the minds of this delegation, therefore needed to be a change the government of New Netherland, removing it from the aegis of the Company and putting it directly under the jurisdiction of the States General, with more say for the patroons in local government they made their views public in the tract, the *Vertoogh van Nieu Nederland*, the *Remonstrance of New Netherland*.

Their attempt came after a number of years of vehement criticism by both the general public and the States General on the West India Company for its mismanagement of the war against the Portuguese in Brazil. It is likely that the delegation was aware of this and tried to use the general opposition to the West India Company to achieve its aims. But soon after the New Netherland delegation submitted its protests the political balance of power within the Netherlands began to change. The supporters of stadholder William II had argued in favor of centralization of colonial administration, thus diminishing the power of the West India Company. William II, however, failed in his attempted coup. His attack on Amsterdam was thwarted and his death through illness late in 1650 left his party leaderless and discredited. The influence of Amsterdam in the States of Holland and therefore in the States General was restored and this provided political protection for the besieged West India Company. At the same time, two of the members of the New Netherland delegation had returned to America, leaving only Adriaen van der Donck as their spokesman in the fatherland. As a result of the political turmoil and the subsequent changes in the political situation in the Dutch Republic, Van der Donck had to return to New Netherland without having achieved anything.[13]

Subsequently, relations between the colonists and the West India Company ameliorated from 1650 onward. The policy of instituting local courts of justice, such as the Court of Fort Orange and Beverwijck [now Albany] in 1652 and the Court of *Burgemeesters* and *Schepenen* in New Amsterdam in 1653, allowed colonists more influence in local affairs as these courts were given administrative authority as well as civil and limited criminal powers, albeit under supervision by the director-general and council, which also served as an appellate court. Some tension remained, but never again would the relations between the colonists and the Company be as sour as in the 1640s.[14]

Emulation and Economy, 1654–1664

The years between the end of the First Anglo-Dutch War in 1654 and the English conquest of 1664 were the heyday of New Netherland: the population increased to 7,000 to 8,000 in 1664, spread out over New Amsterdam, sixteen villages, and two patroonships. This was a quick growth as the colony had only numbered 1,500 to 2,000 inhabitants around 1650. Within fifteen years, then, New Netherland achieved a growth that would take the only other Dutch settlement colony in the early modern era, the Cape Colony at the southern tip of Africa, almost seventy years.[15]

Through this population increase, New Netherland was able to make the transition from an overgrown trading post to a settlement colony with recognizably Dutch features. Public culture in New Netherland was dominated by the colonial elite, consisting of director-general and council, the ministers, the local government officials and chief merchants. Both the colonial elite and the directors in Amsterdam aimed for New Netherland society to emulate the examples set by the Netherlands as much as possible. Thus, for example, the colonial government adopted regulations and institutions from the Dutch Republic almost verbatim and the system of burgher rights was created in Amsterdam in 1652 and introduced in New Amsterdam in 1657; under this system, shopkeepers and artisans had to purchase the small *burgerrecht* to exercise their profession, whereas the large *burgerrecht* was a requirement for magistrates in the city government. Another example is the institution of orphanmasters, who were responsible for looking after the inheritances of minors.[16]

This deliberate emulation could be accomplished relatively easily in public matters of government, justice, religion, and economy, for which official rules were laid down by colonial authorities. It is also recognizable in informal and private facets of life, such as customs surrounding birth, baptism, courtship, marriage, death, and burial, as well as in gender issues. Such details of daily life can be gleaned from the many court cases in New Netherland. These also show a remarkable participation of women in the economy, much more so than in English colonies as Roman-Dutch law allowed Dutch women more opportunities in all aspects of business, even when married, making them equal partners of their husbands in many respects. Court and notarial records also provide us with an insight into slavery in New Netherland. These reveal that enslaved blacks were used primarily on farms and in public works projects in Manhattan. Yet, despite their unfree and low status, they could own property and could testify in court in New Netherland.[17]

While the population of the colony grew, the economy increased and began to diversify. Although the fur trade showed signs of stagnation in the late 1650s, the cultivation and export of tobacco grew considerably. New Netherland tobacco was of inferior quality in comparison with the produce of Virginia and Maryland, a portion of which was shipped to European markets via New Amsterdam, but the cultivation was profitable nonetheless. By 1664 the total value of exported tobacco outstripped that of fur. Other New Netherland products included lumber and wheat, which was grown as a cash crop and exported. Due to this economic growth, the standard of living began to rise and the hardships of pioneer settlements became a thing of the past.[18]

The maturation of New Netherland is also evident in the consolidation of governmental structures in accordance with Dutch practice, of which the increase after 1654 in the number of villages with a court of justice is a sign.

Small benches of justice in New Netherland

Year of establishment	Name
1642	Middelburgh (Newtown)
1644	Heemstede (Hempstead)
1645	Vlissingen (Flushing)
	's-Gravesande (Gravesend)
1646	Breuckelen (Brooklyn)
1652	Beverwijck (Albany)
1653	New Amsterdam (New York)
1654	Amersfoort (Flatlands)
	Midwout (Flatbush)
1656	Oostdorp (Westchester)
	Rustdorp (Jamaica)
1660	Haerlem (Harlem)
1661	Boswijck (Bushwick)
	Wiltwijck (Kingston)
	Bergen
	New Utrecht
1664	Staten Eylandt (Staten Island)

However, the criminal jurisdiction of these courts was limited to minor offences, and director-general and council retained the power to approve, or annul, as the case might be, their local ordinances. As a result, New Netherland had a relatively centralized government, comparable more with rural provinces in the east of the Netherlands than with the relatively autonomous cities in the province of Holland.[19]

In contrast, for ecclesiastical matters the locus of centralization was not colonial but imperial. By 1664, there were six ministers in New Netherland, but that was not sufficient to warrant the institution of a colonial classis, a regional meeting of ministers and elders. Instead the colony remained under the religious supervision of the classis of Amsterdam. In New Netherland, as in other Dutch colonies, the Dutch Reformed Church was the established church. Even so, full church membership was very likely around 20 percent, lower than the 37 percent average in the Dutch Republic around 1650. Among the elite, membership in the Calvinist Reformed Church was more common, as it was a formal requirement for magistrates, as well as an essential ingredient of social status. Supported by local magistrates, the Reformed Church exercised a monopoly on the public exercise of religion. That did not stop Scandinavian and German colonists from trying to obtain a Lutheran minister, an attempt that was suppressed by director-general and council, who considered overt religious pluralism a threat to the stability of colonial society. For the same reason, the colonial government tried to block Jews and Quakers from settling in New Netherland. But the West India Company directors in Amsterdam were of a more liberal mind and rescinded some local decisions. As the power to intervene whenever trouble arose remained with the colonial government, New Netherland as a whole never mirrored the famous tolerance of Amsterdam.[20]

Due to the population increase, the rising need for arable land, and the decline of the trade in peltries, the potential for further conflicts with the Native American groups along the Hudson River increased. In 1655 a short war erupted. Later dubbed the Peach War by Washington Irving, the conflict was started by the murder of an Indian woman caught stealing peaches from the garden of a New Amsterdam colonist. Further troubles took place in the mid-Hudson area, where colonists had founded the village of Wiltwijck [now Kingston, Ulster County]. Twice, in 1660 and 1663, fighting broke out, resulting in a siege of the palisaded village. Yet, in contrast to Kieft's War in the 1640s, the Esopus Wars did not present a danger to the colony as a whole.[21]

While the colonists in the mid-Hudson Valley were thus involved in occasional conflicts with the Munsees, other European countries posed far more serious threats. One of these threats was removed when Stuyvesant in 1655 led a successful expedition to the Delaware River to conquer New Sweden. The English colonies, however, remained a potential enemy. Virginia and Maryland coveted the territory along the Delaware. To the northeast, expansionist-minded New Haveners laid claim to Long Island, including the Dutch-controlled western part, tried to intrude on the Delaware, and eyed the remainder of New Netherland. The Hartford Treaty of 1650 provided a provisional agreement in which the Dutch ceded the eastern part of Long Island, but as it was never fully ratified by the authorities in Europe its impact was negligible. In the end, though, the impetus for the conquest of New Netherland came from not from neighboring colonies, but from England itself.[22]

Restoration and Takeover

In England, the Restoration of 1660 brought an end to the Interregnum. The new king, Charles II, quickly initiated an imperial policy aimed at increasing royal power over the North American colonies and at decreasing the mercantile position of the Dutch Republic by promulgating stricter Navigation Acts against its shipping. The conquest of New Netherland was favored by the faction of the king's brother, James, Duke of York, and in 1664 the king granted him a large part of North America. An English flotilla of four frigates arrived at New Amsterdam in August 1664, carrying the first English governor, Richard Nicolls. There was not much hope for the Dutch colony, as New Amsterdam had only a small garrison, dilapidated defense works, and not enough gunpowder. Thus, as the English offered lenient terms for capitulation, Stuyvesant mounted only a pretense of defense: he acquiesced to capitulation on 5 September, and the agreement of surrender was signed at his bowery a day later. Nine years later the colony was retaken by the Dutch, only to be returned to the English in 1674 in the Treaty of Westminster, which brought the Third Anglo-Dutch War to an end.[23]

English government, however, did not lead to rapid anglicization of the Dutch colonists; the Dutch language was used well into the nineteenth century, especially in rural parts of upper New York State. Most of the Dutch forms of government, though, were abolished by the English. In New York City, the government of *schout*, *burgemeesters*, and *schepenen* was changed to mayor, aldermen, and sheriff in 1664, though this change was temporarily reversed in 1673–1674 during the Dutch Restoration of New Netherland. Outside of New York City, changes came later, but by 1700 the forms of local government had been anglicized. Even so, the Dutch were able to maintain some of their own customs, such as the mutual will, until the beginning of the nineteenth century. Also, the Dutch Reformed Church remained under supervision of the Amsterdam classis until 1772. Thus, in New York City the Dutch remained a distinguishable group until the 1730s, and in Albany the Dutch were the most prominent ethnic group until after the American Revolution.[24]

Assessment

What are we to make of this New Netherland colony and its aftermath? Usually New Netherland is compared—unfavorably—with the surrounding English colonies. That may make sense when looking back from the later development of thirteen colonies into the United States of America, but it reveals a teleological way of thinking, influenced by the rise of nineteenth-century nation-states as the ultimate and unavoidable next stage of human development. From this perspective any form of protest by the colonists is interpreted as a precursor to the American Revolution, and the non-British elements in colonial America, whether French, Spanish, German, Swedish, Finnish, or Dutch, are disregarded. New Netherland from this perspective has been depicted as a failure: insufficiently populated, institutionally weak, economically feeble with an exclusive focus on fur trade; its culture, if there was any, was hardly Dutch. In other words, the Dutch were only there to make a buck and hardly left a trace after the English takeover.[25]

Nowadays, the teleological perspective finds increasingly less credence as new interpretations of New Netherland's history have been put forward, facilitated by the excellent translations of Dr. Charles Gehring of the New Netherland Project. Yet, despite the availability of more information, and despite the subsiding of the teleological perspective, New Netherland is still often comprehended within North American, or at best, Atlantic framework, although focusing on the early modern Dutch Republic and its world wide web of colonies rather than on colonial American history in my opinion provides a more fertile alternative interpretative framework. This allows us to set up a triangular comparison, composed of the Dutch Republic, New Netherland, and other Dutch colonies, whether Asiatic or Atlantic. The first leg of this triangle—the comparison between the Dutch Republic and other Dutch colonies—does not concern us now. The second leg—the comparison between the Dutch Republic and New Netherland—reveals how essentially Dutch this colony was, despite its heterogeneous population: governmentally, religiously, judicially, economically, and sociologically, everything in New Netherland was based on practices in the Dutch Republic. Obviously, it was no carbon copy; factors of scale prohibited that. After all, New Netherland was a small colony of 7,000 to 8,000 colonists, whereas the Dutch Republic was a country of two million people; New Amsterdam had only 2,500 inhabitants, while Amsterdam was a metropolis with well over 100,000 residents.[26]

On to the third leg of the comparative triangle then: several remarkable points come to light when we compare New Netherland with other Dutch colonies. For a start, there are many similarities between early New Netherland governmental structures and the standard government of trading posts, both in the East Indies and, for instance, on the West African coast. Also, Dutch attitudes towards Native Americans or blacks in New Netherland become clearer when considered against the background of what was happening elsewhere in the Dutch overseas empire.[27]

This triangular comparative perspective is also helpful in assessing the push and pull factors of immigration into New Netherland. One of the reasons why New Netherland remained smaller than the surrounding English colonies was the prosperity of the Dutch Republic. The northern Netherlands experienced an economic boom that lasted for most of the seventeenth

century, drawing immigrants from all over Europe. Second, religious toleration made the Netherlands a safe haven for many dissident refugees. The
incentives for migrating out of England—growing religious pressure and a
stagnant economy—were not present on the other side of the North Sea. In
the seventeenth century, the Dutch Republic was an immigration country
rather than an emigration country. On the whole, there were no compelling
reasons for the Dutch to go overseas in large droves. So, the limited success
of the patroonship plan in the late 1620s and the marginal effect of the
abolition of the fur trade monopoly in 1640 can be partly explained by the
booming economy in the Dutch Republic and the availability of alternatives, especially while Brazil was still firmly in Dutch hands. Yet while this
explains the limited immigration, it provides no information on those who
did make the journey. Their motives could vary considerably; especially during
the 1620s and 30s, Dutch colonies were inhabited by the fortune-seekers,
the adventurers, and the restless, who for a large part formed the soldiery
of the East and West India Companies.[28]

As most well-off Dutchmen and women had little reason to leave the
Dutch Republic, the Amsterdam chamber recruited their soldiers and sailors
from the large group of Scandinavian and German immigrants in Amsterdam. The main patroon, Kiliaen van Rensselaer, similarly drew his farmers,
artisans, laborers, and servants from recent immigrants, but he also made
use of the population of the villages in Utrecht and Gelderland provinces,
where he owned land. This largely accounts for why only about half of New
Netherland's total population was born in the Netherlands. Although hired
on a temporary basis, many of these soldiers and farm hands decided to stay
in New Netherland after their contracts expired. They began to set up their
own business and sometimes brought their wives and children over. After
1650 the West India Company turned this into a policy: it recruited soldiers
for only a couple of years, provided for their passage to New Netherland,
and hoped they would turn to farming once their contracts were up. The
company also advanced the cost of the voyage for private immigrants. If the
colonists decided to leave the colony, the sum had to be refunded.[29]

This policy of the West India Company was at least partly inspired by
a feeling of responsibility for those who had lost everything when Dutch
Brazil was evacuated in 1654. Several of the soldiers who had served in New
Holland turned to another trade in New Netherland and brought their wives
with them. An example is Barentje Straetmans, wife of Hans Coenraets,
who was a soldier in Brazil and a baker in Beverwijck. Her sister Teuntje
Straetmans had also been in Brazil and finally settled in Breuckelen with her
fourth German soldier-husband, Gabriel Corbesy. Another Brazilian refugee

was minister Johannes Polhemius, who served the churches on Long Island from 1654 until his death in 1676. It was not his first flight: before going to Brazil in 1636, he had for religious reasons fled the Pfalz in the Rhineland to become minister in Meppel in Drenthe in the eastern Netherlands, the area from where many Long Island settlers originated.

Others with experience elsewhere in the Dutch Atlantic World went to New Netherland as well, showing the interconnectedness of Dutch Atlantic colonies on a personal level. Stuyvesant had served in Brazil and on Curaçao, Jacob Alrichs, vice director on the Delaware in the late 1650s, had been to Brazil. Isaac de Rasière, a West India Company official on Manhattan in the 1620s, later went to Brazil. Minister Everardus Bogardus had served as comforter of the sick on the Dutch forts on the coast of West Africa. Jacob Steendam, the famous poet of New Amsterdam, had been there as well, and went on to become orphanmaster in Batavia, still writing poetry. But on the whole exchanges with the East Indies are rarer than those within the Atlantic basin. Apart from Steendam, the only names of New Netherland colonists that came up in my search were those of Cornelis de Potter, merchant on Manhattan in the 1650s, and his wife Elisabeth, who had earlier been in Batavia, and Margrieta and Rudolphus van Varick, who exchanged Malacca for Long Island in the later seventeenth century.[30]

Conclusion

Only in the 1650s, when the Dutch economy was slowing down and the Portuguese were about to reclaim Brazil, did migration to New Netherland became a viable option for more than just a few. And then New Netherland's population grew at a considerable pace and began to show a distinct social stratification. In a broad sweep, soldiers came from Germany, sailors from Scandinavia, farmers from the eastern parts of the Netherlands, while merchants, ministers, and high officials primarily originated in the province of Holland. Thus, the people who formed the highest layers of the New Netherland society shared a common cultural heritage, derived from Holland.[31]

By this time, after the fall of Dutch Brazil in 1654, New Netherland was the only sizeable Dutch overseas settlement colony. Batavia for example, was not intended to be populated solely by Europeans: it quickly grew into a city of 16.000 inhabitants in 1650, but 20 percent of those were Europeans. And the Cape Colony, founded in the early 1650s, took twice as long to reach a population size that matched that which New Netherland had achieved in forty years. Seen against the background of the Dutch Republic and its other colonies, New Netherland was an astounding success, and the decision of many Dutch to stay, despite having to suffer the yoke of perfidious Albion, is proof of that.[32]

What, then, induced these Dutchmen to stay in New Netherland? Let me return to the example of Jeremias van Rensselaer. Jeremias, as one the sons of patroon Kiliaen van Rensselaer, played a role in the management of the patroonship. He first arrived in New Netherland in 1654, stayed only a short while and went back to the Netherlands. Two years later he traveled to New Netherland again, where he replaced his repatriating brother Jan Baptist as director of the patroonship. Thus, he occupied a position of considerable status in New Netherland. Earlier, I said that Jeremias does not seem to have been a happy colonist in 1663. But appearances can be deceiving, as a fuller quote out of this letter shows; Jeremias promises his brother in Amsterdam that he will send a letter to their mother, who is also living in Amsterdam and then continues:

> I am longing very much to hear from her and should be pleased and happy to know how she reconciles herself to it that I thus entered the married state. However, I doubt not but she will be pleased that the Lord God has granted me such a good partner, with whom I can get along so well and live with peaceably in such a far distant land, separated from all the friends, so that it is the greatest consolation I have. You may perhaps be longing to hear whether we have any baby yet. My answer is no, but my wife is pregnant and will, please God, be in childbed in two or three months at the longest.

So here is the answer to the question how a Dutchman abroad would manage without his relatives. He would marry, start his own family, and thus begin the slow process of detaching himself emotionally from his mother country. Perhaps he was not there to make a buck, but to make a living.

Notes

1. New York State Library, Van Rensselaer Manor Papers, box 50b, folder 49–50, translated in A. J. F. van Laer (trans. and ed.), *Correspondence of Jeremias van Rensselaer 1651–1674* (Albany, NY, 1932), p. 332.

2. So said historian Kenneth Jackson during the image sequence that opens the first episode in Rick Burns' 1999 PBS documentary, *New York: A Documentary*

Film. I obtained this quote from Tom Stabile's article "The Quintessential City: New York City on Film" on <http://www.neh.gov/news/humanities/1999-09/new_york.html> (accessed 31 March 2011). Jackson added "And even today, there's an energy in New York, there's a bustle in New York. That bustle has been there for more than three hundred and fifty years."

3. William T. Reynolds, "Henry Hudson's New World, New World View," in Martha Dickinson Shattuck (ed.), *Explorers, Fortunes & Love Letters: A Window on New Netherland* (Albany: Mount Ida Press, 2009), pp. 10–26; Donald S. Johnson, *Charting the Sea of Darkness: The Four Voyages of Henry Hudson* (New York: Kodansha International, 1995); Simon Hart, *The Prehistory of the New Netherland Company: Amsterdam Notarial Records of the First Dutch Voyages to the Hudson* (Amsterdam: City of Amsterdam Press, 1959); Jaap Jacobs, *The Colony of New Netherland: A Dutch Settlement in Seventeenth-Century America* (Ithaca, NY: Cornell University Press, 2009), pp. 19–30.

4. Jacobs, *The Colony of New Netherland*, pp. 29–31; Wim Klooster, "The Place of New Netherland in the West India Company's Grand Scheme," in Joyce D. Goodfriend (ed.), *Revisiting New Netherland: Perspectives on Early Dutch America* (Leiden: Brill 2005), pp. 57–70; Charles T. Gehring, "New Netherland: The Formative Years, 1609–1632," in Cornelis A. van Minnen, Hans Krabbendam, and Giles Scott-Smith (eds.), *Four Centuries of Dutch-American Relations* (Amsterdam: Boom Publishers, 2009), pp. 74–84; A. J. F. van Laer (trans. and ed.), *Documents Relating to New Netherland, 1624–1626*, in the Henry E. Huntington Library (San Marino, CA, 1924).

5. National Archives, The Hague, archive of the States General, 1.01.04, inv. nr. 5751 (translated in *DRCHNY*, 1:37); Jacobs, *The Colony of New Netherland*, p. 31; Peter Francis, Jr., "The beads that did not buy Manhattan Island," in *New York History* 67 (1986), pp. 5–22; Edmund B. O'Callaghan, *History of New Netherland, or New York under the Dutch*, 2 vols. (New York, 1846–1848), vol. 1, pp. 103–104. Schagen was not just "a Dutch official" nor is it likely he "was on the dock when the ship pulled into port." It is far more likely that he was in attendance at the meeting of the Nineteen in the West India House when the letters, newly arrived with the *Wapen van Amsterdam*, were read aloud, or when the skipper made an oral report; cf. Russell Shorto, *The Island at the Centre of the World: The Epic Story of Dutch Manhattan, The Forgotten Colony That Shaped America* (New York: Doubleday, 2004), pp. 55–56.

6. Maud Wilder Goodwin, *Dutch and English on the Hudson: A Chronicle of Colonial New York* (New Haven, CT, 1919), pp. 70–71.

7. Jaap Jacobs, "Incompetente autocraten? Bestuurlijke verhoudingen in de zeventiende-eeuwse Nederlandse Atlantische Wereld," *De zeventiende eeuw. Cultuur in de Nederlanden in interdisciplinair perspectief* 21 (2005), pp. 64–78; Jacobs, "Migration, Population, and Government in New Netherland," in Van Minnen, et al., *Four Centuries of Dutch-American Relations*, pp. 85–96; Jacobs, *The Colony of New Netherland*, ch. 3; J. A. Schiltkamp, "On Common Ground: Legislation, Government, Jurisprudence, and Law in the Dutch West Indian Colonies: The Order of Government of

1629," in *de Halve Maen* 70 (1997), pp. 73–80; Jacobs, "The Making of the First Minister: Jonas Michaëlius," in Leon van den Broeke, Hans Krabbendam, and Dirk Mouw (eds.), *New World Clergy: Dutch Ministers in the New World, Historical Series of the Reformed Church in America* (Grand Rapids, MI: Eerdmans Publishing Company, 2012), pp. 59–78; Willem Frijhoff, "A Misunderstood Calvinist: The Religious Choices of Bastian Jansz Krol, New Netherland's First Church Servant," in *The Journal of Early American History* 1 (2011), pp. 62–95.

8. Jacobs, *The Colony of New Netherland*, pp. 69–76; Jacobs, "Dutch Proprietary Manors in America: The Patroonships in New Netherland," in L. H. Roper and Bertrand Van Ruymbeke (eds.), *Constructing Early Modern Empires: Proprietary Ventures in the Atlantic World* (Leiden: Brill, 2007), pp. 301–326.

9. *Vryheden by de Vergaderinghe van de Negenthiene vande Geoctroyeerde West-Indische Compagnie vergunt aen allen den ghenen die eenighe Colonien in Nieuw-Nederlandt sullen planten* . . . (Amsterdam, 1630); Oliver A. Rink, "Company Management and Private Trade: The Two Patroonship Plans for New Netherland," *New York History* 59 (1978), pp. 5–26; Jacobs, "Dutch Proprietary Manors in America."

10. Jaap Jacobs, "A Troubled Man: Director Wouter van Twiller and the Affairs of New Netherland in 1635," *New York History* 85 (2004), pp. 213–232; C. A. Weslager, *A Man and His Ship: Pieter Minuit and the* Kalmar Nyckel (Wilmington, DE: Kalmar Nyckel Foundation, 1990); Willem Frijhoff, "Neglected Networks: Director Willem Kieft (1602–1647) and his Dutch Relatives," in Goodfriend, *Revisiting New Netherland*, pp. 147–204.

11. Jacobs, *The Colony of New Netherland*, pp. 72–73, 76.

12. Willem Frijhoff, *Fulfilling God's Mission: The Two Worlds of Dominie Everardus Bogardus, 1607–1647* (Leiden: Brill, 2007); Paul Otto, *The Dutch-Munsee Encounter in America: The Struggle for Sovereignty in the Hudson Valley* (New York: Berghahn Books, 2006); Donna Merwick, *The Shame and the Sorrow: Dutch-Amerindian Encounters in New Netherland* (Philadelphia, PA: University of Pennsylvania Press, 2006); Jacobs, *The Colony of New Netherland*, pp. 76–80.

13. Jaap Jacobs, "Like Father, Like Son? The Early Years of Petrus Stuyvesant," in Goodfriend, *Revisiting New Netherland*, pp. 205–244; Jacobs, "A Hitherto Unknown Letter of Adriaen van der Donck," in *de Halve Maen* 71 (1998), pp. 1–6; Jacobs, *The Colony of New Netherland*, pp. 81–86; Jacobs, "Migration, Population, and Government in New Netherland"; cf. Shorto, *The Island at the Center of the World*.

14. Jacobs, *The Colony of New Netherland*, pp. 86–99; Jacobs, " 'To Favor This New and Growing City of New Amsterdam with a Court of Justice': The Relations between Rulers and Ruled in New Amsterdam," in George Harinck and Hans Krabbendam (eds.), *Amsterdam-New York. Transatlantic Relations and Urban Identities Since 1653* (Amsterdam: VU University Press, 2005), pp. 17–29; Simon Middleton, "Order and Authority in New Netherland: The 1653 Remonstrance and Early Settlement Politics," in *WMQ* 67 (2010), pp. 31–69; Martha Dickinson Shattuck, "A Civil Society: Court and Community in Beverwijck, New Netherland 1652–1664" (PhD diss., Boston University, 1993); Janny Venema, *Beverwijck: A Dutch Village on the*

American Frontier, 1652–1664 (Hilversum: Verloren, 2003); Donna Merwick, *Death of a Notary: Conquest and Change in Colonial New York* (Ithaca, NY: Cornell University Press, 1999); Merwick, *Possessing Albany, 1630–1710: The Dutch and English Experiences* (Cambridge: Cambridge University Press, 1990).

15. Jacobs, "Migration, Population, and Government in New Netherland"; Jacobs, *The Colony of New Netherland*, p. 32–33.

16. Jacobs, *The Colony of New Netherland*, 158–160; Dennis J. Maika, "Securing the Burgher Right in New Amsterdam: The Struggle for Municipal Citizenship in the Seventeenth-Century Atlantic World," in Goodfriend, *Revisiting New Netherland*, pp. 93–128; Adriana E. van Zwieten, "The Orphan Chamber of New Amsterdam," in *WMQ* 53 (1996), pp. 319–340.

17. Shattuck, "A Civil Society"; Susan Elizabeth Shaw, "Building New Netherland: Gender and Family Ties in a Frontier Society" (PhD diss., Cornell University, 2000); Susannah Shaw Romney, "Intimate Networks and Children's Survival in New Netherland in the Seventeenth Century," *Early American Studies* 7 (2009), pp. 270–308; Linda Heywood and John Thornton, "Intercultural Relations between Europeans and Blacks in New Netherland," in Van Minnen, et al., *Four Centuries of Dutch-American Relations*, pp. 192–203; Jacobs, *The Colony of New Netherland*, pp. 55–56, 202–206.

18. Jacobs, *The Colony of New Netherland*, chs. 4 and 7.

19. Ibid., ch. 3.

20. Ibid., ch. 5; cf. Shorto, *The Island at the Center of the World*.

21. Otto, *The Dutch-Munsee Encounter*; Robert S. Grumet, *The Munsee Indians: A History* (Norman, OK: University of Oklahoma Press, 2009); Merwick, *The Shame and the Sorrow*.

22. Jaap Jacobs, "The Hartford Treaty: A European Perspective on a New World conflict," in *de Halve Maen* 68 (1995), pp. 74–79; Richard Waldron, "New Sweden: An Interpretation," in Goodfriend, *Revisiting New Netherland*, pp. 71–90; Charles T. Gehring, "Hodie Mihi, Cras Tibi: Swedish-Dutch relations in the Delaware Valley," in Carol E. Hoffecker, Richard Waldron, Lorraine E. Williams, and Barbara E. Benson (eds.), *New Sweden in America* (Cranbury, NJ: Associated University Presses, 1995), pp. 69–85.

23. Robert M. Bliss, *Revolution and Empire: English Politics and the American Colonies in the Seventeenth Century* (Manchester, UK: Manchester University Press, 1990); Megan Lindsay Cherry, "The Imperial and Political Motivations behind the English Conquest of New Netherland," in *Dutch Crossing* 34 (2010), pp. 77–94; Ronald D. Cohen, "The New England Colonies and the Dutch Recapture of New York, 1673–1674," in *New-York Historical Society Quarterly* 56 (1972), pp. 54–78.

24. Jaap Jacobs, "'It Has Pleased the Lord That We Must Learn English': Dutch New York After 1664," in Deborah L. Krohn and Peter Miller (eds.), *Dutch New York Between East and West: The World of Margrieta van Varick* (New York, New Haven: Bard Graduate Center: Decorative Arts, Design History, Material Culture, The New-York Historical Society, Yale University Press, 2009), pp. 55–66; Roger

Panetta (ed.), *Dutch New York: The Roots of Hudson Valley Culture* (Yonkers, NY: Fordham University Press, 2009); Joyce D. Goodfriend, "The Limits of Religious Pluralism in Eighteenth-Century New York City," in Harinck and Krabbendam, *Amsterdam-New York*, pp. 67–86; David E. Narrett, *Inheritance and Family Life in Colonial New York City* (Ithaca and London: Cornell University Press, 1992); Simon Middleton, *From Privileges to Rights: Work and Politics in Colonial New York City* (Philadelphia: University of Pennsylvania Press, 2006); Goodfriend, *Revisiting New Netherland*; Joyce D. Goodfriend, Benjamin Schmidt & Annette Stott (eds.), *Going Dutch: The Dutch Presence in America 1609–2009* (Leiden: Brill, 2008), and the contributions of Simon Middleton, Joyce D. Goodfriend, David W. Voorhees, Fred van Lieburg and Jan Noordegraaf in Van Minnen, et al., *Four Centuries of Dutch-American Relations*.

25. An example is Robert C. Ritchie, *The Duke's Province. A Study of New York Politics and Society, 1664–1691* (Chapel Hill, NC: University of North Carolina Press, 1977), p. 31. Even more damning is A. Gregg Roeber, " 'The Origin of Whatever Is Not English among Us': The Dutch-Speaking and the German-Speaking Peoples of Colonial British America," in Bernard Bailyn and Philip D. Morgan (eds.), *Strangers Within the Realm: The Cultural Margins of the First British Empire* (Chapel Hill: University of North Carolina Press, 1991), pp. 220–283: "Thus New Netherland was left weak and vulnerable by meager migration into an ethnically diverse colony and the absence of support networks and leaders interested in creating a Dutch culture," at 221; David Hackett Fischer, *Albion's Seed: Four British Folkways in American History* (New York and London: Oxford University Press, 1989) also employs an exclusively Anglocentric perspective; see Joyce D. Goodfriend, "Present at the Creation: Making the Case for the Dutch Founders of America," in *Early American Studies* 7 (2009), pp. 259–269, for the creation of the Anglocentric perspective and the exclusion of others in the grand narrative of American history.

26. <http://www.nnp.org/nnp/publications/index.html> (accessed 21 April 2011); Jacobs, *The Colony of New Netherland*, pp. 251–256.

27. The few examples of this comparative approach include: Marcus P. Meuwese, " 'For the Peace and Well-Being of the Country': Intercultural Mediators and Dutch-Indian Relations in New Netherland and Dutch Brazil, 1600–1664" (PhD diss., University of Notre Dame, 2003); Mark Meuwese, "Dutch Calvinism and Native Americans: A Comparative Study of the Motivations for Protestant Conversion among the Tupis in Northeastern Brazil (1630–1654) and the Mohawks in Central New York (1690–1710)," in James Muldoon (ed.), *The Spiritual Conversion of the Americas* (Gainesville, FL: University Press of Florida, 2004), pp. 118–141; Laurence M. Hauptman and Ronald G. Knapp, "Dutch-Aboriginal Interaction in New Netherland and Formosa: A Historical Geography of Empire," in *Proceedings of the American Philosophical Society* 121 (1977), pp. 166–182; Carmel Schrire and Donna Merwick, "Dutch-Indigenous Relations in New Netherland and the Cape in the Seventeenth Century," in Lisa Falk (ed.), *Historical Archaeology in Global Perspective* (Washington and London: Smithsonian Institution Press, 1991), pp. 11–20; Jaap Jacobs, "Beverwijck, Batavia, and Beyond: Colonial Cities in the Early Modern Dutch

Empire," unpublished research paper presented at the workshop "The Dutch and the World in the Golden Age," Columbia University, New York, NY, 31 March 2007.

28. Jaap Jacobs, "Soldiers of the Company: The Military Personnel of the West India Company in New Netherland," in Herman Wellenreuther (ed.), *Jacob Leisler's Atlantic World in the Later Seventeenth Century: Essays on Religion, Militia Trade, and Networks by Jaap Jacobs, Claudia Schnurmann, David W. Voorhees, and Hermann Wellenreuther* (Münster: LIT Verlag, 2009), pp. 11–31; David S. Cohen, "How Dutch were the Dutch of New Netherland?," in *New York History* 62 (1981), 43–60; Oliver A. Rink, "The People of New Netherland: Notes on Non English Immigration to New York in the Seventeenth Century," in *New York History* 62 (1981), pp. 5–42; Joyce D. Goodfriend, "Foreigners in a Dutch Colonial City," in *New York History* 90 (2009), pp. 241–269.

29. Jacobs, "Soldiers of the Company"; Janny Venema, *Kiliaen van Rensselaer (1586–1643): Designing a New World* (Hilversum: Verloren, 2010); Jacobs, "Dutch Proprietary Manors in America"; Jacobs, *The Colony of New Netherland*, ch. 2.

30. Annette M. Cramer van den Bogaart, "The Life of Teuntje Straatmans: A Dutch Woman's Travels in the Seventeenth-Century Atlantic World," in *The Long Island Historical Journal* 15 (2003), pp. 35–53; Jacobs, "Like Father, Like Son?"; Frijhoff, *Fulfilling God's Mission*; Henry C. Murphy, *Anthology of New Netherland or Translations from the early Dutch poets of New York with memoirs of their lives* (Amsterdam: N. Israel, 1966 [New York, 1865]); John Blythe Dobson, "Cornelis de Potter," *New York Genealogical and Biographical Record* 131 (2000), pp. 260–262; Margriet de Roever, "Grietje Dircks alias Margrieta van Varick. Kind op de Prinsengracht, weduwe in Malakka, domineesvrouw in New York," in Amstelodamum. *Maandblad voor de kennis van Amsterdam* 96 (2009), pp. 169–180; Deborah L. Krohn and Peter Miller (eds.), *Dutch New York Between East and West: The World of Margrieta van Varick* (New Haven: Yale University Press, 2009); Jacobs, *The Colony of New Netherland*, ch. 2.

31. Jacobs, *The Colony of New Netherland*, ch. 2.

32. Hendrik E. Niemeijer, *Batavia. Een koloniale samenleving in de zeventiende eeuw* (Amsterdam: Uitgeverij Balans, 2005); Ad Biewenga, *De Kaap de Goede Hoop Een Nederlandse vestigingskolonie, 1680–1730* (Amsterdam: Samenwerkende uitgeverijen Prometheus-Bert Bakker, 1999).

9

The House of Hope in the Valley of Discord

Connecticut Geopolitics beyond "Anglo-Dutch" Relations (1613–1654)

Lauric Henneton

Introduction

s "we are all Atlanticists now,"[1] it has become a truism that the history of North American settlements (in the present case) is considerably better understood in its wider Atlantic context. Still, a sense of the place, even four centuries after the facts, is central to understanding the opportunities offered, as well as the constraints imposed by geographical features of the landscape in which history unfolded. In other words, historical geography helps us to better understand history as lived. As Timothy Shannon shows in his contribution to this volume, the history of New Netherland, not unlike that of New France, is a history of river systems. The Hudson Valley—or estuary—features prominently, if not centrally, in the history of New Netherland, then New York, but its eastern sister, the Connecticut Valley, may be more relevant in the study of Anglo-Dutch interaction in the decades from the early seventeenth-century explorations (Henry Hudson, Adriaen Block) to the First Anglo-Dutch War (1652–1654).

The relations between the English and the Dutch were initially very cordial, at least on the surface, but soured when the English from Plymouth Colony moved west and set up a trading post on the Connecticut (or Fresh) River in 1633. The Dutch had just founded Fort Good Hope, or the "House of Hope" on the site of present-day Hartford.[2] The Connecticut Valley had become an interface, however rudimentary, a permanent contact zone, as opposed to an occasional place of rendezvous (as Buzzards Bay had been), and an increasingly disputed area (as set out in Figure 14).[3] The settlers from Massachusetts Bay who settled along the river from 1635 on only made matters worse but also contributed by increasing an English population that was immediately too numerous to root out.[4] When the native parameter is added into the geopolitical equation, it becomes clear that regional geopolitics cannot be reduced to mere "Anglo-Dutch" rivalries.

Indeed in the space of just a few years—a decade at the most—the Connecticut Valley became disputed between the Dutch, the English from Plymouth and from the Bay, not to mention the neighboring Native groups. In other words, for both strategic and commercial reasons, the Connecticut Valley had rapidly become what would now be called a geopolitical hotspot. Defining geopolitics is a very thorny task. In this essay, it is used (empirically) as the "politics of the place," the decision-making process that puts one or several sites at the center because of their strategic importance. These sites can

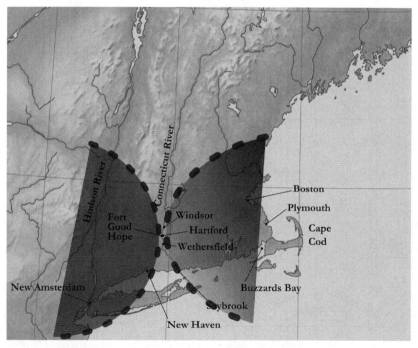

Figure 14. The Connecticut River Interface *(map by author).*

be a cape, an isthmus, an island, a river (as an interface and/or as a boundary), or a mountain pass, for instance. The central issue is control: holding a small site gives the key to access a much larger place and its resources. Famous examples include Gibraltar or Panama and Florida but also, on the way to the riches of the East, Constantinople, the Cape of Good Hope, the island of Socotra, which commanded access to the Gulf of Aden and the Red Sea, the Strait of Ormuz, which commanded entry into the Persian Gulf, or the Strait of Malacca, now Singapore.[5]

If controlling one strategic site commands access to a larger area and its resources, then in no way is the geopolitical prism an anachronistic one.[6] This essay aims at showing to what extent the Connecticut Valley can be considered as a geopolitical hotspot in the early decades of European presence in northeastern North America and how the "Anglo-Dutch" rivalry in seventeenth-century North America revolved around the strategic focus of that valley, broadly conceived. More precisely, geopolitics hinges around the issue of control, either actual or virtual, implying conflicting and disputed titles and claims to the land.

In the 1630s, the Connecticut Valley rapidly became a byword for abundant beaver and fertile soil, as opposed to the relatively barren rocky or sandy soil of coastal, eastern New England. In a preindustrial world, always prone to dearth if not famine, the fertility of the soil had strategic importance, all the more so for settlements otherwise dependent on unreliable supplies from overseas. Moreover, the river was a waterway, more or less parallel to the Hudson River, which provided a connection between the Atlantic Ocean and the markets around the Atlantic basin from the Chesapeake to England to the West Indies to the New England hinterland and its lucrative fur trade.

The proximity and even contiguity of the English and Dutch along the river made competition for the very same resources (fur, but also wampum) and the same middlemen (the local Algonquian tribes[7]) more acute. The intertribal rivalries, in which the Europeans got involved, only added complexity to the situation. This was therefore not simply a neatly binary case of English against Dutch, as the English, like "the Indians," were not united. To these contestants should be added a more distant French parameter as well as the (admittedly occasional) Spanish specter.

This essay, then, will therefore investigate the rival claims to the land and conflicting legitimacies, first looking at naming strategies and the uses of cartography, then at the early stages of the rivalry: first the 1620s through the correspondence between Plymouth Governor William Bradford and New Netherland Secretary Isaac de Rasière, then the successive arrivals of the protagonists along the river in the course of the 1630s.

Henry Hudson, who, as an Englishman working for the Dutch East India Company, famously discovered the river that later came to bear his name, is a good illustration of the disputed status of the Connecticut region, the "valley of discord."[8] The English called it Hudson's River, after the English discoverer, whereas the Dutch called it the North River or, less commonly, the Mauritius (or Mauritse) River, after Maurice of Nassau, then stadholder of Holland and Zeeland.[9] Naming, i.e., imposing a narrative onto landmarks, was a good way of claiming, sometimes by negating former rival claims, and the best way to perpetuate names was to have them put on maps. In 1613, Captain Samuel Argall and the English from Virginia raided the straggling French settlements in Acadia and Mount Desert Island (Maine) and, on the way back, contested the Dutch presence on Manhattan as a violation of the royal charter of Virginia, which claimed for England all lands on the Atlantic coast of America from 34° to 45° N. latitude.[10]

The following year, however, Adriaen Block was the first to use the name "New Netherland" on the map he drew. He named "Noord Zee" what would be later known as Massachusetts Bay and "Zuyder Zee" what the Plymouth settlers called Buzzards Bay, two toponyms directly borrowed from Dutch geography. He also named an island after himself, still known today as Block Island, and was the first European to explore the Connecticut River (which he called the Fresh River). This was then used by the Dutch as a precedent legitimizing the Dutch title to the river.[11]

The same year, Captain John Smith drew a map of the region he called "New England," thereby claiming it explicitly for England. The map was published in 1616. In the accompanying text, he explained that the name "New England" was a tribute and an echo to Drake's "Nova Albyon" (i.e., California), thus named during his circumnavigation, a reminder of the English presence in North America—however ephemeral—long before Hudson's "discovery."[12] Smith's exploration and subsequent map did not include the southern coast of New England: it was limited to the coast north of Cape Cod.

Cartography was used by the Dutch, before and after 1633, to claim land in "eastern" New England (east of the Connecticut Valley). This was far from being a new practice. Cartography was a form of discourse in which marks of sovereignty served as rhetorical devices, if not blatant propaganda.[13] As early as 1617, a map of the Atlantic basin by Willem Jansz Blaeu, had the coat of arms of the United Provinces set between Hudson River and

Cape Cod—right on Connecticut even though it had not yet become a geographic bone of contention.[14]

Anthony Jacobsz (or Antoine Jacques), in a 1621 map, put the Dutch arms on the Hudson but had the name "Nieu Nederland" printed across the region, from the Delaware River to Maine. The Dutch had just begun settling and the map was some sort of published confirmation of their presence as it also recorded the Dutch names given to various geographical landmarks. Publication was a way of publicizing territorial claims, thereby inviting international recognition. Predictably, the English Privy Council complained about that form of appropriation in a letter to Sir Dudley Carleton, the English Ambassador at The Hague.[15]

A decade later, John Mason, who had been granted land in what is now New Hampshire, referred to that map in a letter in which he complained about the Dutch "interlopers" who had "published a Mapp in ye Low Countries of ye sayd sea coaste comprehended betwixt Virginia and Cape Codd, under the title of New Netherlands, giving the name of ye Prince of Aurange [the aforementioned Maurice] to ye Countrie [i.e., Fort Orange, present-day Albany] and river of Manahata, where ye Dutch are now planted."[16]

Mason also resorted to history and historical precedents to prove the anteriority (and therefore the legitimacy) of the English title. North America, he recalled, had been claimed for England as that country "granted to Sir Walter Rawleigh by Queene Elizabeth in Anno 1584 and afterwards to diverse of her subjects under ye title of Virginia." Mason was not the first to use the precedent of Roanoke: Bradford had used it in his correspondence with De Rasière a few years before. Mason then mentioned the Virginia Charter of 1606 and the division between the London and Plymouth Companies. New England had been settled "above 25 yeares since," which is an implicit reference to the short-lived settlement at Sagadahoc in the winter of 1607–1608, i.e., before Hudson entered the river that came to bear his name.[17] With Roanoke, Sagadahoc, and the charter of 1606, Mason was cleverly providing three precedents that unquestionably antedated Hudson's expedition and therefore were thought to dispel the ambiguity about the English explorer working for the Dutch. However, as Jaap Jacobs has recently reminded us, the Dutch West India Company (WIC) objected that "the discovery of the area of the allocation thereof by a government were insufficient legal bases for possession. Only a claim supported by actually occupying an area by populating it with at least fifty colonists was valid."[18]

Blaeu struck again in 1635 with a printed map entitled *Nova Belgica et Anglia Nova*. He used different colors on the coasts and rivers for lands claimed by the Dutch and those left to the English (Figure 17). The land claimed by the Dutch extended from the mouth of the Delaware (or South) River in the southwest to, surprisingly, Cape Cod (included), then north along the White Mountains up to the St. Lawrence River, which served as the northern boundary. Even a misplaced and disproportionate Lake Champlain (extending almost from the St. Lawrence to Narragansett Bay) was claimed by the Dutch, according to Blaeu's map. Claiming Cape Cod was a total fiction, as there were no Dutch settlers there, but Blaeu still chose to keep Block's place names: Massachusetts Bay as the Noord See, Buzzards Bay as the Zuyder See. Connecticut River was still styled the "Versche" River and the English settlements on Connecticut River do not appear—they may have been too recent to be inserted, but they may also have been consciously ignored. What does not appear on the map is therefore as important as what is shown. As Ken MacMillan reminds us, a map is an important political construction, "laden with political and ideological messages."[19]

A 1639 manuscript map of "Nieuw Nederlande," Virginia, and "Nieuw Engeland" attributed to Joan Vinckeboons also used colors to claim lands:

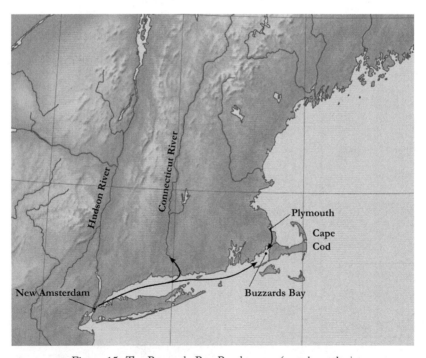

Figure 15. The Buzzards Bay Rendezvous *(map by author)*.

yellow for the Dutch, green for the English, and red for the French.[20] If the absence of the English settlements on the "Versche Rivier" could be understood in 1635, their omission in 1639 had a clear political meaning. More surprising is the absence of the "Fort Good Hope" on the same river. Cape Cod, this time, was acknowledged as belonging to the English, but the whole of Narragansett Bay and even a little beyond was still claimed by the Dutch. The cartography of New England was clearly not up-to-date: it simply followed Smith's 1616 map and failed to show the new villages, some of which had existed for about a decade (Salem, Boston, Watertown, and Dorchester, among others).

As late as 1685, a reprint of Nicolas Visscher's 1655 map entitled *Novi Belgii Novaeque Angliae nec non Partiis Virginiae Tabula* still showed *Nova Belgica / Nieuw Nederlandt / Niew Jorck*, now including Pennsylvania, as claimed by the Dutch; Long Island and Block Island were conceded to New England, which did not extend west of Narragansett Bay. Martha's Vineyard was also claimed by the Dutch (but not Nantucket). The towns of Connecticut were represented, this time, as well as the "Fort de Goede Hoop" but with Dutch names: Windsor appeared as Voynser, Hartford as Herfort and Wethersfield had become Weeters Velt, not to mention Saybrook, now Zeebroeck.

If the English saw the Dutch as "interlopers" and intruders, the Dutch saw things differently, as appears in the 1650 "Representation of New Netherland," attributed to van der Donck, which attempted to prove the English usurpation of lands claimed by the Dutch: "All the islands, bay, havens, rivers, kills and places, even to a great distance on the other side of New Holland or Cape Cod, have Dutch names, which our Dutch ship-masters and traders gave to them. These were the first to discover and to trade to them, even before they had names, as the English themselves well know; but as long as they can manage it and matters go as they please, they are willing not to know it." This was an implicit reference to Block's expeditions—and his 1614 map. To the author, exploring and naming gave a superior title than the theoretical one provided by a royal charter and supplemented by short-lived occupation of a tiny part of land (in the case both of Roanoke and Sagadahoc).[21]

Block's exploration of the "Fresh" River in 1614 was also supposed to give more weight to the Dutch title to the river, as was the purchase of the land "on both sides on the river" from the Indians in 1632. Another sign was the display of "the States' arms" on a tree "in token of possession" on the site that then became Saybrook Point. Yet, this was not enough for the English, as the author notes, as they were said to "have torn them down and carved a ridiculous face in their place."[22] Actual occupation by fifty settlers, however, could never be put forward by the Dutch, as far as the Connecticut/ Fresh River was concerned.

The first English people to settle in the region, in 1620, were those later known as the "Pilgrim Fathers." Any Dutch traders who may have been present on Manhattan at the time did not seem to mind. Those who did settle in the early 1620s, moreover, were themselves considered as intruders in English-claimed "North Virginia."[23] If the "Pilgrims" failed to settle within their allotted patent, they nonetheless did disembark on land claimed by the King of England by virtue of the royal charter of 1606.

The 1620s: "all good neighbourhood and correspondence as far as we may"

The Mayflower passengers, or rather a third of them, had previously lived in the Netherlands, first briefly in Amsterdam, before removing to Leiden from 1609 to 1620. They had declined "large offers" from the Dutch to "go under them to Hudson's River," where they were also supposed to settle according to their initial patent issued by the Virginia Company.[24] After ensuring their survival, they began to look around themselves for trade and in 1623 they went to Buzzards Bay where "the Dutch or French, or both used to come."[25] There, they bartered mainly tobacco from Virginia for cloths. The Dutch secretary, De Rasière, paid a visit to Plymouth in October 1627, which had been preceded by correspondence with Bradford from the preceding March (see Figure 15).

These exchanges, consisting in compliments, offers of mutual help, business propositions and presents, however cordial at first sight, were also an occasion for discussing the legitimacy of the respective titles to the lands they occupied, which is much less known.[26] In his first letter, dated 9 March 1627, De Rasière recalled the geographical proximity of their native countries before evoking the old alliances between the two and striking the Protestant chord by mentioning "our common enemy the Spaniard, who seek nothing else but to usurp and overcome other Christian kings' and princes' lands, that so he might obtain and possess his pretended monarchy over all Christendom, and so to rule and command after his own pleasure over the consciences of so many hundred thousand souls, which God forbid."[27]

In his reply, ten days later, Bradford echoed that tune, to which he was all the more responsive as he had lived in the Low Countries on the eve of the end of the Twelve Years Truce (1609–1621).[28] The English did not fail to convey their gratitude for the "freedom and good content" with which they had lived in Leiden, and they promised they should "not go about to molest or trouble you in any thing, but continue all good neighbourhood and correspondence as far as we may."[29] All this, however sincere, might have served to introduce the "desire" on the part of the English that "you would forbear to trade with the natives in this bay, and river of Narraganset and Sowames, which is (as it were) at our doors." They seem to have been defining a commercial sphere of influence from which they were trying to exclude the Dutch, at a time when, in the East Indies, the Dutch had been doing just the same to the English, only more effectively.[30] Bradford clumsily added that "The which if you do, we think no other English will go about any way to trouble or hinder you." And, we may wonder, what if the Dutch declined the invitation to "forbear" trading in Buzzards Bay?

De Rasière's reply, according to Bradford's account, was "very friendly" but the Dutch maintained "their right and liberty to trade in those parts, which we had desired them to forbear, alleging that as we had authority and commission from our king, so they had the like from the States of Holland, which they would defend." Both titles were beginning to clash. On 14 August, Bradford first thanked De Rasière politely for the cheese he had sent him and professed their "resolution and hearty desire to hold and continue all friendship and good neighbourhood with you as far as we may

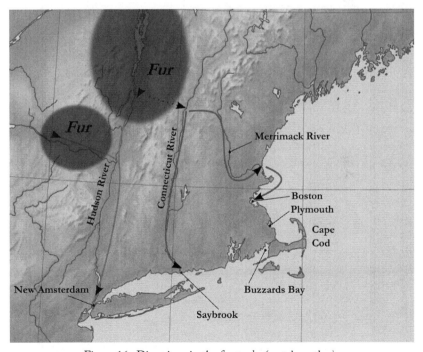

Figure 16. Diversions in the fur trade *(map by author)*.

and lies in our power." Bradford kindly gave warning to his correspondent, "out of our love and good affection toward you, and the trust you repose in us," that "those of Virginia or the fishing ships, which come to New England, peradventure they will make prize of you, if they can, if they find you trading within those limits; as they surprised a colony of the French not many years since, which was seated within these bounds." This was a clear reference to Argall's punitive expedition against the Mount Desert settlement on the coast of Maine in 1613. Bradford countered De Rasière's "allegation" that the Dutch had "navigated and traded in these parts above this twenty six years," therefore (surprisingly) since 1601, with the Elizabethan precedent "well nigh forty years ago," this time a clear reference to the failed Roanoke attempt in the 1580s. As current official sanctions were not enough, the two correspondents were entering the field of historical precedents, and the Dutch could not beat the anteriority of Roanoke—except that it had not lasted.

Bradford assured the Dutch that they had nothing to fear from Plymouth, which must have been a great relief to read, but that he could not answer for his countrymen from other settlements. He therefore advised the Dutch to "solicit the States that they might come to some order and agreement with the king's Majesty and state of England hereabout." De Rasière must not have taken this ill as he told Bradford, during his visit to Plymouth in October 1627 that his "masters," meaning the Dutch West India Company, "were willing to have friendship with us, and to supply us with sundry commodities, and offered us assistance against the French, if need were." Bradford then wrote about the same matters to the West India Company, advising them to "clear the title of your planting in these parts . . . lest it be a bone of division in these stirring evil times, which God forbid." Bradford, however naive, seems to have seen himself as a sincere peacemaker, willing to have the situation settled, not to have the Dutch plantation wiped off the map. He also wrote the Council for New England about these dealings, mentioning in passing that "for strength of men and fortification they far exceed us, and all in this land." He actually did not complain so much about the Dutch as against other English settlers, "who without either patent or license, order or government, live, trade and truck, not with any intent to plant, but rather to forage the country and get what they can, whether by right or wrong and then be gone."

Wampum Revolution[31]

After his visit to Plymouth, De Rasière wrote to Samuel Blommaert, one of the directors of the West India Company, that he worried about the impact of the entry, if not intrusion, of the "Pilgrims" onto the regional geo-economic chessboard: he was afraid that their introduction to "sewant" or "wampum" (white and purple shells used initially used in religious ceremonies and diplomatic meetings, now increasingly as currency in exchange for furs) would lead them to venture inland and discover the trade in furs, "which if they were to find out, it would be a great trouble for us to maintain, for they already dare to threaten that if we will not leave off dealing with that people [?], they will be obliged to use other means; if they do that now, while they are yet ignorant how the case stands, what will they do when they get a notion of it?"[32]

Indeed, Bradford confirmed that their "entrance into the trade of wampumpeag" "turned most to their profit." De Rasière and the Dutch had not measured the risk of introducing the Plymouth settlers to what they had made into a form of currency. Bradford observed how "strange it was to see the great alteration it made in a few years among the Indians themselves." Wampum proved an essential element in the early geopolitics of southern New England. As Mark Meuwese recently noted, the Pequots were eager to supply the Dutch with wampum, in return for which they "were able to secure a steady supply of European trade goods. Additionally, by controlling the flow of these goods into the region, the Pequots were able to exercise growing influence over their indigenous neighbors." The dramatic increase in supply had two prime causes: the Dutch provided the Pequots with metal drills that boosted production and the Pequots subjugated weaker Algonquian groups on both sides of Long Island Sound, including the lower Connecticut River, exacting from them a tribute in wampum.[33] Wampum had initially been used by a few tribes along the coast of Connecticut, but then spread throughout the region, as far north as Fort Orange (Albany), and with the arrival of thousands of Englishmen from 1629 onward and a more systematic use, inflation caused a steep decline in the value of wampum, if not a wholesale "crash."[34]

It was the Dutch who had, somewhat naively, introduced the Plymouth settlers to the use of wampum(peag) as currency, ironically with a view to "maintain control of the wampum trade."[35] Even more naively, in about 1632–1633, the Dutch, "seeing them seated here in a barren quarter, told them of a river called by them the Fresh River, but now . . . known by the name of Connecticut River, which they often commended unto them for a fine place both for plantation and trade, and wished them to make use of it."[36] The Plymouth men, whose trading posts on the Maine coast had been raided by the French in 1632 and who had increasingly numerous rivals settling in Massachusetts Bay, were glad to oblige and turn their eyes to the west, where the Dutch would hopefully be more reliable neighbors.[37] Yet,

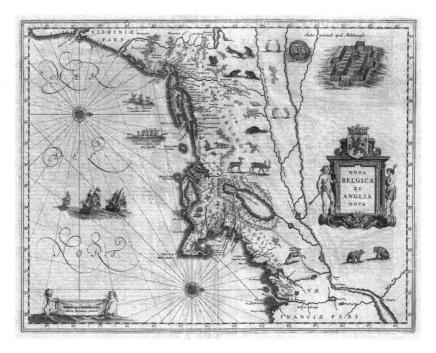

Figure 17. Willem Jansz Blaeu, *Nova Belgica et Anglia Nova* (1635).

when the Dutch realized that the English prepared to build a trading post on the Connecticut River they "began to repent . . . [and] got in a little before them and made a slight fort [Fort Good Hope, now Hartford] and planted two pieces of ordnance, threatening to stop their passage." A deed was signed between the Dutch and Pequot sachem Tatobem on 8 June 1633, securing title for the Dutch and also establishing a free trade zone for "all tribes of Indians," thereby ironically depriving the Pequot of the monopoly they had hitherto enjoyed. The Sequin band, formerly subjugated by the Pequot, was also to be protected by the Dutch.[38] The English, undeterred, managed to pass through, decided on a spot upstream from the Dutch (present-day Windsor), and "palisadoed their house about and fortified themselves better." Since these measures were aimed at ensuring control of the place, and therefore of the river, they have geopolitical significance. Indeed, the Dutch sent troops "in warlike manner, with colours displayed" to root out the English but rapidly gave up when they realized that "it would cost blood."[39] In England, open enemies to the "Godly" were (or claimed to be) afraid that such "discontented persons," "disaffected both to the King's government and to the State

Ecclesiastical" would "seek to fortify themselves by the aid of the Dutch." One of their leaders, Sir Ferdinando Gorges wondered if it were not "more than time these people should be dealt with"[40]: this shows how multilayered the history of one particular valley can become.

The 1630s: The Invasion of the Bay Settlers

If not being able to expel the Plymouth settlers from their post was a disappointment for the Dutch, who were afraid of losing the Indian trade to the English, they had seen nothing yet. The Dutch, indeed, were not alone in enticing the English into the Connecticut Valley. Some of the Connecticut Indians, who had been "driven out from thence by the potency of the Pequots, which usurped upon them," invited the English to settle in the valley, "promising them much trade, especially if they would keep a house [a trading post] there." Bradford adds that "their end was to be restored to their country again," so they hoped to play the English off against the Pequots and their Dutch allies.[41] In April 1631, the "banished Indians"—Wahginnacut, "John Sagamore," and "an Indian, who had lived in England and had served Sir Walter Raleigh" called Jack Straw—also tendered an invitation to the Massachusetts settlers.[42] An initial scheme seems to have consisted of a joint venture between Massachusetts and Plymouth who "should have built and put an equal stock together," but the Massachusetts settlers, being but recently arrived in America, were not ready to trade on such a scale, modest though it may seem to us, since they had virtually nothing to sell as yet.[43]

John Winthrop's account is quite different. If he confirmed that Bradford and Edward Winslow went to Boston to propose "joining in a trade to Connecticut for beaver and hemp," and setting up a joint trading post there "to prevent the Dutch, who were about to build one," he added that the Plymouth offer was declined because Connecticut was not considered "fit for plantation." The reasons given may seem surprising: if "three or four thousand warlike Indians" were not enough, the river was too shallow (not above "six feet at high water") and was not accessible for over seven months a year on account of "the ice" and the "violent stream."[44] In the face of such reluctance, the Plymouth settlers decided to go it alone and set up their own trading post on the site of present-day Windsor, Connecticut.

As already noted, the Dutch first tried to prevent them from passing upstream from them and then besieged them briefly but to no avail. In 1634, the Dutch attempted to divert the Indian trade from the English: "three or four Dutchmen went up . . . to live" with Indians "to get their trade and prevent them for bringing it to the English or to fall into amity with them," but they were stricken "with a great sickness and such a mortality that of a thousand, above nine and a half hundred of them died, and many of them did rot above ground for want of burial" and "the Dutchmen almost starved before they could get away, for ice and snow; but about February they got with much difficulty" to the Pilgrims' trading post and were "refreshed."[45] No doubt Bradford and his brethren would have seen the hand of providential retribution behind this "great sickness."

In 1633, the Plymouth settlers had sent a handful of men to a mere trading post, however "palisadoed." Starting in 1635, the Massachusetts settlers would all but flood the valley. Complaining of "straitness for want of land, especially meadow," they left Watertown, Dorchester and Newtown (later Cambridge) to follow such lay and clerical leaders as Thomas Hooker, John Haynes, and John Warham and founded three villages: Wethersfield, Windsor, and Hartford. From about 800 settlers as early as 1636, their numbers had more than doubled (2,000) and quadrupled by 1654 (3,200).[46] In June 1639, David de Vries discovered that the site known to the Dutch as "Roode-berghs" had recently been settled by the English and renamed New Haven, "where there were about three hundred houses and a fine church built." A few days later, in Hartford, where the "House of Hope" was now located, De Vries saw about a hundred houses (and another "fine church").[47]

Bradford explains that it was the "great mortality," the smallpox epidemic that raged in the winter of 1633–1634, which spurred the Massachusetts settlers to remove to Connecticut. Since their refusal to accept setting up a trading post with the Plymouth settlers, they had kept receiving reports on the valley from traders. The imprecision of these reports led to an inaccurate mental picture of the region and its commercial assets. The Connecticut River was increasingly seen as an avenue to the "Great Lake" (Lake Champlain) where "most of the beaver which is traded between Virginia and Canada" was said to originate. This was estimated to "about ten thousand skins" a year. Controlling the Connecticut River, especially to the North, would mean diverting the fur trade from the Dutch (via the Merrimack River—see Figure 18).[48] The lure of more fertile lands and divergent theological views between such clerical luminaries as Thomas Hooker and John Cotton did the rest. Bradford's narrative has several passages clearly showing his bitterness at being "little better than thrust out" by those whom, however English, he considered as intruders.[49] The dispute can be followed in letters exchanged between the two English jurisdictions.

In July 1635, Jonathan Brewster, the Plymouth agent on the Connecticut, wrote back home to explain the situation: "I hope they [from Massachusetts] will hear reason, as that we were here first and entered with much difficulty and danger both in regard of the Dutch and Indians, and bought the land, to your great charge already disbursed, and have since held here a chargeable possession and kept the Dutch from further encroaching, which would else long before this day have possessed all, and kept out all others, etc. I hope these and such-like arguments will stop them." The Plymouth claim was based on purchase, continuous occupation and anteriority, all of which were considered as solid enough to uphold their title to the lands they were occupying.[50]

In an undated letter to their Plymouth "brethren," the Bay settlers wrote that "God by his Providence cast us" into Connecticut and "in a fair way of Providence tendered it to us, as a meet place to receive our body [i.e., our community]." Against Brewster's arguments, the Massachusetts settlers were playing the providential card, which they believed could trump any other. They also deplored that "you cast a rather partial if not a covetous eye,

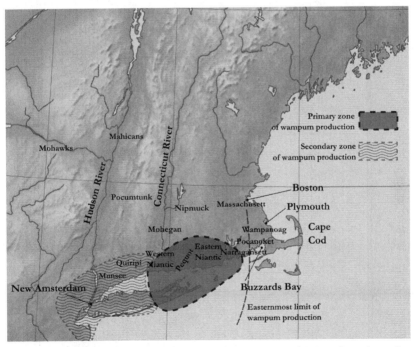

Figure 18. Primary and secondary zones of wampum production *(map by author, with assistance from Paul Otto)*.

upon that which is your neighbours' and not yours; and in so doing, your way could not be fair unto it." A final piece of advice, which the Plymouth magistrates must have found hard to swallow, was that they ought to "Look that you abuse not God's providence in such allegations."[51]

They replied that when they arrived in the valley it was "the Lord's waste," "altogether void of inhabitants." They were therefore entitled to use it "without just offense to any man," all the more so as they intended to employ it "to the right ends for which land was created," an explicit reference to Genesis 1:28, enjoining Man to "replenish the earth, and subdue it." This had become a classic line of reasoning to justify the settlement of Europeans on lands occupied by Amerindians.[52] Eventually, though, the Pilgrims understood they would have to yield "for peace sake."[53]

Meanwhile, in England, the Connecticut Valley was also being coveted by a group of (mostly) puritan noblemen. Indeed, Robert Rich, second earl of Warwick and then president of the Council for New England, had a (very imprecise) patent drafted as early as March 1632, which implies that he and his colleagues—a "Who's who of Puritanism"[54]—had somehow heard of the Connecticut trading opportunities before the removal of the Bay settlers in 1634–1636 and even the erection of the Plymouth trading post in 1633.[55] The governorship of "the riuer Conecticut in New England and of the Harbors and places adioyning" was entrusted to John Winthrop, Jr., in July 1635. He was also charged with the construction of buildings and fortifications "at the River"; while a particular effort was to be made to provide suitable dwellings for "men of qualitie."[56]

Difficulties began as soon as Winthrop arrived on the spot that would later be called "Saybrook," after a combination of the titles of two aristocratic leading lights behind the scheme, Lord Saye and Sele and Lord Brooke. In itself "Saybrook" is another interesting instance of claiming through naming. As early as June 1636, however, Winthrop's illustrious father noted that "the gentlemen seem to be discouraged."[57] Because of the sandbar at the mouth of the river, Saybrook's position made it a strategic point between Long Island Sound and a relatively shallow river. Saybrook would be an interface, the inevitable point of transshipment, thereby commanding the entire trade between the hinterland and the rest of the world.[58]

But this was only theoretical. Indeed, by 1642, Saybrook had long proved a disappointing failure and, if Lord Saye and Sele kept pushing against the Dutch presence (and title), the "Warwick Patent" was nonetheless sold to the Connecticut colony in 1644.[59] In the end, Saybrook was one of several puritan "imperial" ventures in the Atlantic world, the most famous of which was Providence Island, off the coast of Nicaragua, another dismal failure as it was eventually captured by the Spaniards in 1641.[60]

It was also on Connecticut River that Captain John Stone was killed by Pequots seeking revenge against the Dutch, a murder which led to the Pequot War and its (in)famous "Mystic massacre" perpetrated by the English (and their Narragansett allies) against their Pequot enemies in 1637.[61] The war was concluded by the Treaty of Hartford in 1638 that removed the Pequot tribe and re-established the "banished Indians" in their lands. The English were therefore dictating the diplomacy of the region, though not solely on their terms. The same year, a new English settlement called New Haven was founded, this time west of the Connecticut River and closer to the Dutch.[62] In a mere half decade, the Connecticut Valley, once a "pristine wilderness," had changed beyond recognition.[63]

Conclusion

If Massachusetts and more specifically Boston remained the political and demographic center of gravity (as the main port of entry and the most populous town of the region), the Connecticut Valley was becoming more and more populated and was the object of conflicting claims: of rival Native tribes (Pequot, Mohegan, Narragansett, Sequin), whose "loyalties and allegiances" were "rather fluid," of the Dutch who had invited the Plymouth English but now regretted it, and of the Plymouth settlers who were being expelled by the Massachusetts emigrants, even though they had been there first.[64] The Dutch (or at least some of them) explained their failure to keep the English out of what they considered as their land along the "Fresh" River by their failure to "populate" it. This was confirmed by the English: in 1639, John Haynes, then governor of Connecticut, explained to one Dutch guest that "the lands were lying idle" and that it was "a sin to let such rich land . . . lie uncultivated," therefore using, in his turn, the Genesis 1:28 argument.[65]

The period from the Treaty of Hartford (1638) to the outbreak of the First Anglo-Dutch War (1652) was both a period of peace between the Netherlands and England in Europe and one of tension between the Dutch and the English in America.[66] Four English (puritan) colonies—Massachusetts, Connecticut, New Haven and Plymouth—decided to confront the Dutch-Indian threats upon them by creating a defensive confederation in 1643. The English from Connecticut and New Haven kept encroaching upon Long Island, making its eastern part more and more English, whereas the Dutch had not given up their title to Connecticut, especially after Petrus Stuyvesant became director-general of New Netherland in 1647. Finally, a treaty was signed, again at Hartford, in 1650, putting a temporary end to the disputes.[67] However, two years later, the beginning of the First Anglo-Dutch War renewed hostilities, or rather rekindled the fear of Dutch attacks, whether or not in combination with the Indians, especially among the New Haven and Connecticut settlers, who were more exposed. As the Massachusetts authorities did not hark to their calls for preemptive war, the New Haven general court, feeling betrayed by their brethren and testing the limits of the United Colonies, decided to call the Lord Protector to the rescue.[68] As is well known, the fleet sent under the command of former Charlestown (Mass.) settler Robert Sedgwick arrived in New England after peace had broken out in Europe and therefore could no longer (try to) seize New Amsterdam. Acadia, as second-best option, was therefore captured by the English.

Cromwell's "Western Design," however, focused on the West Indies and attacking the Spaniards. The Dutch, in spite of commercial disputes caused by the (first) Navigation Acts (1651) were not seen as a dangerous enemy. New Amsterdam, then, enjoyed a decade of precarious respite on the eastern front until it caught the attention of the Duke of York, who would kindly give it his name (as an English claim) after the Dutch town was finally captured in 1664.

Yet, enlightening and indispensable as it unquestionably is, focusing on a single place, such as the Connecticut River or, in this instance, New Amsterdam, can be misleading and cause us to see Manhattan, quite erroneously, as "the island at the center of the world."[69] As local actors and factors were embedded in increasingly global dynamics, we also need to shift our gaze from microscopic to macroscopic and look at the global picture, i.e., beyond the limits of the Atlantic basin. At the Peace of Breda, which ended the Second Anglo-Dutch War in 1667, the Dutch were not unhappy to agree on the status quo post bellum by which they lost New Amsterdam and its peltries but gained Surinam and its sugar, not to mention, much further, the tiny island of Run (or Polaroon), in the Moluccas, then covered in nutmeg and which they had coveted for decades.[70] Similarly, the event known (in England) as the "Amboyna massacre," when ten Englishmen were tortured and executed in the East Indies in 1623, poisoned Anglo-Dutch relations for the rest of the century, surfacing at each period of tension between the two countries.[71] Resorting to wampum, too, came after "Dutch traders in West Africa during the early seventeenth century [had] recognized that regionally produced goods were often more popular with their native trading partners than European goods."[72] This certainly helps to reconsider the relative importance of such a spot as the New Netherland from a global perspective, but it should also serve as a reminder that the "Atlantic world," if admittedly a useful and stimulating (and fashionable) frame of analysis, should not be considered exclusively or apart from other oceanic worlds.[73]

Notes

1. David Armitage, "Three Concepts of Atlantic History," in idem and Michael J. Braddick (eds.), *The British Atlantic World, 1500–1800* (Basingstoke: Palgrave Macmillan, 2002), p. 11.

2 *NNN*, pp. 202, 203.

3. E.g., "L'interface: contribution à l'analyse de l'espace géographique," *Espace géographique* 37 (2008), pp. 193–208.

4. Mark Meuwese, "The Dutch Connection: New Netherland, the Pequots and the Puritans in Southern New England, 1620–1638," *Early American Studies* 9 (2011), pp. 295–323, at 321–322.

5. My definition does not follow one school in particular. A useful discussion can be found in the introduction to Pascal Lorot and François Thual, *La géopolitique* (Paris: Montchrestien, 1997).

6. See Jean-Michel Sallmann, *Géopolitique du XVIe siècle, 1490–1618* (Paris: Seuil, 2003), for historical geopolitics, or more precisely here the history of international relations. Here, I follow Aymeric Chauprade and Yves Lacoste, who argue that the existence of a national framework is not a prerequisite for geopolitical situations: subnational or prenational geopolitics is conceivable as long as political entities, powers or groups are in existence and in a situation of rivalry. The French school of geopolitics revolves around Yves Lacoste and the Institut Français de Géopolitique he created at the Université Paris VIII–St. Denis (www.geopolitique.net), and the *Herodote* journal, also created and edited by Lacoste. Also to be noted in France is the vast interest in all things *"géopolitiques,"* as shown by the sheer number of titles published with "geopolitics" and "geopolitical" in their titles. In other words, geopolitics sells and consequently the term may be abused. Another manifestation of the interest for geopolitics in France is the growing success of the short weekly television program entitled *"Le dessous des cartes,"* now available as a multi-DVD set and on YouTube, both in French and German. The French "school" of geopolitics, whether or not behind Lacoste, has progressively shed its Marxist overtones, as leading practitioners of the discipline now range across the entire political spectrum.

7. The Mohegan and the small Sequin, Pyquag, and Wangunk bands along the Connecticut River, the Western and Eastern Niantics, Pequot, and Narragansetts between its mouth and Narragansett Bay.

8. Paul R. Lucas, *Valley of Discord: Church and Society along the Connecticut River, 1636–1725* (Hanover, NH: University Press of New England, 1976).

9. Benjamin Schmidt, "Mapping an Empire: Cartographic and Colonial Rivalry in Seventeenth-Century Dutch and English North America," *WMQ* 54:3 (July 1997), pp. 549–578 at 568; *NNN*, pp. 102, 103; *DRCHNY*, 1:128–129.

10. Beauchamp Plantagenet, *A Description of the Province of New Albion* (London, 1648), p. 16; G. Folsom, "Expedition of Captain Samuel Argall, afterwards Governor of Virginia, Knight, &c., to the French Settlements in Acadia, and Manhattan Island, AD 1613," *Collections of the New-York Historical Society*, 2nd ser., 1, pt. 9 (1841), pp. 333–342. On Hudson and Argall, also see Schmidt, "Mapping an Empire," p. 567n.

The former French Acadia is now Nova Scotia, but the Acadia National Park (on Mount Desert Island) is in Maine. Mount Desert Island, on 44°N was included into the land claimed by the English in the Virginia charters, whose northern limit (45°N) actually ran through Acadia/Nova Scotia.

11. As in the 1650 "Representation of New Netherland," *NNN*, p. 309.

12. John Smith, A Description of New England (1616), in Philip L. Barbour (ed.), *The Complete Works of Captain John Smith*, 3 vols. (Chapel Hill, NC and London: University of North Carolina Press, 1986), 1:324.

13. Ken MacMillan, "Sovereignty 'More Plainly Described': Early English Maps of North America 1580–1625," *The Journal of British Studies* 42, no. 4 (2003), pp. 413–447; see also Patricia Seed, *Ceremonies of Possession in Europe's Conquest of the New World, 1492–1640* (Cambridge and New York, Cambridge University Press, 1995).

14. W. J. Blaeu, *Paskaart van Guinea, Brasilien en West Indien, 1617*, New York Public Library Digital Gallery: <http://digitalgallery.nypl.org/nypldigital/id?54660>; see also Schmidt, "Mapping an Empire," p. 559.

15. *DRCHNY*, 3:6.

16. *DRCHNY*, 3:16–17.

17. *DRCHNY*, 3:16.

18. Jaap Jacobs, *The Colony of New Netherland: A Dutch Settlement in Seventeenth-Century America* (Ithaca, NY and London: Cornell University Press, 2009), p. 30.

19. MacMillan, "Sovereignty 'More Plainly Described'," p. 413.

20. *Pascaert van Nieuw Nederlandt, Virginia, ende Nieuw-Engelandt verthonendt alles wat van die landin by See, oft by land is ondect oft Bekent*, Library of Congress, Henry Harrisse Collection, vol. 2, map 7. Available on the American Memory database, <http://memory.loc.gov/ammem/gmdhtml/dsxphome.html>.

21. *NNN*, p. 306. That Sagadahoc was abandoned was duly noted in a long memorandum addressed to the States General by the directors of the Dutch West India Company in 1632 which caused Mason to write his aforementioned letter mentioning Sagadahoc as a legitimizing precedent, E. B. O'Callaghan, *History of New Netherland, or New York Under the Dutch* (New York, 1848), 2 vols., 1:133.

22. *NNN*, p. 309.

23. *DRCHNY*, 3:6, 8.

24. William Bradford, *Of Plymouth Plantation 1620–1647*, Samuel Eliot Morison (ed.) (New York: Knopf, 2001), pp. 37, 60; Edward Winslow, *Hypocrisy Unmasked . . .* [London, 1646], in Alexander Young (ed.), *Chronicles of the Pilgrim Fathers of the Colony of Plymouth from 1602 to 1625*, 2nd ed. (Baltimore, MD: Genealogical Publishing Co. 1974 [1844]), p. 385.

25. Edward Winslow, *Good Newes from New England* [London, 1624] in Young, *Chronicles of the Pilgrim Fathers*, p. 306; Bradford, *Of Plymouth Plantation*, pp. 192–193.

26. "Correspondence between the colonies of New Netherlands and New Plymouth, AD 1627. From the letter-book of William Bradford, governor of New-Plymouth, etc.," *Collections of the New-York Historical Society*, 2nd ser., 1, pt. 11 (1841), p. [355]–368.

27. Bradford, *Of Plymouth Plantation*, p. 378. Also see Benjamin Schmidt, "The Dutch Atlantic: From Provincialism to Globalism," in Jack P. Greene and Philip D. Morgan (eds.), *Atlantic History: A Critical Appraisal* (Oxford and New York: Oxford University Press, 2009), pp. 163–187.

28. In *Of Plymouth Plantation*, Bradford explained that the fear of the Spaniards' cruelty was one of the reasons why the Pilgrims chose to emigrate, at p. 23. In 1620, a Dutch as well as a French edition of Las Casas's text was published in Amsterdam to denounce Spanish cruelty: *Le Miroir de la cruelle et horrible tyrannie espagnole perpétrée au Pays Bas par le tyran duc de Albe et aultres commandeurs de par le roy Philippe le deuxiesme . . . –Le Miroir de la tyrannie espagnole perpétrée aux Indes occidentales and Den Spiegel der spaensche tÿrannÿe geschiet in West-Indien, . . . in't spaensch beschreven door den E. bisschop Don Fraey Bartholomé de Las Casas, . . . – Tweede deel van de Spieghel der spaensche tÿrannÿe gheschiet in Nederlandt* (Amsterdam, 1620).

29. "Correspondence from letter-book of Bradford," p. 361. The final qualification is interesting; we may wonder what to make of it. The following paragraphs are based on the same set of letters.

30. Vincent C. Loth, "Armed Incidents and Unpaid Bills: Anglo-Dutch Rivalry in the Banda Islands in the Seventeenth Century," *Modern Asian Studies* 29 (1995), pp. 705–740.

31. Neal Salisbury, *Manitou and Providence: Indians, Europeans and the Making of New England, 1500–1643* (Oxford and New York: Oxford University Press, 1982), pp. 147–152.

32. *NNN*, p. 110. Wampum was initially used as "a means of effecting vital social transactions. It served as the insignia of chiefs and commanded the services of shamans," it "consoled the bereaved and celebrated marriages," and it "was offered in compensation for crimes and could be used to end blood feuds. In diplomacy, wampum exchanges sealed treaties of peace and alliances of war," and as the Dutch also found out, it could ransom captives, Alfred A. Cave, *The Pequot War* (Amherst, MA: University of Massachusetts Press, 1996), p. 53.

33. Meuwese, "The Dutch Connection," p. 309; Cave, *The Pequot War*, p. 50.

34. Bradford, *Of Plymouth Plantation*, p. 203; Salisbury, *Manitou and Providence*; Jacques Rousseau, "Histoire monétaire comparée: le krach du marché du wampum," *Annales. Histoire, sciences sociales* 21 (1966), pp. 1073–1079; Mary W. Herman, "Wampum as Money in Northeastern North America," *Ethnohistory* 3 (1956), pp. 21–33, Claudia Schnurmann, "Wampum as cultural broker in Northeastern America, 1620–1660," in Sünne Juterczenka and Gesa Mackethun (eds.), *The Fuzzy Logic of Encounter: New Perspectives on Cultural Exchanges* (Münster: Waxmann, 2009), pp. 85–206, along with Paul Otto's, Jon Parmenter's and Claudia Schnurmann's contributions to this volume.

35. Meuwese, "The Dutch Connection," p. 309.

36. Plymouth had already been trading at the mouth of the Kennebec River since 1625 and got a patent to establish a trading post in 1628 on the site of present-day Augusta, Maine.

37. Bradford, *Of Plymouth Plantation*, pp. 244–246.

38. *DRCHNY*, 2:139–140; Meuwese, "The Dutch Connection," p. 311; Salisbury, *Manitou and Providence*, p. 207.

39. Bradford, *Of Plymouth Plantation*, pp. 257–259. Contrary to what Oliver Rink points out, the "amicable" relations between New Plymouth and New Amsterdam were not broken in 1632 when the ship *Eendracht*, seeking refuge from poor weather into Plymouth (Devon) harbor, was seized by the English "at the suit of New England Company, on a charge of having traded to, and obtained her cargo in countries subject to His Britannic Majesty"; Rink read "Plymouth, England" for "New Plymouth." It was more probable that the Council for New England that ordered the seizure to protest against the Dutch presence (seen as usurpation) between Virginia and New England. The administrative argument that followed, and of which Mason's aforementioned complaints were part, included territorial claims and counter-claims on both sides, Oliver A. Rink, *Holland on the Hudson: An Economic and Social History of Dutch New York* (Ithaca and London: Cornell University Press, 1986), p. 118n, and O'Callaghan, *History of New Netherland*, 1:130–136 (and not 143–145 as appears in Rink). I would like to thank Jaap Jacobs for pointing out the confusion in Rink. Interestingly, the directors of the Dutch West India Company attributed the decision to seize the *Eendracht* to "the intrigues of the Spanish ambassador in London," ibid., p. 132 and *DRCHNY*, 1:45, 49. All the relevant documents are in *DRCHNY*, 1:45–60. See also *CSPC*, vol. 1, 1574–1660 (London, 1860), pp. 141, 143, 144, 154, 156.

40. *CSPC*, vol. 1, pp. 191–192.

41. Bradford, *Of Plymouth Plantation*, p. 258; Meuwese, "The Dutch Connection," p. 310. In 1642, William Fiennes, Lord Saye and Sele, questioned the Dutch title to Connecticut: he acknowledged that they had purchased land from the Indians, on which purchase they based their title, but added that "it is very well know[n] that the Pequots had no just, but an usurped, title" to the land they were occupying, thereby making the Dutch claim void, *DRCHNY*, 1:128–129.

The story of the "invasion" of the Pequots, long the standard explanation of the Pequot War, has been questioned by Alfred D. Cave, "The Pequot Invasion of

Southern New England: A Reassessment of the Evidence," *The New England Quarterly* 62 (1989), pp. 27–44. Yet, Cave's argument is not entirely convincing as he took no account of mentions of the Pequot "usurpation" earlier than William Hubbard's in the 1670s. Meuwese, "The Dutch Connection," makes a persuasive case for the role of the Pequots, or more precisely of the Dutch-Pequot alliance, in the diplomatic process leading to the "Pequot War." For the classic picture of the geographical distribution of Amerindian tribes in northeastern North America, Alden T. Vaughan, *New England Frontier: Puritans and Indians, 1620–1675*, 3rd ed. (Norman, OK: University of Oklahoma Press, 1995), pp. 50–58.

42. John Winthrop, *The History of New England from 1630 to 1649* (Boston, 1853), 2 vols., 1:62–63. Winthrop then learned that Wahginnacut was "a very treacherous man" and he did not want the straggling colony of Massachusetts to become embroiled in a feud between rival tribes. The "River Quonehtacut" was said to lie "not above five days' journey from us by land."

43. Bradford, *Of Plymouth Plantation*, p. 258.

44. Winthrop, *History of New England*, 1:125.

45. Bradford, *Of Plymouth Plantation*, p. 270.

46. Winthrop, *The History of New England*, 1:157; Francis J. Bremer, *The Puritan Experiment: New England Society from Bradford to Edwards* (New York: St. Martin's Press, 1976), p. 78; Cave, *The Pequot War*, pp. 76–98.

47. *NNN*, pp. 202, 203.

48. Winthrop, *The History of New England*, 1:134–135. Decision-making was therefore based on a spatial misconstruction originating in the imprecision of intelligence based on hearsay and unreliable translations from Amerindians, James Horn, "Imperfect Understandings: Rumor, Knowledge, and Uncertainty in Early Virginia," in Peter C. Mancall (ed.), *The Atlantic World and Virginia, 1550–1624* (Chapel Hill: University of North Carolina Press, 2007), pp. 513–540.

49. Bradford, *Of Plymouth Plantation*, pp. 258–259. About the "great mortality," see also Winthrop, *The History of New England*, 1:137, 138, 146–147.

50. Ibid., p. 281.

51. Ibid., p. 282.

52. Ibid., p. 282; [Robert Cushman], "Reasons and Considerations touching the lawfulness of removing out of England into the parts of America" (1621), in Young, *Chronicles of the Pilgrim Fathers*, pp. 243–244; John Winthrop, "Reasons to be considered for justifying the undertakers of the intended Plantation in New England, and for encouraging such whose hearts Gods shall move to join with them in it," in *The Winthrop Papers*, 6 vols. (Boston: The Massachusetts Historical Society, 1929–92), 2:139.

53. Bradford, *Of Plymouth Plantation*, p. 283. The removal of so many people from Massachusetts to the Connecticut valley did not go without saying and caused a major division in the General Court in 1634, and was the cause behind the attribution of a veto power to the magistrates.

54. Robert C. Black III, *The Younger John Winthrop* (New York and London: Columbia University Press, 1966), p. 87.

55. Reprinted in B. B. Trumbull, *A Complete History of Connecticut*, 2 vols. (Hartford, 1818), 1:423–424, Black, *The Younger John Winthrop*, p. 373n.

56. Black, *The Younger John Winthrop*, p. 87; *Winthrop Papers*, 3:198–199.

57. Ibid., p. 96.

58. Ibid., p. 375n for references in the Winthrop Papers dealing with transshipment.

59. Ibid., pp. 96, 163; for Lord Saye and Sele's efforts against the Dutch, already mentioned above, see *DRCHNY*, 1:128–129.

60. Karen O. Kupperman, *Providence Island 1630–1641: The Other Puritan Colony* (Cambridge, Cambridge University Press, 1993).

61. Bradford, *Of Plymouth Plantation*, pp. 294–297. Sassacus, the "chief sachem" of the Pequots, was beheaded by the Mohawks, to whom he had supposedly fled. Bradford, a little more than a decade after the war, wrote that the Mohawks wanted to "satisfy the English, or rather the Narragansetts"; Cave, *Pequot War*, passim; Meuwese, "The Dutch Connection," pp. 313–315. Interestingly, the Pequots acknowledged they initially made no difference between the Dutch and the English, who were "both strangers to us," cited in Meuwese, "The Dutch Connection," p. 315.

62. F. J. Bremer, *The Puritan Experiment*, p. 78. In Britain, the late 1630s saw an escalation in the tension between Scotland and the crown over the introduction of the Scottish Prayer Book (June 1637). The breaking up of the First Bishops' War in June 1639 spelt the definitive end of machinations orchestrated by Sir Ferdinando Gorges and the Council for New England (with the support of Archbishop Laud) to annul the Royal Charter granted for Massachusetts Bay in 1629. During the 1630s, Gorges and his circle tried to completely reorganize New England, geographically and politically, along lines that were much less unorthodox than the puritans'. See *CSPC*, vol. 1, passim, notably a "Digest of an Ecclesiastical Government for the Church of New England," March 1635, p. 199.

63. Rink, *Holland on the Hudson*, p. 121.

64. Cave, *The Pequot War*, p. 66.

65. *NNN*, p. 203. David de Vries, the aforementioned guest, had been born at La Rochelle in the 1590s. That the Dutch "neglected to populate the land" was also argued by the author of the "Representation" (1650) in *NNN*, p. 306.

66. It was also, famously, a period of war(s) in the British Isles.

67. The Treaty of Hartford (1650) was ratified by the Dutch States General in 1656 but never was in England, Black, *The Younger John Winthrop*, pp. 164, 390n.; *DRCHNY*, 1:459, 611–612 and Jaap Jacobs, "The Hartford Treaty: A European Perspective on a New World Conflict," *de Halve Maen* 68 (1995), p. 74–79.

68. Charles J. Hoadly (ed.), *Records of the Colony or Jurisdiction of New Haven from May, 1653 to the Union* (Hartford, 1858), pp. 37–38 (12 Oct 1653); *A Collection of the State Papers of John Thurloe, volume 1: 1638–1653* (1742), pp. 721–733. <http://www.british-history.ac.uk/report.aspx?compid=55294> Date accessed: 06 September 2009. 1:721ff.

69. Russell Shorto, *The Island at the Center of the World: The Epic Story of Dutch Manhattan and the Forgotten Colony that Shaped America* (New York: Doubleday, 2004).

70. Loth, "Armed Incidents and Unpaid Bills." Thomas Bender has recently reminded us that "Americans and American histories tend to put the Dutch settlement of New York at the start of a linear development of what would become the American metropolis. But that appropriates for American history what in fact belongs to Dutch history and to the history of oceanic commerce and capitalism. New Amsterdam was part of a global Dutch commercial strategy, and the settlement on Manhattan was on the periphery of the periphery of the empire. Not only were the East Indian interests more valuable and more visible from the Dutch point of view, but even in the Americas, Manhattan was minor compared with the far more important and profitable Brazilian sugar colony of Pernambuco, which they had wrested from the Portuguese," Thomas Bender, *A Nation among Nations: America's Place in World History* (New York: Hill and Wang, 2006), pp. 39–40. On the exchange of New Amsterdam for Surinam and Run/Polaroon (the latter being more often than not overlooked), see Gijs Rommelse, *The Second Anglo-Dutch War: International Raison d'État, Mercantilism and Maritime Strife* (Hilversum: Verloren, 2006), 184–188; Steven A. Pincus, *Protestantism and Patriotism: Ideologies and the Making of English Foreign Policy, 1650–1668* (Cambridge: Cambridge University Press, 1996), pp. 403–405; Francis G. Davenport, Charles O. Paullin, *European Treaties Bearing on the History of the United States and Its Dependencies* (Clark, NJ: The Lawbook Exchange, 2004 [1917]), pp. 119–122.

71. Karen Chancey, "The Amboyna Massacre in English Politics, 1624–1632," *Albion: A Quarterly Journal Concerned with British Studies* 30 (1998), pp. 583–598. When the Dutch ambassador complained to Secretary Sir John Coke about the seizure of the *Eendracht* in (old) Plymouth in 1632, Coke replied only: "AMBOINA," *DRCHNY*, 1:48. In a letter to their "High Mightinesses" of the States General, Ambassador Joachimi deplored that "So long as this stumbling block be not removed, everything shall turn to our prejudice." *DRCHNY*, 1:54. In London as in The Hague, the seats of decision-making at central (as opposed to local/regional) level, events in both East Indies and the Americas were impossible to dissociate. Historians' vision is artificially impaired by, among other reasons, the split of (English) archives, or at least the colonial series of the State Papers (and their Calendars), into "East Indies, China and Japan" on the one hand and "America and West Indies" on the other; see Alison Games, "Beyond the Atlantic: English Globetrotters and Transoceanic Connections," *WMQ* 63:4 (October 2006), pp. 675–692, and Philip J. Stern, "British Asia and British Atlantic: Comparisons and Connections," ibid., pp. 692–712.

72. Meuwese, "The Dutch Connection," p. 308.

73. "Atlantic history, then, is a slice of world history. It is a way of looking at global and regional processes within a contained unit, although that region was not, of course, hermetically sealed off from the rest of the world, and thus was

simultaneously involved in transformations unique to the Atlantic and those derived from global processes." Alison Games, "Atlantic History: Definitions, Challenges and Opportunities," *The American Historical Review* 111:3 (June 2006), pp. 741–757 at 748. See also Peter A. Coclanis, "Beyond Atlantic History," in Greene and Morgan, *Atlantic History*, pp. 337–356.

IV

THE FORMATION OF ATLANTIC WORLDS

10

Religion and Toleration in Old and New Netherland

Willem Frijhoff

The Atlantic Perspective

*A*dopting the Atlantic perspective supposes a major change of view, not only in America but also in Europe. We do not have to think any more in national communities (the U.S.A., the Netherlands), or even in regional or local bodies (New Netherland, New York), but in transnational and indeed transatlantic networks, in other words: in cultural areas, founded much more on physical than on national space. Such cultural areas embrace, for instance, the countries bound to the North Sea, or to the Mediterranean Sea, or to the Atlantic Ocean. Since classical antiquity there has been a common Mediterranean civilization comprising southern Europe, northern Africa, Asia Minor (present-day Turkey) and what we commonly call the Near East (the Asian countries bordering the Mediterranean Sea). Similarly, since the conquests of the late fifteenth and sixteenth centuries, a Spanish and Portuguese civilization has existed on both sides of the southern half of the Atlantic Ocean. And we may speak of a common "Western civilization" spanning the Ocean's northern half and including not only the Germanic, Scandinavian and Anglo-Saxon nations but also most of the French-speaking communities. Ever since the beginnings of civilization, oceans and seas have united people by trade, migrations, and curiosity, and create a shared cultural universe. Therefore, cultural history has to become trans-cultural history or, still better, cross-cultural history.

At first sight, the Atlantic perspective may not really seem fit for the topic of religion. Is not religion about truth? And does not truth radically transcend geographical distances, national qualities, and social distinctions? Besides, is there any particular reason to comment upon religion in New Netherland, since in the Dutch period there was formally only one church, the Dutch Reformed Church? Not only did this public church survive the takeover of the colony by the English in 1664–1673, but in front of the Anglican Church of the new English rulers it monopolized the Dutch community more and more, becoming in later centuries typically the Dutch church and excluding in fact other Christians from the sense of a common Dutch ethnicity. However, at second sight there is room for a closer analysis and for discussion, because there are always several ways of looking at religion. Beside a theological vision or a political view, there is for instance an historical or cultural approach. Indeed, religious experience can only express itself through the culture of a given community and its members, and culture changes according to the conditions of time and space.

Church Monopoly and Religious Diversity

Just as in the European Netherlands, there was in New Netherland only one publicly authorized church, the Reformed Church of Calvinistic persuasion. That Church followed the rules and doctrine fixed by the national Synod held in the Dutch city of Dordrecht (commonly called Dort) in 1618–1619. There were however several linguistic varieties within the one Dutch Reformed Church: Dutch of course, but also French (called the Walloon Church but comprising also the French Huguenot refugees), English (Presbyterian), and even German. Many people in the Netherlands and its overseas colonies confessed, however, in private, in their homes, other Christian creeds: Lutheran, Catholic, Mennonite, Baptist, Quaker, etc. In fact, a considerable number of the inhabitants of the colony of New Netherland may have confessed other religions. That was the case of the Natives, probably also of a fair number of the African slaves—though many of them may already had been baptized by the Roman Catholic Portuguese colonizers in their African homelands—and even of some of the immigrants themselves, such as the early settlers Anthony "the Turk" and Abraham van Salee, the famous sons of an Islamic mother, and in the 1650s of the first Jewish immigrants to the colony

Obviously, for the immigrants in New Netherland, the Christian creeds must have been less self-evident and were much more challenged by non-Christians in their new fatherland than at home. From the start, the West India Company in charge of the colony showed a keen awareness of the obligations this religious diversity imposed on the immigrants. According to

Article 2 of the Provisional Regulations for the very first colonists, issued on 30 March 1624, they should "by their Christian life and conduct seek to attract the Indians and other blind people [i.e., non-believers] to the knowledge of God and his word."

These facts put us in presence of some important questions. First, what does religion really mean in the early modern period, and specifically in the New Netherland context? Was it about truth? About spiritual experience? About liturgy and ceremonial services? About moral values and peacefully living together? About social gathering and civic ritual? Second, up to what point was religion in New Netherland a copy of that in the European homeland? And when exactly did it start to follow its own way in the colony, in interaction with its new American context? Think for instance of American Pietism and the Great Awakening of the eighteenth century. Third, if there were Christians other than those pertaining to the Reformed Church, how did they live together? In other words: was there a form of peaceful coexistence, or even of formal toleration? What shape did it take, and how was it motivated or legitimized?

Toleration and the Sense of Identity

We cannot tackle all of those themes together. I prefer limiting the analysis to the theme of religious toleration. There is a clear and important reason for this, which precisely has to do with the transatlantic bonds between the Dutch and American Reformed communities. Let me summarize it in a few words. Traditionally the Dutch Republic is known as a Protestant nation. Hence Calvinism has become a major feature of Dutch ethnicity in America indeed. It is true that people with other creeds or persuasions, for instance Lutherans, Mennonites, Catholics or Jews, have also migrated from the Netherlands to America, especially during the nineteenth century, but also in the centuries before. The prevailing historical image of the Netherlands itself, however, is quite clearly that of a Protestant, and even a strictly Calvinist, nation. Yet, as a national community in Europe the Dutch people boast at the same time of a strong tradition of toleration, in particular religious toleration.[1] Toleration is at the heart of the self-image of the Dutch.[2] Taken in the sense of permissiveness for otherwise forbidden things or actions, or of openness to new, unofficial trends and movements, toleration is one of the most important tools the Dutch use for the regulation of their national community: remember such diverse developments of the last decades as the early rise of the anti-nuclear peace movement in the Netherlands, gay pride and gay marriage, voluntary abortion, drugs consumption, euthanasia, etc. People may object to Dutch permissiveness in such matters but they testify of a strong collective toleration for diverging ideas, attitudes, and persuasions. Toleration is a value that the Dutch are proud of and consider to be at the heart of their historical identity.

But toleration has a very precise sense in the American context too, in particular in this geographical area formerly possessed and shaped by the Dutch. For some American historians such as Russell Shorto and others involved in New Netherland history, for example, the Dutch period was the real start of religious toleration as a basic American value.[3] In September 2009, the then-Prince of Orange, heir to the Dutch throne, when visiting New York stated it clearly: the American value of toleration is a Dutch legacy. Is toleration therefore a Dutch virtue, something deposited in the genetic material of the Dutch and brought by them to the New World? That is apparently the opinion of Shorto in whose important book on New Netherland we read the following crucial passage on this theme:

> Tolerance was more than just an attitude in the Dutch Republic. Following the bloody religious persecution of thousands in the previous century at the hands of the Spanish, the Dutch provinces had broken new ground in writing into their 1579 de facto constitution the guarantee that 'each person shall remain free. Especially in his religion, and that no one shall be persecuted or investigated because of their religion.' This sentence became the ground on which the culturally diverse society of the seventeenth century was built. But as in so many societies—think of the early United States, a slaveholding nation that believed itself to be rooted on the principle of freedom—the guiding rule was often broken. In the 1620s a debate on the meaning and wisdom of tolerance had raged through the Dutch provinces. [. . .] Out of this struggle came an elaborate written rationale for tolerance of religious diversity. Its climax—really, a watershed in human thought—came with Arminius's follower Simon Episcopius declaring in a series of carefully reasoned arguments that the strength of a state derived not from maintaining a single, firmly held faith, as was almost universally believed in Europe, but from allowing its citizens freedom of worship and intellectual inquiry. It is impossible to imagine how revolutionary this was, how intoxicating it felt to those who championed it, and how deeply it affected Adriaen van der Donck and his generation

of scholars. By Van der Donck's time at Leiden, the tolerance advocates held sway, and the staggering successes of the Golden Age only strengthened their case.[4]

Yet, my impression is that Shorto, in his willingness to celebrate the Dutch as the champions and founders of American toleration, privileges the ideas above the facts. Indeed, the followers of the liberal theologian Jacobus Arminius were quickly defeated by the orthodox wing of the Reformed Church and forced to resign their ministry. Many had to flee the country for a while, and their political chief, the Grand Pensionary (the equivalent of a present-day prime minister) Johan van Oldenbarnevelt, was beheaded after a mock trial under the auspices of the stadholder, Prince Maurice of Orange-Nassau. Besides, the celebrated lawyer Van der Donck certainly was not an Arminian, but a militant Calvinist who married the daughter of a stern Presbyterian minister, Reverend Francis Doughty. On the other hand, his hated opponent New Netherland Director Willem Kieft came from a family with Remonstrant Arminian sympathies. Yet it is precisely Kieft's memory that was soiled by his cruelty and intolerance during the first Indian War of 1643–1645.

From an Atlantic perspective, this apparent contradiction between the intolerance of a monopolistic church and the toleration that a whole national community ascribes to itself, needs discussion and clarification. To put it simply: Is (religious) toleration a typical Dutch attitude, introduced in America by the Dutch themselves? Is it an American value developed in the specific conditions of American society? Or is it perhaps something in between, neither typically Dutch nor essentially American, but the fruit of a historical process of community-building? It is useful to distinguish between forms (which are transmissible over the oceans) and meanings (which may be old, new, or mixed, but are always bound to precise situations, communities, and territories)? Ultimately this issue refers to vital questions about the relation between values, ideas and practices in history. In order to get things clear, we must first focus on the key terms, the tools for the debate.

Religion

The first key term is religion. How do we approach religion, especially in New Netherland?[5] There are many ways of looking at religion. My approach differs from the usual perceptions of religion by the professionals of church history. I want to start from the people's religious needs and practices, instead of focussing on the established Reformed Church or on the formal religious policy of the State. I look at religion not so much top-down as, preferably, bottom-up. Of course, other approaches are legitimate, but for the moment I keep to this one. Through this approach we will be able to diversify our vision of the seventeenth-century colony's religion, link it to religious practices in the immigrants' homelands, analyze their transformation in the new world, and understand them thereby in a fuller meaning. This may be called the sociocultural or anthropological view. Religion is not opposed to culture, nor is it a category aside from culture, but from the point of view of the humanities, in particular of history, religion fundamentally is a form of culture, a dimension, or a variety of culture. In order to express itself and to make itself recognizable in a given community, religion adopts the cultural forms and practices—which we may call the "cultural repertoires"—of that community as it has evolved in time and space. This fact entitles us to a properly cultural look at religion.

Religion always was a distinguished feature of early modern societies, because until far into the eighteenth or nineteenth century people remained unable to think of a world without God: God as the maker of the universe, as the motor of history and of evolution, as the judge of our actions, thoughts, emotions, and motives, and indeed of our souls. Normally, for the early modern European or American Christians the religious motive came first, before the commercial, political, or social arguments. For us this has become unfamiliar. Even when we are gifted with a very religious mind, we know that at least some of the world's events and developments have their own rationale and that God's interference quite often may be at most indirect. This difference between the religious argument in former times and nowadays is a clear example of the cultural dimension of religion.

As a cultural approach, religious history covers in fact three great research fields which in everyday practice may overlap, yet are governed by different chains of causality, reflect different views of rationality, and correspond to different forms of experience.[6] In order to grasp what in the past was happening in religion, we must respect the analytical distinctions between these fields without using the historical sources at face value or taking current historiography uncritically for granted. We may summarize these three research fields under the three concepts of religion, faith, and church. Religion refers to the order of the sacred, the common perception of the divine and of higher forces, of sacred corporate bonds, of holiness, and of the supernatural. Faith is the basically a personal, and individual, belief in and experience of the bond between man and God, of whatever nature this may be. It refers to a person's duties in his or her individual life and in society, as derived from this bond. Church is the essentially communitarian and institutional organization of common interests in religion and faith. Church includes their intellectual legitimization by theological discourse, their emotional expression in the spirituality of a given group, and the common ethical concerns of the community.

Toleration

The second key term is toleration. The Republic of the Seven United Provinces, currently called the Dutch Republic (i.e., roughly the present-day Kingdom of the Netherlands), offers the rather special case of a State which called itself mono-confessional and Protestant while at the same time organizing the civic community along the lines of religious diversity. There was a clear tension between these two aspects of collective life and its representation: confessional pluralism and coexistence was unusual, if not out of place, in a state that claimed to be monolithically Calvinistic. This tension explains the contrasting images of the United Provinces—and of New Netherland—that we find not only in the contemporary sources but also in more recent literature: was it a Protestant state, or a Calvinistic nation, or a liberal community? The huge variety of solutions adopted in the single provinces of the Dutch Republic, reputed to be autonomous where religion was concerned, adds still more to the opacity of the general picture. Public toleration as it is claimed (or supposed!) by present-day American authors for the early modern Netherlands existed only in the province of Holland itself, and more precisely in Amsterdam and in some of the larger cities, like Haarlem, Gouda or Rotterdam, but much less in most of the other towns of Holland and virtually nowhere in the other provinces, at least during the New Netherland period in the seventeenth century.

Opinions can obviously diverge as to which term is the most apt to qualify the persisting religious pluralism that existed in Holland in the seventeenth century, but the diversity itself was a unanimously established fact, avidly commented on by contemporaries. However, diversity or pluralism does not necessarily mean "toleration." Toleration at the very least is the tacit admission of this diversity as permissible. In fact several degrees of toleration can be defined, which cannot easily be distinguished in modern idiom. Toleration in the active sense was about the legal freedom to be different, but as such it involved hardly more in early modern society than freedom of conscience, most often without any right to express these convictions in the public space of the national community, let alone to public worship.

Toleration in the passive sense of the term, though, was more widespread. It may be defined as a more or less systematic form of connivance (in Dutch *conniventie* or *toelating*) with convictions or actions that were not allowed, the wilful non-application of legally prescribed practice, or the will to turn a blind eye on them (literally *oogluiking*, in Dutch). It is in this passive sense that toleration usually involved freedom of public worship, mostly however not in the public space but simply as a form of *religio domestica*, religious service at home, for the family members alone.

As a concept of political philosophy, the term "toleration" appears in Europe only after the takeover of New Netherland by the English, yet always in close relation to the Dutch Republic. First in the writings of the Amsterdam Jewish philosopher Baruch de Spinoza (1632–1677); then in those of John Locke (1632–1704), an English refugee at Rotterdam who wrote to his Dutch friend Philippus à Limborch a public "Letter concerning Toleration" (1689) that passes for the very first systematic treatise on that matter; and in the works of Pierre Bayle (1647–1708), who as a French refugee at Rotterdam opposed sharply the intolerant anti-Huguenot policy of the French King Louis XIV (reigned 1643–1715).[7] Locke rigorously distinguished between the civil society, to which one is obliged to belong and that is therefore forced to accept the diversity of religious opinions, and the religious society which is purely voluntary and may therefore reject other persuasions.[8] In this strong sense of the word, the term toleration appeared only after Holland had elaborated its particular form of political acceptance of religious diversity in spite of the legal inequality of the different churches involved.

In the Dutch Republic, a mix of both formulas, active and passive, was observed, but rather differently according to the towns and provinces. Freedom of conscience was ensured for all, at least in principle, but freedom of worship was variously allowed, according to the attitude of the civil authorities and their degree of social or cultural consensus with the dissenting faithful. In fact, in the colonial societies of the Dutch, such as New Netherland, where the immigrants were obliged to keep tightly together in an often hostile environment, the religious monopoly of the Reformed Church normally was enforced with greater strength than in the home country. On the other hand, the level of public toleration of the East and West India Companies' religious policy remained rather low, at any rate lower than in their homeland. The Reformed Church acted overseas first and foremost as the adhesive of the Europeans' community and the ferment of immigrant cohesion. Doctrinal purity most often was a matter of lesser concern.

The Origin of Dutch Toleration: Political or Religious?

Because religion was present everywhere in society, the problem of toleration was always urgent in Europe, and it took a violent stance many times: think of the wars of religion, endemic in Europe until the end of the seventeenth century and remember that for eighty years, until the 1648 Peace Treaties of Münster and Osnabrück in Westphalia, the Dutch Republic was formally at war with Spain. Religion was one of the two major issues of the Revolt that the inhabitants of the Low Countries had started around 1568 for their political and religious freedom against their Habsburg sovereign, of Roman Catholic persuasion. In fact, the Dutch Revolt created a new field of political application for the old concept of "toleration"—precisely because the new State emerged simultaneously with the rise of a fiercely defended religious pluralism.[9] The Revolt was as much about the freedom of thinking as about the liberty to confess a different religious creed. Freedom of conscience for all, beyond the right to existence of the Calvinist Church, remained therefore a crucial issue for the emerging nation. The right to religious dissent (i.e., the Revolt *religionis ergo*, according to the maxim of the time) justified the desire for political liberty (i.e., the Revolt *libertatis ergo*). But many did not want to exchange the tyranny of a sovereign for the tyranny of a church, be it the Calvinist Church that called itself the only "Truly Reformed Church" (*de ware gereformeerde kerk*). Had not the leader of the revolt, William of Orange himself, made a strong plea for freedom of conscience together with freedom to worship for the various confessions?

In the Dutch Republic often voices were raised to exclude particular religious groups from the political life of the new State. Without forgetting the violent Anabaptists at the beginning of the sixteenth century and their peaceful successors, the Mennonites, we may particularly refer to the fate of the Catholics from the end of the sixteenth century onward, of the Lutherans rejected by their Calvinist successors, of the Arminians (the liberal variant of the Reformed creed) at the beginning of the seventeenth century, or of the Socinians (the followers of Faustus Socinus who rejected the Holy Trinity) a little later on. In fact, only members or sympathizers of the Reformed Church were admitted to public offices in the State. The adherents of all the other churches and religious communities were second-range citizens, deprived of the full exercise of their civic rights. However, the principle itself of a passive but legitimate difference of private opinion and of personal religious persuasion was never really challenged. It was not even questioned by the most orthodox and the most demanding Calvinist ministers who were at the height of their power after the Peace of Westphalia (1648). After all, that peace treaty recognized a State that claimed to be founded on religious dissent. In fact, all forms of diversity, of pluralism and of toleration practised in the Republic of the United Provinces were included in the fundamental principle of freedom of conscience, formulated in Article 13 of the Union of Utrecht, the founding charter of the Republic.[10] The article stated that "each person shall remain free, especially in his religion, and that no one shall be persecuted or investigated because of their religion." It protected therefore the so-called *forum internum*, i.e., the freedom of any person to adhere to the religion of one's own choice. This article was and remained the philosophical base, as it were, of the new State.

Indeed, the particular position of the Reformed Church in the Dutch Republic was closely linked to the evolution of the Dutch State itself.[11] In 1579 the Seventeen Provinces of the Low Countries, which in 1548 had been united in the so-called Burgundian Circle of the Habsburg territories, split into two. In the South the provinces formed the Union of Arras which remained faithful to the sovereign (6 January 1579), and in the North the Union of Utrecht (23 January 1579) that abjured the authority of Philip II on 22 July 1581. Although not more than slightly affected by Calvinism, the Northern Provinces were pushed by Holland into the hands of the rebels. To that end, Holland used the Reformation for political reasons, as the only way of rallying the hard and fast Calvinists who were so numerous in the Southern Provinces and would came over to the North after the final surrender of Antwerp to the Spanish army in 1585. The united front against the king was henceforth founded on an ambiguity, because a large part of the rebellious population of the North was not automatically won over to Calvinism, not even to the Protestant Reformation as such. They simply wanted freedom, either to maintain the specific federal organization that characterized the political structure of the Low Countries, or to be able to exercise freely their own form of religion. But its ecclesiastical or doctrinal outlines did not necessarily correspond to the religious order favored by the Calvinists.

Freedom of Conscience and Religious Claims to Universality

By adopting the principle of individual freedom of conscience, understood not as freedom of religious practice for the community, but as a personal freedom of thought, the United Provinces automatically became a distinctive case in the European landscape. Throughout Europe, territorial or community limitations of religious conscience by the ecclesiastical and civil authorities remained the rule, even in places where edicts of toleration for a particular confession had been issued, as was the case in France or in some German states and Central European territories. The distinctive feature of the Dutch solution was precisely a generalized but purely individual practice of toleration that had nothing to do with legislation for particular groups. Its limits remained therefore inevitably vague and changeable. It was based on a new and largely implicit relationship between the ecclesiastical and the civil authorities, which was itself vested in a new idea of the civic body.[12]

After the formal introduction of the Confession of Heidelberg as the "dominant" religion in the last quarter of the sixteenth century, the militant Calvinists were not long finding out that, for many of their compatriots attracted to their Church, religious life remained just as much an outside show as in the days of Catholicism. So the Protestant elites themselves formulated a dual claim. First the new doctrine had to be imposed publicly by making the Reformed Church a real State Church; this was the Geneva-bound model of the *civitas Dei*, where the Church dominates the State, as opposed to the pluralist evangelical model, where the State dominates the Church. At the same time it was necessary to reform the life of the community by a new practice of piety. *Reformatio vitae* (the reformation of life) and *praxis pietatis* (the practice of piety) were henceforth the key words of the efforts at Christianization.

Quite rapidly, however, the Reformed Church had to deal with the refusal of its theocratic desires on the part of the authorities. The latter were quite happy with a popular church, marked by Protestantism, but they did not want a theocracy under the control of ministers. The publicly recognized church certainly enjoyed privileges but no longer lived in symbiosis with the State as state churches in the proper sense of the term did elsewhere in Europe, as in neighboring France or England. The desired union of the public, Reformed Church with the entire Dutch society soon proved to be a chimera. Instead, a plurality of denominational churches, old and new, with more or less clandestine forms of worship, imposed itself against the wish of the ruling church but with the connivance of many among the secular authorities. While continuing to defend its point of view in the pulpit, the Reformed Church had in fact to resign itself to a position of limited power and a reduced number of members. It therefore gave up its ambition to form a great popular church, coextensive with the nation in the way the medieval church had been before. Instead, it developed the idea of a church for the Saved, the Elect, an *Ecclesia purior* (a pure church) of true believers. This idea was founded on the new dogma that was taking shape (the predestination of a limited number of chosen people) and on a newly emerging disciplinary practice which preferred a small perfect community easy to control rather than a religiosity of "sociological Christians" interested only in the rites of passage of individual life (baptism, marriage, funeral) and the social ministry of the diaconate for the poor and helpless.

The new theological doctrine was sanctioned in 1618–1619 by the National Synod of Dordrecht (or Dort). It corresponded well with the simultaneously emerging spiritual movement of the Further Reformation, i.e., the in-depth reformation of manners and morals by the members of the Reformed Church. The pretension of the Church to universality was gradually abandoned and transferred to the secular community, in which everybody should be welcome—even complete outsiders such as the Jews, who were supposed to hate the Christians and vice versa. By stripping the urban landscape of all its religious elements, Catholic and Protestant alike, the town itself, in its role as body politic, became the new sacred community, with its own history, its legends, its symbolism, and its ritual which ensured a civic peace that went beyond differences of convictions. It was so, for instance, in Haarlem. From the early seventeenth century the myth of the courage of its Crusaders, shared by all when conquering the Egyptian town of Damiette in 1219, in the medieval days of undivided Christianity, was actively propagandized by the town council among its citizens in order to conjure the religious and ethnic tensions that menaced the town's population irremediably.[13]

At the end, this evolution resulted in what I would like to call "cultural Calvinism," that is, a society in which the secular authorities adopted the values of the public, Calvinist church as a cultural yardstick for social behavior without however committing themselves forcibly to the Calvinist creed, and in which, on the other side, the laity adopted those Calvinist values as their own, regardless their denominational position.[14] In fact, cultural Calvinism sprang from confessional diversity. But at the same time, political authorities could always strengthen the Calvinistic outlook of public life without infringing on the basic principle of individual freedom of conscience.

That is what happened in New Netherland under Director-General Petrus Stuyvesant (1647–1664). He used all the available political instruments to reinforce the religious conformity and the Calvinistic imprint of the colony's public order, yet the principle of freedom of conscience obliged him to allow the existence of dissenting communities, at least in private. Both parties, i.e., the director-general who represented the political authorities and the public monopoly of the Reformed Church on the one hand, and the faithful of competing creeds on the other hand, sought for expedients to extend the limits of what was legally permitted. Stuyvesant tried to prevent the public expression and the institutional establishment of all other confessions than the Dutch Reformed: his victims were successively the Lutherans (1653), the Jews (1654), and the Quakers (1657).[15] The dissenters on their part looked for the margins of the law which, in the context of religious pluralism, would allow them to achieve growing forms of public community-building. That is for instance the background of the famous "Flushing Remonstrance" of 27 December 1657, by which 31 inhabitants of the village of Flushing on Long Island opposed Stuyvesant's harsh policy toward the Quakers, who qualified as an "abominable sect" and whose activities were strictly forbidden by a recent law.[16] The petitioners tried to justify a legalization of their meetings, the "conventicles," and asked for an exemption from the law, but to no avail, since Stuyvesant arrested the main petitioners and the others had to retract their petition. But the episode shows how much leeway people could try to find grey areas in the legal dispositions, and how much the effective execution of policy could depend on the balance between legal violence and social negotiation.

Religious Pluralism

Before the Dutch Republic went through a process of growing bipolarization between Catholics and Calvinists, during the last decades of the seventeenth century and in the course of the eighteenth century, religious diversity persisted therefore largely within the country and its establishments overseas.[17] And it did so during the whole existence of New Netherland. Catholics formed the most problematic group, but for unclear reasons they never were quite numerous in New Netherland. Indeed, soon after the Revolt and the adoption of the Union of Utrecht the Dutch had to cope with the fact that Catholicism remained culturally and socially important in their country, because many opponents to the king's policy simply had not joined the Reformed Church. But Catholicism was all the same the political enemy outside, and outside meant not only the power of the Pope in Rome, decried as the Anti-Christ by the Reformed ministers, but the Catholic territories just across the frontiers of the Dutch State in the Southern Netherlands and Germany: Flanders, Brabant, Liège, Cologne, Cleves, Münster. The Protestant state of the Dutch Republic remained surrounded by a chain of Catholic territories that put a constant strain on its Calvinization effort by providing opportunities for public worship, Catholic education across the border, and protection of the rights of Dutch Catholics.

In fact, between the final reduction of Antwerp by the Spanish in 1585, and the second quarter of the seventeenth century, the Revolt and the war caused within the Low Countries a mass migration for religious as well as economic reasons from the South to the North, and, reversely but on a smaller scale, from the North to the South. Around 1625, about 20 percent of the population of the provinces of Holland and Zeeland consisted of immigrants from the Southern provinces, Dutch-speaking Flemish and French-speaking Walloons alike, many of them Calvinists or Lutherans, but some others just Catholics following the economic mainstream to the North. Globally, their integration into Dutch society reinforced its Calvinistic outlook, and many ministers, teachers, and other members of intellectual professions were refugees of a strongly orthodox Calvinistic persuasion.[18]

Among the native population as well as the immigrants, freedom of conscience favored, in turn, the emergence of a host of small, locally based, dissenting religious communities, called "conventicles," outside or in the margin of the established churches. Because there was no compulsory state church but just an officially admitted public church, enjoying a monopoly position in the public sphere but destitute of any power of enforcement, many hesitated to embrace one church or another. Until far into the seventeenth century, one could find in the Dutch provinces many inhabitants who had not been baptized at all. They remained "seekers" or agnostics, or they went, as it were, shopping around for their practical religious needs among the established churches, either Protestant or Catholic. The internationally best known Dutchman of the seventeenth century, the painter and engraver Rembrandt van Rijn is a good example of such an independent religious seeker. Though not opposed to Protestantism, he kept during his whole life to his own, Bible-inspired religious persuasion, without committing himself to a particular church.[19]

Next to the approximately 30 percent of the Dutch population who finally remained Roman Catholic, there were many Mennonites. In the coastal provinces they could form locally up to 25 percent of the inhabitants. Lutherans were especially numerous in towns where Scandinavian and German immigration was important, like Amsterdam, Utrecht, or Rotterdam, or in the numerous garrison towns on the eastern and southern borders of the Republic, since the army recruited essentially in the Holy Roman Empire— that is, by the way, the reason why most soldiers in New Netherland were of German origin. After a short period of persecution in the 1630s and 1720s, the (liberal) Arminians came back and soon installed themselves in many towns as an alternative Reformed community. It is not difficult to retrieve in the literature of that period many ardent defences of religious pluralism seen as constituent of Holland's identity. Take, for instance, a poem by Jan van der Veen (1578–1656) on the freedom of preaching. He himself had been educated in the Mennonite community with its repeated splits. In his list of groups allowed to express themselves in the Republic, he included not only the Roman Catholics with their numerous religious orders, each with different tendencies, the Lutherans, Mennonites and Arminians, Zwinglians, Puritans and Arians, Libertines and Perfectists, Socinians and Sophists, but also some popular lay preachers with flowery names ("Robbert Tobbertsen den Flouwer"), the members of the Pietist conventicles ("Jan Taurens in 't Suchtent-huys," Jan Taurens in the House of Moaning), the Rosicrucians, and finally the Jews, the Turks (probably the Armenian Christians, who had a church in Amsterdam, or Muslim merchants from the Ottoman Empire or the Mediterranean Barbary Coast, who had settled in the city), and the Gipsies (Heidens, heathen). This poem's success can be seen in its reprinting in a pamphlet during the 1672 war against France and England, where the text appears as an apologia for general toleration against the religious intolerance of the invader, the king of France.[20]

Few visitors to the United Provinces made such an accurate assessment of the country as Sir William Temple (1628–1699) in his *Observations upon the United Provinces of the Netherlands*, published in the year 1673, during the Second Anglo-Dutch War. In his chapter on religion, Temple clearly described the notable differences he observed, while he was there as ambassador (1668–1670), in the treatment and the public status of the different religions present in Holland. But he also stressed the freedom of conscience that, in his eyes, was the distinctive characteristic of the Dutch Republic:

> the great Care of this State has ever been, To favour no particular or curious Inquisition into the Faith or Religious Principles of any peaceable man, who came to live under the protection of their Laws.[21]

If despite all this the Catholic religion seemed exempt from the pervading toleration it was because of the suspicion of political treason which had weighed on Catholics since the Revolt. Temple, himself an orthodox member of the Church of England, took note of the fact that Catholics apparently formed "a sound piece of the State and fast joined in with the rest," and that they had never shown any desire for revolution or treason. As for the other religions, Temple insisted on the freedom which existed to practise any religion within private houses, the so-called *religio domestica* with no danger of being questioned or spied upon. Moreover, he stated, if the followers of any Sect grow so numerous in any place, that they affect a publique Congregation, and are content to purchase a place of Assembly, to bear the charge of a Pastor or a Teacher, and to pay for this Liberty to the Publique; They go and propose their desire to the Magistrates of the place, where they reside, Who inform themselves of their Opinions, and manners of Worship, and if they find nothing in either, destructive to Civil Society, or prejudicial to the Constitutions of their State, And content themselves with the price that is offer'd for the purchase of this Liberty, They easily allow it; But with the condition, That one or more Commissioners shall be appointed, who shall have free admission at all their meetings, shall be both the Observers and Witnesses of all that is acted or preached among them, and whose testimony shall be received concerning any thing that passes there to the prejudice of the State; In which the Laws and Executions are as severe as against any Civil Crimes.[22]

Despite the limits of his perception, Temple saw exactly where the remarkable nature of the United Provinces was: in the autonomy of public order and of political reason. The sacred principle of personal and individual liberty, effectively defended by a State that knowingly occupied a purely secular position as regards religion, was violently opposed to any hint of theocracy. It was civic society and more particularly civic peace, libertine and republican order that appeared as the yardstick of toleration, not just a religious principle of whatever tendency or order.

Religion in New Netherland

The Dutch colonies followed closely the laws and ordinances of the fatherland. They were therefore bound to present themselves as part of a Protestant State but to organize their community, in fact, as a plural, multi-confessional society.[23] Our basic texts are quite clear on that point. Consider the paragraph on religion and toleration in the 1624 Provisional Regulations for New Netherland:

[Article 2.] While conducting their affairs they [the 1624 colonists] shall practice no other form of divine worship than the one of the reformed religion in the manner as currently performed here in this country, and thus by their Christian life and conduct seek to attract the Indians and other blind people [non-believers, Christians other than Calvinists?] to the knowledge of God and his word without, on the other hand, persecuting anyone for reason of his religion but to leave every person the freedom of his conscience. However, in case any one among them [the colonists] or living under their authority [i.e., servants, other Europeans, or perhaps Africans] should wilfully slander the name of God, our Saviour Jesus Christ or commit blasphemy, he shall be punished according to severity by the Commander and his Council.[24]

In fact, during the first decades of New Netherland's existence, virtually all our documents on the colony were produced either by the Protestant State (that is, the West India Company, the Directors, and the Council) or by the Reformed Church that cared for its morals, and their representatives, but only very seldom by or from within the community itself or its individual lay members. The Flushing Remonstrance is one of the rare examples of the latter. Therefore, our vision is necessarily biased. However, in the Netherlands people of different denominations lived together in what I have called a form of "ecumenicity of everyday life" (*omgangsoecumene*), this basic civic harmony, on the borderline between public and private space, which decided what the measure of religious toleration should be.[25] As long as no vital elements of Christian doctrine or ethics were at stake, religion in everyday life was deconfessionalized. In the public space of the Dutch Republic, unwritten rules of social behavior prevented people from discussing religious matters with neighbors of other persuasion, or in public places like taverns, ships, or barges, or only in terms of general Christian values. Basically, the same holds for everyday life in the Dutch colonial empire. The East and West India Company regulations tried to maintain civic harmony beyond religious pluralism aboard ship by expressly forbidding religious disputes. The Reformed Church itself functioned basically as an agent of social cohesion and cultural conformity much more than as an instrument of religious indoctrination, and the available sources make it quite evident that, for lack of religious services of other confessions, non-Reformed Christians attended the public church without much denominational scruples.

Until quite recently, New Netherland religious history has often been read in a rather normative, sometimes even teleological way, interpreting it backwards from the outcome to the start. Following the final surrender of the colony to the English crown in 1674 and the establishment of the English state church as the church of the new rulers, the Dutch Reformed Church became emblematic for ethnic "Dutch" in a restrictive, conservative, denominational sense, with the connotation of the religion of the first occupants.[26] After the takeover, Lutherans, Catholics, and others virtually disappeared from the self-understanding of the heirs of New Netherland. Henceforth, Dutchness meant "everybody Reformed."

But consider now the religious composition of the colony. The official records of the colony's council and the Company directors have created together a strong impression of a Calvinistic bulwark under construction. That may have been the case indeed of the Walloons in the very first year of colonization (1624), but soon the religious landscape was diversified. Beside the occasional European Catholic or Mennonite, not to speak of the temporary influx of Jews from Brazil, two great non-Reformed groups of inhabitants can be distinguished among the immigrants from the very start of the colony: an important contingent of Lutherans coming from the German, Scandinavian and Central European territories, and a population of enslaved blacks coming mostly from the Portuguese colonies on the African West Coast and the realm of Congo and therefore imbued with a minimum of Catholic worship and spirituality.

In fact, religion was experienced on two levels: on a first, broad, community level, religion stood for the European cultural code shared by all, especially vis-à-vis the natives; it was only after the 1640s that the black population was gradually excluded from this general consensus. This first, rather open, popular church model was largely inclusive, since it considered religion as the common expression of the culture of the whole community. During the first Indian War, however, the community was split up and director Kieft's faction expressly rejected community with the others, by ostensibly refusing participation at the Lord's Supper—a liturgical ceremony that initially was also the supreme aggregation ritual of the civil community.

On a second level, religion stood for denomination, for a particular creed or church, its doctrine and morals. Ministers were of course supposed to preach their confessional wisdom and to unite in the service of their church those who had committed themselves to that particular confession, the directors having to support them in this Christianizing task. But the first directors were barely confessing Calvinists, and director Willem Kieft, as noted above, came from a liberal Arminian background.[27] He used the church to discipline the colony but does not appear as a passionate Calvinist himself. On the contrary, when founding the first church in the fort, in 1642, he showed a typical patrician, secular attitude: the church was a building of the Company, not of the congregation, and it had to serve the whole population, not only the Reformed community. It was the public church open to all, regardless of confession. It was only under Stuyvesant that the Reformed Church and the director's policy found each other in a similar concern for the Calvinization of the whole community.

Religious Pluralism and Civic Unity

When we compare New Netherland to nearby New England, the paradise of the godly, it is quite obvious that the Company's policy insured not a religious unity but a real cultural cohesion within the colony. In the perception of the English Puritans in Europe, the Dutch Republic in Europe was a Calvinist nation and a bulwark of the true religion besieged by the Papists. It was God's own sanctuary, an idealized refuge for all persons persecuted for the true faith: from Bohemia, France, the Palatinate, and occasionally even from England. Yet, just the reverse image prevailed overseas. For the colonists from Massachusetts and the surrounding area, New Netherland was a den of iniquity, a land without law and order. The English colonists who in August 1642 presented the States General with their claim to the territory of Connecticut, formally owned by the Dutch, put forward two decisive arguments: there were too few Dutch colonists to exploit the land; "furthermore they live there without rule, in a godlessness unbefitting the Gospel of Christ."[28] This was hardly a Puritan Valhalla!

It must however be emphasized that the twofold cultural value of religion—that is as civil religion, or cultural Calvinism, on the one hand, and as a creed, or confessional religion, on the other—had been provided for from the start by the Regulations of the West India Company. The basic document for all Company employees was the Articulbrieff of 1624.[29] These Articles included a clear paragraph about religion and servants of the church. The rules of conduct were in the first place intended for ships, but by extension also applied to the colonies themselves. Cursing, swearing, and slander were forbidden and carried a 10-stiver fine. No one was allowed to "reprimand, scold, or upset the minister or admonisher [mostly a comforter of the sick], or hinder him in any way in the exercise of his office or calling" (Art. 16). At morning or evening prayers and during Bible readings everyone without exception—that is, including Lutherans, Mennonites, Catholics, or people without confessional ties—was required to listen respectfully (Art. 17) and no one was allowed to be absent (Art. 18). Finally, it was expressly forbidden "to raise any issues or disputed points of religion" (Art. 19). The ship was a religiously neutral space, and although religion played a pivotal role there in maintaining a community, it was without ecclesiastical ties. The minister or admonisher was officially the public preacher for the entire group, not the representative of a specific church, even though he used the books and rites of the dominant church.

These rules of conduct adhered closely to the freedom of conscience as upheld in the Dutch Republic. As long as the colony of New Netherland had no legislation of its own, it was similarly a neutral space in which the minister of God's Word was much more the representative of an undivided religious sphere than of a particular church. But the minister did have to restrict himself to the religious sphere! The instructions for ministers that the West India Company adopted in Middelburg in late 1635 state explicitly that they must occupy themselves exclusively with religion (Art. 6). They should express criticism of captains, skippers, commissioners, and other authorities "neither in their preaching nor in public, or with such indication and particularization of the fact, persons, or office," for the authorities may not become objects of "ridicule or disparagement by such rough folk as our sailors and soldiers are" (Arts. 10–11). Clearly there was no room for theocracy in the Dutch colonies.

An Inclusive Public Church

The Reformed congregation initially was not only spread out over a large area of New Netherland, it was also much more diverse than those in comparable towns and villages in the fatherland.[30] In rough and increasingly dangerous New Netherland the congregation at first functioned as an important social, binding agent. This is evident from the relatively large number of Reformed church members among the few thousand colonists who belonged to a wide range of denominations, whereas in the fatherland formal membership remained scarce in the early decades of that century. Although the earliest membership list of New Amsterdam's Reformed community dates only from 1649, whole pages of it are filled with names of persons whom we recognize from the sources as long-time residents of the town. In 1648 Reverend Backerus spoke of 170 members. And certainly not all of them could have been drunkards and blockheads, as the rigid minister maintained. It is actually more surprising that after years of war, dissension, and lawlessness, and with so many dissenters in the colony, the core congregation was still that large. In a colony where almost everyone acted out of selfish interests, one could at first expect only "few churchwardens" (*kerckmeesters*, i.e., pious churchgoers), "but instead people who are good at lining their pockets," as Van der Donck commented sardonically.[31] This means that the ministers must have been very active in building up their congregation, and that they had strong grassroots support.

Living in New Netherland were not only whites but also a great many native Indians, while the number of blacks, mostly slaves, increased steadily as well. The Reformed minister's congregation comprised mainly whites and blacks. But even among the whites he could not take his authority for granted. During his visit to Manhattan in 1643 the Jesuit refugee Isaac Jogues noted that formally only the Reformed religion was practiced in New Netherland, and he thought—mistakenly—that officially only Calvinists were admitted to the colony.[32] But in fact, he added, those rules were brushed aside, and there were many religious minorities: Catholics, Lutherans, English Puritans, and Mennonites, among others. Kieft had proudly told him that the inhabitants spoke eighteen different languages. Some of those languages implied linguistic varieties of Reformed church membership, like the French-speaking Walloons (and perhaps some Huguenots), present since the very beginning in 1624, and the English Presbyterians.

In 1640 the Presbyterian minister Francis Doughty was already living in New Amsterdam. As a non-conformist, Doughty had been forced to flee first to Massachusetts in 1637, then to Rhode Island because the hard-line Puritans judged his statements about baptism to be less than orthodox, and finally to New Netherland. There he in fact served the growing group of English-speaking colonists, including probably the non-Presbyterians. But in March 1642 Kieft granted him permission to found, together with the people of his denomination, an English colony, named Newtown, at Maspeth on Long Island. During the war with the Indians it was burnt to the ground the very next year. The English fled to New Amsterdam, whereas Doughty stayed on. Kieft allowed him to act as minister for the English on Manhattan, without a mandate from the West India Company. As a Reformed sister congregation the English were allowed to hold their own public services. But because the group was too small to support its own minister, collections were taken up among the Hollanders as well.

Public Church and Lay Religion

To what extent was the Company church also a binding agent for such linguistic varieties and even for dissenters? Did dissenters call on the public minister for baptisms and marriages? In many cases they did, that much is clear from the names of known Lutherans in the baptismal and marriage registers of the Reformed Church. At any rate, the pastoral structure of the Reformed congregation, scattered over a huge territory, was much more complicated than the formal sources of Reformed origin suggest, and religious pluralism was a rule under the seemingly uniform heading of the public church. Brandt van Slichtenhorst, who was appointed director of Rensselaerswijck in 1647, for example, insisted in his instructions of January 1650 that on Sundays and holidays the leaseholder of Rensselaerswijck at Catskill read to his household and employees from the Bible or a house Postil, recite prayers, and sing psalms.[33] As more land was cleared and more settlements were added, similar practices of prayer services without a minister must have developed elsewhere. But even in New Amsterdam itself the situation was more complicated. By law, public worship services and private religious meetings were both the exclusive right of the Reformed religion. But the Reformed were not a homogeneous group.

In fact, the lay practice of group reading of the Bible and other religious books was very common in the Dutch Republic, often to the despair of the Reformed consistories who, afraid of losing grip on the congregation, fought steadily against the "conventicles," either the regular or the alternative religious gatherings of the lay people who were unwilling to recognize clerical authority as a matter of course. The Reformed Church tried to control this movement by setting clear and strong regulations. But, as Father Jogues's remarks seem to imply, the principle of freedom of conscience prevented both the civil and the ecclesiastical authorities from infringing on the right to organize forms of domestic worship and Bible reading in private settings. Small wonder that, when in August 1657 the first Quakers, expelled from Boston, established themselves in New Netherland and started their "conventicles," the ministers and civil authorities reacted violently, fearing the danger of sectarianism and lay religion.[34] Our sources suggest that there was reason to do so indeed, since the cultural practice of Bible reading and of worshipping outside the formal, public church was not at all unknown among the dissenters, if not among the faithful of the Reformed congregation itself.

Under such circumstances the value of attending church services lay less in what one could learn in the church—because that could as well be learnt at home—than in the particular way the Holy Word was preached in church, and in the people one could meet there. The church was perhaps more important as a public meeting place for residents of all denominations than as an institute for religious instruction. Church building and church community were places of socialization where the necessary aggregation rituals of the community were performed. In those rituals the Reformed Church played a significant but certainly not the only part. Just as in the homeland, doctrinal and ethical questions divided the population, but at the same time a shared, supra-confessional, basic spirituality united many of them creating a common mentality in which they could recognize their concerns.

But around 1650, in the Stuyvesant era, fundamental changes in the relations between secular society, church, and religion occurred in New Netherland. They correspond perfectly with what happened in patria. The watershed here is the Great Assembly of the States General of 1651. Following the Peace of Westphalia (1648) that had formally and finally recognized the independence of the nation, the Great Assembly was meant to regulate definitely the matters of state, church and army.[35] Although the monopolistic claims of the theocratic faction of the Reformed Church (which in fact included the New Netherland ministers) were rejected, the Assembly inaugurated a process of confessionalization of Dutch society during which all existing religious communities, either full-grown churches or smaller groups (the "conventicles"), gradually took a more distinct, denominational outlook, whereas civil society organized public rituals and community life in a more secular way.

Civil society pushed forward as its own the norms and values defined by the public church, without, however, granting to that church permission to sanction them publicly for others than its own confessing members. From a cultural point of view, this meant that Calvinist culture became the common social norm for virtually all religious communities, although it was imposed along secular ways, as a civic culture. But it meant also that Calvinism was perpetually forced to prove itself in front of the secular power as a valuable moral authority. That precisely made Dutch society so paradoxical in the eyes of foreign observers: whereas the state proclaimed itself Protestant, many among its leaders showed a fundamental distrust toward the claims of the Reformed Church. Stuyvesant's policy followed closely the events in his fatherland, but due to his strong personal commitment to Calvinism, in agreement with the theocratic views of the Reformed ministers in the colony, the Reformed Church managed to impose its views in America with much greater force then in the Dutch Republic itself. At the 1664 takeover, the colony seemed more Calvinistic and less tolerant than ever.

Conclusions

At this point, we may seem to have moved quite a distance away from our central theme: toleration. Yet, what I want to show is how much confessionalization, church building, and toleration are embedded in social practices of a broader scope. The important concept is not "religion," or even "church," but "public church," i.e., a church appropriated by a specific cultural group and recognized as such by the public authorities; a church that had its own rights and pretensions in the public space, and therefore provoked thoughts, symbolic action, and opposition by others. On the other side, however, there are the actors of history: people who believe in something, either a full-fledged confessional creed or a religious persuasion they have sought and discovered all by themselves, like there were many in the Netherlands.

New Netherland, then, was a Protestant colony, but enjoyed individual freedom of conscience as far as the regulations of the homeland permitted it, at the judgment of the director and his council. That did not always include freedom of public expression, however, as the Lutherans and the Quakers learnt by force in the 1650s. It is precisely this political and sociocultural dimension of New Netherland's evolution that makes it possible to distinguish between three periods, perfectly parallel to the evolution in the European Netherlands. The first period is the founding phase, from the start of the colony's settlement in 1624 until approximately 1650: everything is then under construction. There were rules, but the rules were much more meant to ensure public cohesion and harmony in a divided community, menaced by enemies on virtually all the borders, than to warrant the true Reformed faith. The Reformed Church itself patiently constructed its predominant, public place in New Netherland society, as it did in the homeland, still recognizing the rights to dissent in the personal sphere.

After 1650 a second phase started, characterized by a more rigorous internal mission policy: Dutch society had to be reformed in depth. It is the phase of the Further Reformation, or moral rearmament and formal pietism, the triumph of the practice of piety and ethics above doctrine and learning. However, real, socially compelling piety and morality were only accessible to the elite of the faithful. The triumphal Reformed Church therefore at the same time had to withdraw from the idea of a broad, popular, general, and national church. Sustained by the theology of predestination, it adopted the ideology of the few elect and contents itself with a smaller group of true faithful. From that moment on, the initial, social acceptance of religious diversity might have developed into an intellectual variety of toleration, based upon the acknowledgment of the church's limits and the acceptance of other creeds, considered as of lower intrinsic value of course, but still acceptable because fundamentally Christian. We see this evolution quite clearly reflected in Stuyvesant's policy. As a representative of the pure church with a clear-cut moral mission in his colony, he was forced and was finally inclined to accept a minimum version of religious pluralism, but not without a persisting missionary attitude toward the dissenters and the other religions.

A third phase started with the takeover of New Netherland by the English in the decades of the 1660s and the 1670s. The Reformed Church lost its monopoly in the public space and had to share its privileged position with the church of the new rulers, the Church of England. The bi-public regime that followed really must have been the true school of toleration, because for the first time two full-fledged churches had to live together and to work out ways of coexistence in a shared society. The Dutch Reformed Church, now a private institution, counterbalanced its losses by closing the ranks and accentuating its Dutch embedding, as a form of Dutch ethnicity. But I would contend that American toleration as a social value really started at that very encounter between intellectually related, yet socially opposite, churches.[36]

We have therefore to look at toleration in a less intellectual, more dynamic way than we used to do. Toleration is not an essential quality of whatever population or nation, but it develops as a social and cultural practice within a community that needs solutions for diversity, helped by the intellectual and moral discourse on the virtues of toleration. That means also that toleration is never totally achieved or definitely acquired: it has to be recovered, regained and re-tested over and over again. A lesson in humility for all of us!

Notes

1. Willem Frijhoff, "Religious toleration in the United Provinces: from 'case' to 'model,'" in R. Po-Chia-Hsia and Henk van Nierop (eds.), *Calvinism and Religious Toleration in the Dutch Golden Age* (Cambridge: Cambridge University Press, 2002), pp. 27–52.

2. Cf. Willem Frijhoff, "Dutchness in fact and fiction," in Joyce D. Good-friend, Benjamin Schmidt, and Annette Stott (eds.), *Going Dutch: The Dutch Presence in America, 1609–2009* (Leiden and Boston: Brill, 2008), pp. 327–358.

3. Russell Shorto, *The Island at the Center of the World. The Epic Story of Dutch Manhattan and the Forgotten Colony That Shaped America* (New York: Doubleday, 2004), pp. 96–97, 274–275. See also the website of Joep de Koning: www.tolerancewalk.com.

4. Shorto, *The Island at the Center of the World*, pp. 96–97.

5. Willem Frijhoff, "Seventeenth-Century Religion as a Cultural Practice: Reassessing New Netherland's Religious History," in Margriet Bruijn Lacy, Charles Gehring, and Jenneke Oosterhoff (eds.), *From De Halve Maen to KLM: 400 Years of Dutch-American Exchange* (Münster/Westphalia: Nodus Publikationen, 2008), pp. 159–174.

6. For this distinction, cf. Willem Frijhoff, *Embodied belief. Ten essays on religious culture in Dutch history* (Hilversum: Verloren, 2002).

7. Jonathan I. Israel, *Radical Enlightenment. Philosophy and the Making of Modernity 1650–1750* (Oxford: Oxford University Press, 2001); idem, "The Intellectual Debate about Toleration in the Dutch Republic," in Christiane Berkvens-Stevelinck, Jonathan Israel and G. H. M. Posthumus Meyjes (eds.), *The Emergence of Tolerance in the Dutch Republic* (Leiden, New York, and Cologne: Brill, 1997), pp. 3–36; idem, "Locke, Spinoza and the Philosophical Debate Concerning Toleration in the Early Enlightenment (c. 1670–c. 1750)," in *Koninklijke Nederlandse Akademie van Wetenschappen, Mededelingen van de Afdeling Letterkunde (Amsterdam)*, n.s., 62:6 (1999), pp. 5–19.

8. John Locke, *Epistola de tolerantia* [1689], William Popple trans., *A Letter concerning Toleration* [1689]; Latin and English texts revised and edited by Mario Montuori (The Hague: Martinus Nijhoff, 1963); Pierre Bayle, *A Philosophical Commentary on these Words of the Gospel, Luke 14:23, 'Compel Them to Come In, That My House May Be Full'* [1686], John Kilcullen and Chandran Kukathas (eds.) (Indianapolis, IN: Liberty Fund, 2005); Voltaire, *Traité sur la tolérance*, introduction and notes by John Renwick (Oxford: Voltaire Foundation, 1999). Cf. John Marshall, *John Locke, Toleration and Early Enlightenment Culture* (Cambridge: Cambridge University Press, 2006); John Kilcullen, *Sincerity and Truth: Essays on Arnauld, Bayle, and Toleration* (Oxford: Clarendon Press, 1988).

9. A. Pettegree, "The politics of toleration in the free Netherlands, 1572–1620," in O. P. Grell and B. Scribner (eds.), *Tolerance and Intolerance in the European Reformation* (Cambridge: Cambridge University Press, 1996), pp. 182–198.

10. See the English text of the Union of Utrecht in E. H. Kossmann and A. F. Mellink (eds.), *Texts concerning the Revolt of the Netherlands* (Cambridge: Cambridge University Press, 1974), 165–173; A. Th. van Deursen, "Between unity and independence: the application of the Union as a fundamental law," *The Low Countries History Yearbook* 14 (1981), pp. 50–65.

11. Alastair Duke, *Reformation and Revolt in the Low Countries* (London: The Hambledon Press, 1990); Martin van Gelderen, "Politics and religion (1572–1590): the debates on religious toleration and the substance of liberty," in idem, *The Political Thought of the Dutch Revolt 1555–1590* (Cambridge: Cambridge University Press, 1992), pp. 213–259.

12. On this subject see also Wiebe Bergsma, "Church, state and people," in Karel Davids and Jan Lucassen (eds.), *A Miracle Mirrored: The Dutch Republic in European Perspective* (Cambridge: Cambridge University Press, 1995), pp. 196–228.

13. Willem Frijhoff, "Ritual acting and city history: Haarlem, Amsterdam and Hasselt," in Heidi de Mare and Anna Vos (eds.), *Urban rituals in Italy and the Netherlands: Historical contrasts in the use of public space, architecture and the urban environment* (Assen, Neth.: Van Gorcum, 1993), pp. 93–106; idem, "Damiette appropriée. La mémoire de croisade, instrument de concorde civique (Haarlem, XVIe–XVIIIe siècle)," in *Revue du Nord* 88 (January–March 2006), pp. 7–42.

14. Willem Frijhoff, "Was the Dutch Republic a Calvinist Community? The State, the Confessions, and Culture in the Early Modern Netherlands," in André

Holenstein, Thomas Maissen, and Maarten Prak (eds.), *The Republican Alternative: The Netherlands and Switzerland Compared* (Amsterdam: Amsterdam University Press, 2008), pp. 99–122.

15. James Homer Williams, "'Abominable Religion' and Dutch (In)tolerance: The Jews and Petrus Stuyvesant," in *de Halve Maen* 71, no. 4 (1998), pp. 85–91; Leo Hershkowitz, "By Chance or Choice: Jews in New Amsterdam 1654," in *de Halve Maen* 77, no. 2 (2004), pp. 23–30.

16. For recent discussions of the Flushing Remonstrance, see the 2007 papers by David William Voorhees and Evan Haefeli on: <http://www.flushingremonstrance.info/documents/Flushing_Remonstrance_DV.rtf>, and >http://www.bownehouse.org/pdf/Evan_Haefeli_Flushing_Remonstrance.pdf>.

17. See for an overview Benjamin J. Kaplan, *Divided by Faith: Religious Conflict and the Practice of Toleration in Early Modern Europe* (Cambridge, Mass.: Harvard University Press, 2007); C. Scott Dixon, Dagmar Freist, and Mark Greengrass (eds.), *Living with Religious Diversity in Early-Modern Europe* (Farnham, Surrey: Ashgate, 2009).

18. J. Briels, *Zuidnederlanders in de Republiek 1572–1630: Een demografische en cultuurhistorische studie* (Sint-Niklaas, Belgium: Danthe, 1985); Jan Lucassen and Rinus Penninx (eds.), *Newcomers: Immigrants and their Descendants in the Netherlands 1550–1995* (Amsterdam: Het Spinhuis, 1997); Willem Frijhoff, "Migrations religieuses dans les Provinces-Unies avant le second Refuge," in *Revue du Nord* 80 (July-December 1998), pp. 573–598.

19. S. A. C. Dudok van Heel, *De jonge Rembrandt onder tijdgenoten. Godsdienst en schilderkunst in Leiden en Amsterdam* (Nijmegen: Nijmegen University Press, 2006).

20. *t'Samen-spraeck, Voor-gestelt van vier Persoonen: Twee Hollanders, Pieter en Klaes. Een Fransman. Een Bovenlander* (s.l., 1672), fol. B2r.

21. William Temple, *Observations upon the United Provinces of the Netherlands*, Sir George Clark (ed.) (Oxford: Clarendon Press, 1972), p. 103.

22. Ibid., pp. 104–105.

23. For a synthesis, Fred van Lieburg, "The Dutch and Their Religion," in Hans Krabbendam, Cornelis A. van Minnen, and Giles Scott-Smith (eds.), *Four Centuries of Dutch-American Relations 1609–2009* (Albany: SUNY Press, 2009), pp. 154–165. On toleration in New Netherland, Jaap Jacobs, "Between Repression and Approval: Connivance and Tolerance in the Dutch Republic and in New Netherland," in *de Halve Maen* 71, no. 3 (1998), pp. 51–58.

24. Original text: "Sullen binnen haer bedryff anders geen Gods dienst pleegen als die vande gereformeerde religie in manieren tegenwoordich hier te lande gepleecht wort, ende soo door hun Cristelyck leven ende wandel de Indianen ende andere blinde menschen tot de kennisz Godes ende synes woort sien te trecken, sonder nochtans ijemant ter oorsaecke van syne religie te vervolgen, maer een yder de vrijch[eyt] van sijn consciencie te laten, doch soo jemant onder [hen] ofte [onder] haeren gebiet staende, de naeme Godes ofte onses Zalichm[aeckers] Jesu Christi moetwillich lasterde ofte blasphemeerde sal den selven near gelegentheyt door den Commandeur ende

synen Raet gestraft worden," published in F. C. Wieder, *De stichting van New York in juli 1625. Reconstructies en nieuwe gegevens ontleend aan de Van Rappard documenten* (Zutphen: Walburg Pers, 2009 [1925]), p. 112.

25. Willem Frijhoff, "The threshold of toleration: Interconfessional conviviality in Holland during the early modern period," in idem, *Embodied belief*, pp. 39–65; Frijhoff and Marijke Spies, *1650: Hard-Won Unity*, Myra Heerspink Scholz (trans.) [Dutch Culture in a European perspective] (Assen, Neth.: Royal Van Gorcum / Basingstoke U.K.: Palgrave Macmillan, 2004), pp. 50, 381–382, and register in voce.

26. Randall Balmer, *A Perfect Babel of Confusion: Dutch Religion and English Culture in the Middle Colonies* (New York and Oxford: Oxford University Press, 1989) has set the tone sharply for such approaches.

27. Willem Frijhoff, "Neglected networks: Director Willem Kieft (1602–1647) and his Dutch relatives," in Joyce D. Goodfriend (ed.), *Revisiting New Netherland: Perspectives on Early Dutch America* (Leiden and Boston: Brill, 2005), 147–204.

28. National Archives (The Hague), States General, no. 5756, exh. 9 August 1642; cf. *DRCHNY*, 1:127–135.

29. The full title is *Articulen ende ordonnantien ter vergaderinge vande Negenthiene der Generale Geoctroyeerde West-Indische Compagnie geresumeert ende ghearresteert* (Amsterdam: s.n., 1641).

30. For what follows, see Frijhoff, "Seventeenth-Century Religion as a Cultural Practice," pp. 159–174.

31. Adriaen van der Donck, *Beschryvinge van Nieuw-Nederlant*, 2nd ed. (Amsterdam, 1656), p. 97, Diederik Willem Goedhuys (trans.); *A Description of New Netherland*, Charles T. Gehring and William A. Starna (eds.) (Lincoln, Neb. London: University of Nebraska Press, 2008), p. 138.

32 *NNN*, p. 260.

33. A. J. F. van Laer (trans.), *Register of the Provincial Secretary*, 3 vols. (Baltimore: Genealogical Publishing Co., 1974), 3:212–215.

34. Jaap Jacobs, *New Netherland: A Dutch Colony in Seventeenth-Century America* (Leiden and Boston: Brill, 2005), pp. 305–311.

35. Frijhoff and Spies, *1650: Hard-Won Unity*, pp. 77–82.

36. See for this thesis Evan Haefeli, *New Netherland and the Dutch Origins of American Religious Liberty* (Philadelphia, PA: University of Pennsylvania Press, 2012).

11

Indian-European Networks and Atlantic Trade in the Seventeenth Century

Claudia Schnurmann

$\mathcal{W}$ hile the Englishman Henry Hudson was trying to close a gap between Europe and Asia through his search for a Northwest Passage in 1609, he took Europe and its ways of life to America: he behaved as the typical Renaissance man; he followed traditional European patterns with regard to racial and cultural arrogance; and he used methods of colonialism which would dominate European involvement in Atlantic trade, politics, and economics for decades to come. Correspondingly, the complement of his international crew (notwithstanding the many conflicts that occurred among its members) demonstrated the strong influence of supranational cooperation in non-European environments in open contrast to their governments' national interests. The employment of the Englishman Hudson by the Dutch East India Company (VOC) demonstrated his perceived national loyalty held little importance compared to his personal interests, while Hudson's voyages in the service of the VOC gave the Dutch Republic a claim to North American territory and thereby enabled the transfer of European conflicts to North America.

In doing so, Hudson, his first mate Robert Juet, and the VOC ignored rival European claims, as well as the rights of Native Americans and evidence of the presence of European rivals in North America, when they described the land as an abandoned paradise and its inhabitants like godless savages, thereby allowing the Europeans to take possession of America's lands and peoples. Thus, from the beginning Hudson and his crew had no sense of the cultural "other"; the mixed Dutch-English crew was subjected to European prejudices and treated the American Indians accordingly.

At the same time, Hudson followed certain patterns with regard to trade and the valuation of America. He exchanged European manufactured goods for resources from America's waters and lands: tobacco, furs, fish, oysters, lobsters, and wampum, which was used both by Europeans and Native Americans to create and maintain their involvements in an Atlantic trade system and which was useful to both for many decades.[1]

Native American Interests in Wampum

White wampum or zeawant is made from sea snails called periwinkles; black or dark purple wampum is made from quahog clams.[2] Within Native North American societies, wampum was used long before Europeans reached American shores.[3] The so-called "true" wampum and "wampum" with its several variations were used by peoples who belonged to different linguistic families: The term wampum—a shortened version from wam pumpeage/wom pomp e ak—was created by Algonquian-speaking Native Americans who lived close to the shell-rich North American salt marshes of the Atlantic Ocean. The Algonquians collected sea snails and clams in the shallow waters of the Atlantic, then feasted on those tasty shellfish or dried them for further trade. They turned the shells into decorative jewelry to adorn their bodies and dresses.[4]

Slowly wampum acquired other functions as its glow and glamour was in high demand with the Iroquois who belong to another language group from their cousins, the Algonquians, upon whom their wampum supply depended. To the Iroquois living in the forests, wampum acquired a special value. Together with the Algonquian product the Iroquois integrated the Algonquian term "wampum" into their culture and used those beads as symbols of friendship, peace, for declarations of either war or peace, or as mere gifts.[5] Before the Europeans came to America, the amount of Algonquian wampum supplied to the Iroquois was probably small. That would change soon.

Like the Frenchmen Jacques Cartier[6] and Samuel de Champlain,[7] the Englishmen[8] in Dutch service came into contact with the true kind of wampum when they interacted with Indigenous people. They were, however, so much enmeshed in their own cultural perceptions of value that they failed to notice the difference between the mass-produced glass beads they had brought from Europe and had exchanged as "trifles" for those goods they cherished and the true wampum cherished by the Native Americans; Hudson and his chronicler Juet especially did not have a clue about the potential of true wampum ("stropes of beades") that was presented to them in September 1609 by some Algonquians who had recovered from strong hangovers and returned to the *Halve Maen* either for more alcohol or to excuse their indecent behavior from the previous day.[9]

European Interests in Wampum

It was due to the cleverness of Dutch merchants of the New Netherland Company that the economic potential of wampum for the colonial as well as for the Atlantic trade was discovered. The change of perception could have been triggered by the experience of 1617 when a wampum belt was presented by the Mohawks to Dutch merchants. The lesson that wampum could be used for ransom also was not lost. Between 1617 and 1622, influenced by Dutch-Mohawk bonding, both Dutch demand for peltries and Dutch sense for commercial wampum acquired a new quality insofar as they successfully connected Native Americans and Europeans in an economic and cultural Atlantic system from which all participants could satisfy their particular demands. Algonquians exchanged first-class manufactured wampum with European settlers for manufactured European goods; the Europeans used that wampum to obtain furs from the Iroquois which were transported to Europe. Under those circumstances wampum acquired a new function: it was a commodity to the Algonquian which was exchanged for goods they valued more, it was a cheap substitute for bullion, a cashless payment in a European sense, and was used as a go-between by different Native American cultures and became an object of cultural yearning for the Iroquois. Wampum helped to support the enterprise of "New Netherland."

Indeed, the Dutch West India Company soon recognized the importance of wampum for its well-being; the design of 1630 for a coat of arms for New Netherland reflects the important elements of the colony's existence: beavers and wampum sketched in happy harmony.[10]

Figure 19. Seal of New Netherland (1901). http://commons.wikimedia.org/wiki/File:seal_of_new_netherland.jpg.

Between 1624 and 1630, 42,000 beaver furs were sent via New Amsterdam to the Netherlands. The value of those freights amounted to at least 330,000 guilders.[11] Since the fur-bearing animals near the European colonies in the northeast soon were quickly exterminated, nearly all those furs came to *patria* through trade with the Iroquois.

Over several decades, Europeans, first in New Netherland and after 1627 in Plymouth, supported by Dutch traders like Isaac de Rasière, convinced the hesitant New Englanders to participate in the wampum trade.[12] They would load this American artifact made by Algonquians, this symbol of power, myth, and religious meaning to the Iroquois, with European notions of money, and declare it a substitute and a legal tender as well as a trade commodity. In his journal of the first three decades of Plymouth Plantation, the colony's governor William Bradford continuously regarded wampum as a "current commodity," i.e., a trade item for the Narragansetts and Pequots who "grew rich and potent by it."[13] In the meantime De Rasière had already come to the conclusion that wampum could be used as a substitute for money, "since one can buy with it [wampum] everything they [the Native Americans] have."[14]

As Europeans tended to regulate things, they tried to organize trade within North America in the way to which they were accustomed. One way to do so was by regulation, standardization, and control of the quality of goods which they used as substitutes for cash. There were simultaneously several kinds of monies in use: rare Dutch, German, English, and Spanish currency, bills of exchange, and trade goods such as beaver pelts, tobacco from the Chesapeake colonies, even cacao beans in the South, and finally shell beads, both true wampum and crude European fakes.[15]

Shell beads made by Algonquians as well as European manufactures, such as textiles, metal wares, rifles, and alcohol, were the only goods Native Americans sought. Europeans regarded the Indian contribution to American trade, their locally produced beads, as mere trifles and crude trash which could by European will and design be transformed into currency. On the other hand, Iroquois who harbored strong urges for Algonquian wampum and European goods (not incidentally they called the Dutch "knife makers") had readily available (at least at first) beaver pelts to offer, something they, in turn, considered trifles.[16]

Many colonists, whether they originated from the Netherlands, from the German territories, from France, or from the British Isles, mixed their deep prejudices about and disgust for those "savages," "heathens" and wild men—those "other" cultures and ways of life they could not comprehend—with their keen desire to obtain beaver pelts from those "heathens." Even though Europeans used wampum as a money substitute until the 1670s and knew of places, like Gardiners Bay near Long Island, where wampum was produced by Native Americans ("the mine" of New Netherland[17]), the colonial governments missed one basic effect that for Europeans defined currency: they lacked control over the production of wampum (35–48 beads per person per day), so they lacked control both over the amount of wampum in circulation and over the distribution process. The tool to help Europeans control the trade with Native Americans de facto was controlled by the "mintmakers," the Pequots and Narragansetts. Thus, these Native Americans were able to turn the table on European arrogance and racial prejudice.

Metropolitan authorities tried in vain to import European control techniques and implant European concepts of exchange rates on the wampum producers and the settlers who had their own matters to which they had to attend. The result of this governmental weakness and the hard-headedness of certain people was a long list of ordinances, acts, and court decisions designed to organize the hotchpotch of exchange rates, qualities, and commercial behavior.[18] Notwithstanding his dislike of the situation, New Netherland Director-General Petrus Stuyvesant had to declare to his employer, the Dutch West India Company, on 21 April 1660, "wampum is the source and the mother of the beaver trade, and for goods only, without wampum, we cannot obtain beavers from the savages."[19]

Wampum as a Bone of Contention in Intercolonial and Interethnic Relations

The fight for control over wampum supply not only shaped the politics of New Netherland and New England; it made the different Native American nations in the northeastern region part of the power constellations. The tribes were not always suffering and exploited objects, torn between European interests; they were actors with their very own interests and aims. The Mohawk-Mahican wars of the 1620s, which were won by the Mohawk, provide just one example of active Native Americans who followed their own agendas and considered the Europeans as servants to their interests.[20] It was a question of manpower until Europeans got the upper hand and subdued the Algonquian mintmakers: in the 1630s New England subdued the Pequots and forced them to pay fees in form of wampum. More than nine million pieces of wampum thereby entered the New English system, which helped New England's own economic growth without support from a metropolis that was heading toward civil war (1642–1651).[21]

The bickering between New Netherland and New England over Long Island during the 1640s–1650s, which ended with the Hartford convention of 1650, provides a further illustration. The Euro-Americans in New Netherland and Connecticut not only agreed on colonial political issues, but they also came to terms about the shell resources and the makers of wampum, the mintmakers, especially the Narragansetts.[22] The Algonquian word for Long Island, one bone of New Netherland/New England contention, resembled "Sewanhackey," which means "place of seawan." The creation of the term itself demonstrates that the Algonquian knew the meaning of Long Island and its potential for their interests, too.[23]

Effect of Wampum on the American Northeast and the Atlantic Economy

For four decades, from the 1620s to the 1660s, wampum was crucial to New Netherland/New England, the European-Indian, and the Indian-European-Indian trade in northeastern North America. To a certain degree wampum survived the political changes from New Netherland to New York first in 1664, then in 1674. While the New England colonies gave up wampum as a money substitute rather quickly, the Dutch inhabitants of New York stuck to the formerly little-loved *zeawant* for petty commercial transactions. It still seemed so profitable within the colony that one of the most influential merchants in the New York-Holland trade, the Frisian-born Frederick Philipse, tried in 1668 to control wampum circulation by putting European-Caribbean fakes on the market. To finance his extensive fur trade to Holland—perhaps to finance his efforts to get a hold on the trade with East African slaves and enlarge his profits by reducing his overhead—he imported conches from Bermuda and employed Native Americans and Europeans alike to manufacture a kind of "mass produced" wampum with European tools,[24] something the Iroquois detested because this type of Europeanized wampum lacked the aesthetics and glow they cherished in true wampum.

Wampum thus connected Europeans and Native Americans first in an American system of trade. The Algonquians "sold" wampum as a trade item. The Iroquois "took and kept/bought" it. Only the Europeans "sold" *and* "bought" it and turned wampum into a currency like beaver pelts and tobacco that temporarily, in times of low flow of cash, fulfilled the same purpose.[25]

In a second step wampum became a tool that helped to create an Atlantic economic trade network which worked in different directions.

Wampum that was used to acquire furs for Europe's consumers incorporated Europeans in America and Europe, Algonquian and Iroquois into one Atlantic system of cultures, trade, and economics. Surely different concepts of function/meaning/value/use of wampum existed but wampum helped to support New Netherland/New England in their difficult beginnings when the impact of government was poor and the financial means even poorer. In a way, New Netherland resembled pretty much today's third-world countries. In their drive to make a living and even profits colonists relied on methods still used by weak economies—they circulated substitute currencies in all possible forms. Thus, access to the production, ownership and distribution of wampum/*zeawant* defined power constellations between Native American nations, between those nations and European colonies, and between the colonies. At the beginning of the seventeenth century due to their control of the production and input of wampum into the northeastern American markets the Algonquian profited until they were subdued by Europeans and Iroquois; Mohawk and Europeans prospered on different levels and at different times.

By the time colonists acquired a better supply of coined money, the beaver populations in New Netherland's hinterland had been destroyed and the Mohawk had to rely on business partners within the Iroquois League to supply the colonists with peltries as the most important means of obtaining wampum. When New Netherland changed into New York, and Mohawk-French relations improved in the 1660s, conditions changed.[26] The fewer furs brought to the market, the more wampum was produced and inflation set in. Supplied with millions of beads from the 1640s[27] the Mohawk, Oneida, and other members of the Iroquois League relied more and more on the traditional use of wampum belts as objects of diplomacy. William N. Fenton and webpages produced by people within the Six Indian Nations describe the prolific use of wampum belts in the later seventeenth century.[28] While the Euro-Americans on the east coast of the North American continent lost their interest in wampum, wampum did not lose its importance in the intercourse of nations and peoples of North America. Its instrumentalization as commodity, cultural item, diplomatic messenger, and means of exchange followed the Euro-American westward expansion in the centuries to come. Now true wampum has become an artifact, an object of art—a value it really earns while tourists sometimes are satisfied with its cheap copy, beads made out of plastic and sold to them by Native Americans for greenbacks: a late turn of the tables? The value is in the eye of the beholder.

Notes

1. See the essay by Paul Otto in this volume for a further discussion of the use and significance of wampum.

2. Typical for the casual use of spelling there existed many ways to write zeawant; possible variations are sewant, seewan, and sewan to name but a few. Wampum is a contraction from the Algonquian word *wampumpeage* (pronounced wom pom pe ak) or white shell beads. Historical wampum consists of small, usually cylindrical, white and purple beads, hand polished, drilled, and strung into strings, <http://www.nativeweb.org/resources/crafts_indigenous_technology/beads_beadwork/>; for the archaeological evidence, discussing the prehistoric, proto- and postcontact wampum, see Lynn Ceci, "Native wampum as a peripheral resource in the seventeenth-century world system," in Laurence M. Hauptman and James D. Wherry (eds.), *The Pequots in Southern New England: The Fall and Rise of an American Indian Nation* (Norman, OK: University of Oklahoma Press, 1990), pp. 48–63. Specialists differentiate between proto-wampum in northeastern North America from circa 200–1510 AD, and the so-called true wampum in the contact period of the sixteenth century and the first decades of the seventeenth century. A most important contribution to the extensive literature on wampum is Lois Scozzari, "The Significance of Wampum to Seventeenth-Century Indians in New England," originally published in *The Connecticut Review*, <http://www.hartford-hwp.com/archives/41/037.html>.

3. William N. Fenton, *The Great Law and the Longhouse: A Political History of the Iroquois Confederacy* (Norman: University of Oklahoma Press, 1998), pp. 224–239; Lynn Ceci, *The Effect of European Contact and Trade on the Settlement Pattern of Indians in Coastal New York, 1524–1665* (New York and London: Garland, 1990).

4. Frank G. Speck, "The Functions of Wampum among the Eastern Algonkian," *Memoirs of the American Anthropological Association* 6 (January–March, 1919), pp. 3–71; Ceci, "Native Wampum as a Peripheral Resource," p. 49.

5. In all these cases mentioned wampum was considered as a commodity which was given and taken in an exchange also called presentation and acceptation of gifts. This Native American perception of an exchange of goods as an exchange of gifts should live on for many years to come. At the base of this exchange lay the notion that only things were presented, given, and taken that carried value for both sides. The more abstract value was connected with an object, the more importance was conveyed by it as it proved the value of the object itself; the person who gave it up and the value the giver saw in the person who enjoyed the present. This idea, however, could hold on only within an exchange of goods by people who cherished the same cultural notions, Claudia Schnurmann, *Europa trifft Amerika. Atlantische Wirtschaft in der Frühen Neuzeit 1492–1783* (Frankfurt am Main: Fischer, 1998), passim; the reports by Samuel de Champlain in 1603, about ornaments of matachias, which are beads and braided cords made of porcupine quills, dyed in various colors, David B. Quinn, et al. (eds.), *Newfoundland from Fishery to Colony: Northwest Passage Searches*, vol. 4 in *New American World: A Documentary History of America to 1612*, 5

vols. (New York: Arno Press, 1979), pp. 397–398, or, with regard to Jacques Cartier, idem, *America from Concept to Discovery: Early Exploration of North America*, vol. 1 in *New American World*, p. 300. See <http://www.rosaryworkshop.com/Historyjournal-ingBead.htm> [accessed 6 April 2006].

6. About the use of wampum as ransom, gift, trifle, means of corruption, and penance see for example the remarks of Jacques Cartier on his second journey in J. Franklin Jameson (ed.), *Original Narratives of Early American History: Early English and French Voyages, 1534–1608* (New York, 1906), p. 82, or see "sewan" in <http://www.gutenberg.org/dirs/etext00/mohwk10.txt>: "Donnacona . . . gave him [the French captain] a present of foure and twenty chaines of Esurgny, for that is the greatest and preciosest riches they have in this world, for they esteeme more of that, then of any gold or silver." He also provided his audience with gruesome description about the disgusting methods of selecting those molluscs which were needed by the Native Americans of Hochelaga to produce wampum. In 1535, Cartier remarked about the inhabitants of Hochelaga, before they were driven away by the Iroquois, and about their use of freshwater shells: "of them [shells] they make beads, and wear them about their necks, even as we doe chains of gold and silver, accounting it the preciousest thing in the world . . . no care of any other wealth or commodities in this world. For they have no knowledge of it, and that is, because they never travel and go out of their country," in Jameson, *Narratives*, p. 60; Cartier put an end to the local perspective of some of the inhabitants of Hochelaga when he took or probably kidnapped some of them for France. Still today, some moccasins decorated with porcupine quills that once had graced their feet belong to the exhibits of the Musée de l'Homme in Paris, Mathé Allain, *The Image of the Indians in Early French Atlases and Travel Accounts* (Chicago, Ill.: The Newberry Library 1989), <http://www.newberry.org/smith/slidesets/ss13.html>, p. 1.

7. Report of Samuel de Champlain and François Gravé du Pont on an expedition to the Saint Lawrence River in September 1603, and a visit to the Algonquians and the Montagnais, standing between Algonquian and the Iroquois: "suddenly all the women and girls proceeded to cast off their mantles of skins, and stripped themselves stark naked, showing their privities, but retaining their ornaments of matachias, which are beads and braided cords made of porcupine quills;" prisoners of war, the Montagnais and Etechmins had to sacrifice their belongings to the victorious Algonquians "each of them took what seemed proper to him, such as matachias, tomahawks, swords, kettles . . . seal . . . every one had a present, which they proceeded to give to the Algonquians," Quinn, *Newfoundland from Fishery to Colony*, p. 397f.

8. Marcus P. Meuwese, "For the peace and well-being of the Country: intercultural mediators and Dutch-Indian Relations in New Netherland and Dutch Brazil, 1600–1664" (PhD diss. University of Notre Dame, 2003), p. 45.

9. "Juet's Journal," <http://s3.amazonaws.com/nytdocs/docs/216/216.pdf>; Pierre Biard, "Canadian Mission [*Mission Canadensia. Epistola ex Porturegali in Acadia, transmissa ad Praepositum Generalem Societatis Jesu.*]," in *JR*, 2:57–123 at 73: "the savages who have neither copper, iron, hemp, nor manufactured articles of any kind . . . they

have no arts." See <http://ia300215.us.archive.org//load_djvu_applet.cgi?file=1/items/jesuits02jesuuoft/jesuits02jesuuoft.djvu>. Although the French noticed the existence of wampum in Algonquian societies from the 1530s onward to the first decade of the seventeenth century, they neither recognized nor used the commercial potential of wampum when it could have been offered to the Iroquois in exchange for furs. The French Jesuits who sent letters home in the 1610s, in which they reported their experience with Algonquians on the Saint Lawrence, did not mention anything that resembled wampum, porcelain, and the like as worthy of their notice, while they paid much attention to beaver pelts as trading items.

10. Jaap Jacobs, *New Netherland: A Dutch Colony in Seventeenth-Century America* (Leiden and Boston: Brill, 2005).

11. For precise numbers, Ceci, *The Effect of European Contact and Trade*, p. 194, table 9.

12. Isaack de Rasière to Blommaert, 1628, in Sydney V. James (ed.), *Three Visitors to Early Plymouth: Letters about the Pilgrim Settlement in New England during its first seven years by John Pory, Emmanuel Altham and Isaack de Rasières* (Plymouth, MA: Plimoth Plantation, 1963), pp. 63–80; for the role of De Rasière, Ceci, "Wampum as a Peripheral Resource," p. 58.

13. Samuel Eliot Morison (ed.), *Of Plymouth Plantation 1620–1647 by William Bradford* (New York: A. A. Knopf, 2001), p. 203.

14. James, *Three Visitors to Early Plymouth*, p. 70.

15. John J. McCusker, *Money and Exchange in Europe and America, 1600–1775* (Chapel Hill, NC: University of North Carolina Press, 1978), p. 157.

16. In this context the "Schagen letter" requires some attention; normally this letter written 5 November 1626 is taken as a proof for the buying of Manhattan as there is hardly any other evidence of this big deal in history which is taken as a proof of tough European bargaining—to think of it: all of Manhattan just for goods worth 60 guilders or $24? However, the letter gives room to misinterpretation as the Lenape did not sell land but only the temporary usage of the land, and with regard to wampum the letter is the more interesting as the beads which were part of the bargain must have had come from Europe. It hardly makes any sense to give a product back to its producers, W. Keith Kavenagh (ed.), *Foundations of Colonial America: A Documentary History*, 3 vols. (New York: Chelsea House, 1973, 2:755, or with a photo of the famous letter of Pieter Schagen to the States General in The Hague in: <http://www.newnetherlandinstitute.org/nnp/documents/schagen_main.html>.

17. Secretary van Tienhoven, quoted in Fenton, *Great Law*, p. 227; to demonstrate the impact of Native Americans on the developments and constellations in North America and to get away from the usual imaging Indians as victims, see the term "Indians were the mintmasters," Francis Jennings, *The Invasion of America: Indians, Colonialism, and the Cant of Conquest* (New York: W. W. Norton & Co., 1976), p. 93.

18. <http://www.coins.nd.edu/ColCoin/ColCoinIntros/NNWampum.html>.

19. <http://www.coins.nd.edu/ColCoin/ColCoinIntros/NNWampum.html>.

20. Lee Sultzman, *Mahican History*, in <http://www.dickshovel.com/Mahican.html>.

21. "[T]he records do indicate that payments between 1634 and 1664 to English colonists amounted . . . to over 21.000 fathoms of wampum—almost 7 million beads . . . beads worth about 5.000 pounds in English currency entered colonial coffers . . . more if double-valued purple beads were included. Thus, a second outcome of the Pequot War was, in effect, the partial underwriting of New England colonization costs by the conquered natives. A third outcome was the creation of a new, English trade triangle," Ceci, "Wampum as a Peripheral Resource," p. 61 and table 1: wampum payments by New England-Long Island Indians, 1634–1664, 62. # 21.043,4 FATHOMS = 6.94 Mill beads.

22. <http://www.coins.nd.edu/ColCoin/ColCoinIntros/NNWampum.html>.

23. Ibid.: "The significance of the area was brought out during discussions of the realignment of the borders between New Netherland and the English colonies, which took place at the Hartford Convention in September of 1650. The secretary of New Netherland, Cornelis van Tienhoven, wrote several communications on the disputed lands. In a description of the boundaries of New Netherland written on 22 February 1650, Van Tienhoven included a discussion of Long Island, in which he stated, "The greatest part of the Wampum, for which the furs are traded, is manufactured there by the Natives." In a supplemental letter written less that two weeks later, on 4 March 1650, he further explained the importance of the area: "I begin then at the most easterly point of Long Island . . . This point is also well adapted to secure the trade of the Indians in Wampum, (the mine of New Netherland,) since in and about the abovementioned sea and the islands therein situated, lie the cockles whereof Wampum is made, from which great profit could be realized by those who would plant a colony or hamlet at the aforesaid Point, for the cultivation of the land, for raising all sorts of cattle, for fishing and the wampum trade." The lawyer Adriaen van der Donck was more emphatic with regard to the importance of Long Island in his diatribe against the province's border concessions to the English. His paper was written in reaction to the not yet ratified Hartford Treaty of 1650 by which Long Island was divided into two parts, the English took the eastern portion up to the westernmost point of Oyster Bay, while the Dutch took the remainder of the island. Concerning this concession of part of Long Island, Van der Donck firmly stated the entirety of the island should be retained by New Netherland, "otherwise the trade will suffer great damage, because the English will retain all the Wampum manufacturers to themselves and we shall be obligated to eat oats out of English hands," <http://www.nativeweb.org/resources/crafts_indigenous_technology/beads_beadwork/>, 1.

24. Robert C. Ritchie, "Piracy, Trade, and the Law in the Early British Empire," in Claudia Schnurmann and Hartmut Lehmann (eds.), *Atlantic Understandings: Essays on European and American History in Honor of Hermann Wellenreuther* (Hamburg-Münster: LIT Verlag, 2006), pp. 61–75 at 61f.; see too *RNA*, 2:114–117.

25. Ceci, "Wampum as a Peripheral Resource," p. 50f.

26. William N. Fenton and Elisabeth Tooker, "Mohawk," in Bruce G. Trigger (ed.), *Northeast*, vol. 15 in William C. Sturtevant (ed.), *Handbook of North American Indians*, 17 vols. (Washington, D.C.: Smithsonian Institution, 1978), pp. 466–480.

27. Ceci, "Wampum as a Peripheral Resource," p. 50. At two Seneca sites more than 350,000 beads and 23 wampum belts have been found that dated from 1640–1675.

28. Fenton, Great Law; <http://www.mohicanpress.com/mo08017.html>.

12

Merging the Two Streams of Migration to New Netherland

Joyce D. Goodfriend

$\mathcal{T}$wo ships. The *Roseboom* (The Rose Tree) and the *Musch* (Sparrow). Each sailed into New Amsterdam's magnificent harbor loaded with people eager to disembark after an arduous and perilous voyage. The passengers on *De Roseboom*, which arrived in 1663, are enumerated in an account book kept by Dutch West India Company officials.[1] Most had left Europe in hopes of bettering their situation in the fledgling Dutch colony of New Netherland. One woman was coming to rejoin her husband, a blacksmith in Esopus. Accompanying her was her four-year-old daughter. Another man was returning to his home in New Netherland. Every other passenger presumably was immigrating to the Dutch colony. In the majority of cases their place of origin is indicated in the accounts, places ranging from Amersfoort to east Friesland to Liège to Hamburg.

Nineteen people were traveling alone, seventeen men and two women. The remaining passengers were grouped in eleven family units. Seven families contained a husband, wife, and children, while three consisted of a father and children, and one a mother and child. One family included a husband, wife, six children, and a nephew. Scrutiny of passenger lists from other ships heading to the colony reveals that occasionally a servant was attached to a family grouping. The information on these European immigrants to New Netherland was not comprehensive since not every individual's name was given. Following seventeenth-century custom, the names of wives and children were not noted. Although children's names were not given, their ages were, thus making it possible for genealogists to identify them with the help of baptismal or family records in the Netherlands or other parts of Europe.

The people who crossed the seas on the other vessel, the *Musch*, which arrived in 1664, remain nameless.[2] Although we have clues to their origins in Africa, no specific information identifies any African on this ship or any other vessel carrying slaves. These men and women, in all likelihood captured and enslaved in Africa, embarked on their voyage in Curaçao, a Caribbean island belonging to the Dutch West India Company, and were transported to the Company's North American colony as slaves. A few were kept by the Company, but most were sold at a public auction in New Amsterdam in May 1664. The record preserved of this auction describes them as "Negroes" or "Negresses" but does not designate them by name.[3] In one instance there is a "Negress and child." Those whose names are inscribed on the document are the slaves' purchasers, a veritable roster of well-known burghers including Paulus Leendertsz van de Grift, Nicolaes de Meijer, Isaac Bedloo, and Jacob Leisler. Also carefully noted on this document are the prices paid for the enslaved Africans—prices that bespeak the value that New Netherlanders of European descent attached to the slave newcomers, now fully transformed into human property.

The people on the *Roseboom* and the *Musch* represent the two streams of migration to New Netherland over the forty or so years of its existence, yet their odysseys have not been interlaced in the annals of the colony. In a historiography that privileges European colonizers, the subject of immigration to New Netherland has been confined to the transatlantic voyagers—Dutch, Germans, French, English, Norwegians, and others—who sailed directly from Europe to New Amsterdam.[4] The arrival of Africans in New Netherland has been treated as a separate strand of the colony's history, usually subsumed under the topic of slavery.

The 400th anniversary of Dutch beginnings in North America is an appropriate time to confront the inequity at the heart of standard accounts of colonization that conceive of European migrants as people and African migrants as commodities. I wish to suggest here that we make a conceptual leap in our interpretation of the subject of migration to New Netherland and couple the stories of the European and African migrants to the Dutch West India Company's North American colony in one narrative. My proposal is rooted in a broader conversation about creating a national narrative that is more inclusive and that reflects the makeup of the United States in the twenty-first century. Arguably, the most intractable problem involved in constructing a genuinely pluralistic version of the nation's past that holds appeal for school children and the general public yet is consonant with the work of academicians, is finding a satisfactory way to incorporate slavery into the narrative. Because standard renditions of early American history invariably have highlighted the accomplishments of European-descended peoples, many Americans have been averse to inserting African slaves into the narrative as historical actors.

In the particular case of New Netherland, the question of discursive restitution is even more vexed, since the topic of migration to New Netherland impinges not only on the national narrative of the United States but on that of the Netherlands as well. Dutch scholars who have endeavored to reframe their country's history in the postcolonial era have been forced to come to terms with the residues of the slave societies over which their nation presided. Complicating the task of revision has been the deep-rooted disposition to train the historical spotlight on the Dutch East Indies, which purportedly were relatively untouched by the grim reality of slavery. As a consequence, the Dutch public acquired little knowledge of their countrymen's involvement in slavery or the egregious disinterest of the Dutch in the abolitionist movement that crested in the nineteenth century. Dutch enterprises in Africa and the Americas, when they could be overlooked no longer, were saddled with the stigma of slavery.

Much of the opposition to placing slaves on the same conceptual level as free immigrants can be traced to the widely prevalent assumption that coerced and voluntary migrants had nothing in common. In the United States, there has been a long-standing tendency to define immigrants as Europeans. Oscar Handlin, who first cast the story of American immigration in grand terms in his 1951 book, *The Uprooted: The Epic Story of the Great Migrations that made the American People*, seemingly fixed the conceptual framework for the immigrant story.[5] Starting from the premise that "the immigrants *were* American history," Handlin proceeded to focus exclusively on the waves of nineteenth- and early twentieth-century immigrants from Europe, in essence reinforcing the entrenched belief that the experience of enslavement disqualified those of African descent from being considered immigrants. Handlin's disregard of the African migratory stream can be attributed, at least in part, to the fact that *The Uprooted* was written in a segregated America.

Once the Civil Rights Movement gathered momentum in subsequent decades and the institutional props of a segregated society were gradually dismantled, the way was cleared for historians to address the problem of asymmetry in the national narrative. During the last fifty years, with continuing pressure from African-American constituencies and the widespread adoption of multicultural curricula, the visibility of enslaved Africans in accounts of the country's history has been magnified. Perhaps equally significant, the Founding Fathers, once safely ensconced on a pedestal, have come to be deemed appropriate subjects for investigation regarding their relations with enslaved Africans. No longer is it considered sacrilegious to think of George Washington, Thomas Jefferson, and Benjamin Franklin and slavery in the same breath.

In this refreshed atmosphere of inquiry, historians have begun to situate coerced and voluntary migration under the same conceptual umbrella. James Horn and Philip Morgan, in a 2005 essay pointedly titled "Settlers and Slaves: European and African Migrations to Early Modern British America," make clear how essential it is to adopt an Atlantic framework to study migration in the sixteenth, seventeenth and eighteenth centuries.[6] "To aim at Atlantic history," they contend, "is to grapple with the complex forces that shaped migrant experience, no matter what the type, and it must encompass population movements from all parts of the Atlantic rim."[7] Their meticulous analysis of a wide range of data narrows the distance between coerced and free migrants by documenting what they had in common. Ira Berlin, who also juxtaposes the stories of African and European migrants to America in his 2010 book, *The Making of African America: The Four Great Migrations*, attaches great weight to the distinctiveness of the experiences of African Americans, noting "their unnatural injection into America society and contested incorporation."[8] Yet he presses us to consider "[t]he global perspective and the long view of human history [which] call into question distinctions between coerced migrations and voluntary migrations."[9] Viewed from this angle, he asserts, the conditions under which many free migrants moved "strained the very meaning of human volition."[10] A recent survey of the history of European migration to Dutch territories similarly calls attention to "gradations of intentionality in 'Dutch' migration and colonization."[11]

While it is unwise to exaggerate the receptiveness of the American public to the revisions to the national narrative proffered by academics, there is little doubt that a more inclusive storyline has penetrated mainstream American history books during the last few decades. Buttressed by an enormous amount of research on the Atlantic slave trade, treatments of the migration of Africans to the Americas display a precision and nuance that stand in sharp contrast to the impressionistic studies of former generations. American historical memory, though still tilted toward the valorization of men and women of European ancestry, now reserves ample space for African Americans and Native Americans, not to mention a variety of other non-Europeans. By contrast, historians in the Netherlands have struggled to stretch the historical canvas to accommodate the perspectives of colonized peoples in the East and West Indies.[12]

As the Netherlands mutated into a postcolonial society following World War II, assumptions of European superiority embedded in accounts of the Dutch Empire proved hard to dislodge. Even as native peoples moved toward self-determination, scribes in the fatherland continued to privilege colonizers. The Dutch East Indies, assumed to be the centerpiece of the Dutch colonial empire, remained in the forefront of national thinking, as Indonesian independence failed to subdue nostalgia for the glory days of Dutch East India Company rule. The determination of politicians to preserve Dutch influence in Indonesia, though ill-advised and ultimately unsuccessful, also impeded efforts to rethink the history of Dutch colonialism. One fateful consequence of continuing to dwell on the positive outcomes of Dutch colonization in the East Indies, particularly in the realm of international commerce, was the relegation of the Dutch West India Company's activities, and specifically its involvement in the transatlantic slave trade, to the margins of national history. Overlooking the evidence of Indian Ocean slavery, keepers of the Dutch past found little incentive to inflect the national narrative with discussion of Dutch slave trading and slave holding.[13]

It was not until streams of immigrants from the former Dutch colonies in the West Indies altered the makeup of the Netherlands' population in the final decades of the twentieth century that the inattentiveness to Dutch slaving enterprises began to be remedied. Pressure from Caribbean activists, particularly immigrants from Surinam, to weave enslaved Africans into the narrative of national history accelerated the efforts of Dutch academics to bring greater recognition to the Dutch role in the slave trade and slavery. Another strand of research concerning the lack of Dutch participation in the antislavery movement added further layers of proof to the increasingly somber picture of Dutch colonialism and its aftermath.[14]

Progress in constructing revisionist narratives of the history of the Netherlands was soon coupled with government-sponsored initiatives for making amends for past deeds. Ironically, the common belief that territories in the West Indies were not at the heart of the Dutch colonial empire may have made it less wrenching to admit Dutch complicity in the slave trade and the West Indian plantation societies that depended on slave labor. In the late 1990s, the Dutch government, goaded by Caribbean militants, inaugurated a program aimed at atoning for the atrocities committed during the slave trade and granting dignity to its victims and their descendants. Decisions to erect a national monument to memorialize those who had suffered through slavery and to found an institute for research on slavery set off an unprecedented public dialogue on the implications of the assumptions underlying these resolutions. As it turned out, policymakers, Afro-Caribbean migrants, Dutch intellectuals, and the national press held divergent views not only on the design and location of the national monument, but on the principles of integration and multiculturalism that were integral to the vision of the twenty-first-century Dutch nation held by the government. In short, the contest over the place of slavery in Dutch national memory instigated a wide-scale public debate on the coordinates of Dutch identity that escalated after the assassination of the anti-immigrant political figure, Pim Fortuyn, in Hilversum in May 2002.[15] The prospect of reaching a consensus on the inclusion of the descendants of slaves in Dutch society and Dutch history books is now slimmer and is just one of the casualties of the current course of Dutch politics.

Still, the dedication of the national monument erected in Amsterdam to memorialize those who suffered as a result of the slave trade on 1 July 2002, the 139th anniversary of the abolition of Dutch slavery, with then-Queen Beatrix and Prime Minister Wim Kok in attendance, made clear the commitment of those at the head of the Dutch government as well as the royal family to this modified version of Dutch history.[16] To erase any doubts about the official stance on slavery and its victims, then-Crown Prince (now-King) Willem Alexander personally visited the site of the Dutch slave-trading fortress at Elmina in present-day Ghana in 2002 and enunciated the key elements in this new position: "We look back with remorse to that dark age of human relations. We pay tribute to the victims of this inhuman trade."[17] Nevertheless, the potent symbolism inhering in this public expiation for the sins of the fathers in their dealings in Africa and the West Indies left unaddressed the question of responsibility for the harms inflicted on the ancestors of present-day Indonesians.

Dutch historians intent on revising scholarship on colonial Dutch possessions in the Americas, notably Suriname and the Dutch Antilles, have readily acceded to demands to accord the enslaved peoples of the Caribbean region a more prominent place in their studies. Yet the possibility of redressing the balance in standard accounts of the Dutch West Indies hinges on the yet-to-be-determined shape of counter narratives grounded in the point of view of the enslaved.[18] Those retelling the stories of the more transitory Dutch colonies of Brazil and New Netherland may be even less forthright in evaluating the impact of slavery on the societies created there.[19] Based on his assessment of the work of Russell Shorto and Jaap Jacobs, Gert Oostindie asserts that "the African dimension of early Dutch settlement [in New Amsterdam] was recently rediscovered, but certainly not as a defining characteristic."[20] Shorto, an American journalist, perhaps moved by idealism, chose to emphasize New Netherland as an example of the much-vaunted Dutch toleration of the seventeenth century, thereby glossing over the legacy of slavery in the colony.[21]

A more interesting case is that of Jaap Jacobs, the Dutch scholar who has written the now authoritative history of New Netherland. Evidence from successive editions of Jacobs' book suggests that he has monitored intellectual currents on both sides of the Atlantic. The initial English language version of his work, *New Netherland: A Dutch Colony in Seventeenth-Century America* (2005), contained a long chapter called "The Peopling of Such Empty and Unfurnished Lands" that focused exclusively on the characteristics of the Europeans who settled in the Dutch colony.[22] Jacobs reserved his examination of New Netherland's enslaved Africans for a section of the book called "The Periphery of the Community: Jews and Blacks." However, in the revised and abbreviated edition of his study, *The Colony of New Netherland: A Dutch Settlement in Seventeenth-Century America* (2009), Jacobs took a major step toward reconceptualizing the subject of migration to the colony, changing the title of the relevant chapter to "Population and Immigration" and inserting a one page section on "Enslaved Blacks" toward the end of it.[23] Nonetheless, his perfunctory treatment of African immigrants, whom he considers numerically insignificant in the colony as a whole, fosters the impression that their story is at best a footnote to the historically significant story of the European immigrants who form the protagonists of the chapter. Moreover, by labeling these people as blacks rather than Africans, he minimizes the chance to detect any equivalence in the experiences of migrants from Africa and migrants from Europe.

Examining the patterns of African and European migration to New Netherland in tandem brings into view the commonalities of experience of these two groups of New Netherland pioneers. To think of the African men and women who arrived in the colony not simply as slaves but as voyagers whose travel histories were often longer and more circuitous than those of their European counterparts is a means to disavow the dehumanization of Africans that occurs whenever the linkage between "African" and "slave" is made by teachers and students of the early modern world.

Reorienting our perspective on the flows of people to the New Netherland colony by charting the ocean voyages of those who journeyed to the North American Dutch colony from Africa with stopovers in Curaçao or perhaps Brazil directs our attention to the pivotal role played by Dutch slave traders in the seventeenth-century Atlantic world. It helps us to understand the alacrity with which New Netherland's European settlers responded to the cues in their environment by seizing the opportunity to participate in the commerce in slaves that stretched from Europe to Africa to the Americas. To satisfy the local Company's need for slave labor (and subsequently the desire of private individuals for slaves) enslaved Africans were procured in

Curaçao, the Dutch slave entrepôt in the Caribbean, and even in Africa.

By weaving the story of African migrants to New Netherland into the master narrative of its history, and especially that of New Amsterdam, the colony's nerve center where the great majority of enslaved Africans resided and where their numbers were far from insignificant, the singularity of New Netherland's development is brought into relief. Steadily increasing reliance on slave labor distinguished New Amsterdam from Boston, for example, where very few slaves were found before 1664, the year that New Netherland was surrendered to the English.[24]

The Dutch colonial city's distinctive demographic profile highlights its biracial character from an early stage. Although historians invariably fix on New Amsterdam's heterogeneity as its defining characteristic, their gaze too often has been trained on the diverse makeup of the European immigrant population.[25] Conceiving of New Amsterdam as a society in which blacks and whites coexisted, albeit on unequal terms, leads us to approach the issue of community building in a fresh light. Judging from the frequency with which "Negroes" are mentioned in civil and ecclesiastical records pertaining to New Amsterdam, Africans and Europeans regularly mingled in this small urban space on Manhattan. The city became a crucible in which attitudes toward others were formed and re-formed as the composition of the population evolved.

Reframing New Netherland's immigration history to incorporate Africans as well as Europeans not only allows us to appreciate the common humanity of all pioneers but sharpens our perception of how the experiences of the two groups of immigrants varied. The most fundamental difference between African and European immigrants to New Netherland was that Europeans chose to board the ships that crossed the ocean while the Africans were compelled to climb onto the vessels. In other words, the Africans who came in chains were involuntary immigrants and the Europeans were voluntary immigrants, even the orphans who were shipped to the colony by officials in the fatherland. New Netherlanders of European ancestry migrated to the Dutch North American colony of their free will. Enslaved Africans, by contrast, had fallen prey to European slavers in Africa, or perhaps a Spanish or Portuguese colony, and were taken to the Dutch slave-trading entrepôt of Curaçao for reshipment to New Amsterdam. They were captives who found themselves transformed into merchandise. Their experiences sharply differentiated them from voyagers from Europe.

Not surprisingly the demographic characteristics of the African immigrants entering the port were shaped by market considerations.[26] Potential buyers of slaves customarily wanted strong laborers and therefore placed a premium on young men and to a lesser extent, young women. However, the economics of the Dutch slave trade were such that New Netherland was not a primary destination for slaves, and buyers there had to be satisfied with slaves who were not saleable in Curaçao or elsewhere. Director-General Petrus Stuyvesant described the male and female slaves who had been transported to the colony on the *Musch* in 1664 as "on an average, pretty old, and as the skipper alleges, rejected by the Spaniards."[27] Still the majority of enslaved Africans who reached New Netherland must have been relatively youthful, and the women certainly were of childbearing age. In this respect, the age structure of the colony's African population resembled that of the European migrants to New Netherland, who were far from a cross section of Dutch society, given the fact that older segments of the population rarely emigrated from the homeland. Notwithstanding the similarity of the age structure of these seventeenth-century immigrant populations—the bias toward the young—the composition of the European immigrants differed greatly from that of their African counterparts.

Immigrants from Europe tended to come in family units, a fact well-documented by historians using the abundant data in passenger lists and other sources. However, to assume from the void of information on the family background of African immigrants to New Netherland that captive Africans, bereft of kinfolk as a consequence of the imperatives of slave trading, did not prize family life as much as the Europeans who stripped them of their family ties is erroneous. In this alien environment men and women of African descent recreated families once given the opportunity to do so. Families were a welcome anchor for people uprooted from their birth families in their homelands. The records of New Amsterdam's Reformed Church beginning in 1639 contain numerous examples of slave baptisms and some marriages that attest to the Africans' drive to form and maintain families while under Dutch rule in New Netherland.[28] Their willingness to use a Dutch institution and conform to Dutch religious practices to accomplish their goal is striking, and even more remarkable are their continuing efforts to have their offspring baptized even after local Dutch ministers virtually halted the practice on the pretext that worldly motives impelled the Africans to seek baptism for their children.[29] The fact that African New Netherlanders had concluded that Christianization was a key step on the road to emancipation does not mean that they were not amenable to the Dutch Protestantism they encountered on Manhattan. Many Kongo people would have already been exposed to Christianity in its Catholic form in their homelands or in Iberian colonies. The salience of Christianity in the complex of cultural values they brought with them to New Netherland is critical to understanding their adaptation to the variant of Dutch society that developed in the West India Company's North American colony.

As a rule, historians have regarded only European immigrants as capable of importing values and traditions from their homelands to New Netherland. Their intramural scholarly debates have centered on how successfully Dutch culture was transplanted to the colony. By default, African immigrants have been deemed devoid of culture as defined by Europeans and considered mere receptacles for Dutch culture, whether deliberately instilled or casually absorbed. The findings of specialists in African history concerning the cultural background of West Central African migrants to New Netherland cast doubt on this line of thinking and, by doing so, narrow the distance between African and European migrants.[30] Even though much more is known about their lives after they were inserted into the role of slave in New Netherland, the fact that transplanted Kongolese people brought distinctive cultural baggage with them is no longer in question. If the Africans who found their way to New Netherland were not deracinated individuals but rather bearers of fundamental elements of the vibrant cultures of West Central Africa as filtered through experiences in Spanish or Portuguese colonies, then the experiences of African and European migrants may have been more analogous than previously admitted. Members of each group came with a cultural compass, which they used to orient themselves to their new environment. Indeed, it is plausible to contend that at least the initial generation of African immigrants to New Netherland was more culturally homogenous than the Europeans who commanded their labor.

The diverse cultures of New Netherland's European settlers can be traced to the flows of European migration to the Dutch colony. Some have argued for the inexorability of the process of cultural blending among Europeans in New Netherland (and particularly New Amsterdam), but a survey of the sources of cultural difference in the settler population suggests that caution is warranted in this respect. The variety of languages spoken in New Netherland is a clue to the diversity of European cultures represented in the colony. Although it may be beyond our power to verify Director Willem Kieft's report to Father Isaac Jogues that there were "men of eighteen different languages" on Manhattan in the early 1640s, the documentary record of the colony is studded with references to the varied tongues used by European settlers.[31] Immigrants spoke in the customary languages of their native region, and these languages and dialects provide evidence of their origins in places across the map of western Europe—the United Provinces, the German states, Norway, Sweden, France, England and even Bohemia and Italy.

Not all who disembarked in New Amsterdam came directly from the Netherlands, and those who did were not all natives of the United Provinces. In the early seventeenth century the Dutch Republic was the primary destination for migrants from all over Europe seeking sanctuary from religious persecution or opportunities to better themselves economically.[32] Some of these sojourners in the Netherlands (or their children) elected to continue their journeys to Dutch America in hopes of improving their economic position.[33]

While the majority of New Netherland's settlers of European ancestry came directly from the Netherlands, some came by way of other American colonies. Secondary migration in the Americas is not usually featured in histories of migration to New Netherland, but it accounts for the presence of a good number of the colony's European immigrants. A small number came from other Dutch colonies as, for example, those who moved north after Dutch Brazil fell back into Portuguese hands in 1654. This included employees of the Dutch West India Company as well as settlers, notably Jews, who traveled to New Netherland. Others came from Curaçao, but migrants from other Dutch American possessions were not the only secondary migrants to arrive in New Netherland. The English men and women who founded communities on Long Island in the 1640s and 1650s started out in the neighboring New England colonies of Massachusetts and Connecticut. Dissatisfaction with the decisions made by their towns' Puritan rulers in religious matters prompted their exodus and their settlement in New Netherland occurred at the invitation of Director Kieft. Lady Deborah Moody's Baptist followers who settled in Gravesend are perhaps the most famous example of people who originally were part of the Great Puritan Migration (1629–1640) and who later cast their lots with the Dutch in New Netherland. In sum, European migrants to New Netherland originated in a variety of towns and cities in Western Europe, including the British Isles. Most migrants were funneled through the Netherlands, but others moved to New Netherland from assorted places in Dutch and English America.

Differences among New Netherland's settler population stemmed not only from their diverse regional origins but from their adherence to different religious traditions. The most obvious separation was between Christians and Jews. The vast majority of New Netherland's Europeans were Christians, specifically Protestant Christians, but there were a few Jewish migrants, most coming from Brazil in 1654 after the Portuguese takeover, but a few came directly from the Netherlands. One was Jacob Barsimson who was a passenger on the *Pereboom* (the *Pear Tree*) in 1654.[34] These Jews, largely Sephardim, have garnered deserved recognition as pioneers and there is an abundant literature on their role in the history of the diaspora in the Americas.[35] In addition, their icy reception from Director-General Stuyvesant has elicited much comment from scholars of religious toleration.[36] Their numbers were small, however, and their community transitory.

Far more important than the separation between Christians and Jews in New Netherland were the divisions among Protestants. Reformed Protestants from England and the Netherlands shared a good deal in common and it was Stuyvesant's goal to forge links between these two constituencies even though they did not have identical practices. It was the Protestants outside the Calvinist umbrella, most notably the Lutherans and the Quakers, who stood as greater obstacles to New Netherland's religious harmony. Despite Stuyvesant's concerted effort to bring Lutherans into the Reformed fold by denying them the privilege of public worship, many remained adherents of the Augsburg Confession.[37] Their subterranean Lutheran congregation surfaced in New York City once English governance commenced.

Still there was a common denominator in New Netherland's religious life—Christianity—that bound virtually all the population of immigrants together. (The few Jews, of course, were the exception.) Remarkably, the earliest generation of Africans and many of their offspring joined with Reformed Protestants in Christian worship in New Amsterdam. Earlier exposure to Catholicism and a growing familiarity with Western religious institutions combined to bring them to the Reformed Church and to motivate them to offer their children for baptism there. (A handful gravitated to the Lutherans, who also welcomed them.) Most significantly, it was Dutch Reformed ministers who closed the church door to African New Netherlanders. Nevertheless, this shift in Reformed policy should not obscure the fact that people with roots in West Central Africa and Western Europe managed for a couple of decades to fit under the Christian umbrella in New Netherland. This thread of a common Christianity is crucial to the construction of a unified story of migration to the Dutch North American colony.

Everyone in New Netherland except the Native inhabitants of the region (and this, of course, is a mighty exception) was an immigrant or the child of an immigrant. For far too long historians imbued with a Eurocentric view of the colonization of Dutch America have treated immigration to New Netherland as synonymous with European immigration, unthinkingly defining immigrants solely as people who chose to come across the ocean of their own volition. For writers whose antecedents lay in Europe and who were inculcated with the notion that an African was equivalent to a slave, placing African migrants who arrived in shackles on a par with European immigrants was inconceivable. Now, four centuries after the Dutch colonial project in North America commenced, we are poised to retroactively grant the status of immigrant to scores of people who were brought to New Netherland against their will as captives of colonizers intent on transforming them into commodities.

Scanning the records of New Netherland reveals how well documented the lives of people of African descent in the colony are. We can view them at work, at church, and in taverns and once given a measure of freedom, as tillers of the soil on their own farms on land allotted to them. Surely it is time to identify these men and women as immigrants and not just slaves. Thinking of the human cargo that arrived in New Netherland more expansively, as I have advocated, does not lessen our obligation to contrast the situations of European and African migrants and assess the consequences of the advantages enjoyed by immigrants from Europe. What matters is that we not allow the perceptions of earlier generations of historians, both professional and amateur, to limit our conceptual horizons and dictate who should or should not be considered an immigrant. If we think of each ship sailing into New Amsterdam's harbor as bringing migrants who worked and played, ate and drank, loved and lamented, and at least occasionally prayed, we will have a truer picture of the peopling of New Netherland and a firmer foundation on which to graft the history of New York and the nation.

Notes

1. "Passengers to New Netherland," *Holland Society Year Book, 1902* (New York, 1902), pp. 1–37.

2. E. B. O'Callaghan (ed.), *Voyages of the Slavers St. John and Arms of Amsterdam, 1659, 1663; Together with additional Papers illustrative of the Slave Trade under the Dutch* (Albany, NY: 1867), pp. 202–205.

3. Ibid.

4. The early study of migration to New Netherland in Bertus Harry Wabeke, *Dutch Migration to North America 1624–1860* (New York, 1944) has been superseded by the discussion in Jaap Jacobs, *New Netherland: A Dutch Colony in Seventeenth-Century America* (Leiden and Boston: Brill, 2005).

5. Oscar Handlin, *The Uprooted: The Epic Story of the Great Migrations that Made the American People*, 2nd ed. (Philadelphia. PA: University of Pennsylvania Press, 2002 [1951]).

6. James Horn and Philip D. Morgan, "Settlers and Slaves: European and African Migrations to Early Modern British America," in Elizabeth Mancke and

Carole Shammas (eds.), *The Creation of the British Atlantic World* (Baltimore, MD and London: Johns Hopkins University Press, 2005), pp. 19–44.

7. Ibid., at p. 19.

8. Ira Berlin, *The Making of African America: The Four Great Migrations* (New York: Viking, 2010), p. 42.

9. Ibid., p. 44.

10. Ibid., p. 45.

11. Gijs Kruijtzer, "European Migration in the Dutch Sphere," in Gert Oostindie (ed.), *Dutch Colonialism, Migration and Cultural Heritage* (Leiden: KITLV Press, 2008), p. 107. David Eltis has illuminated the underpinnings of the customary antithesis between slavery and freedom in "Slavery and Freedom in the Early Modern World," in Stanley Engerman (ed.), *Terms of Labor: Slavery, Serfdom and Free Labor* (Stanford, CA: Stanford University Press, 1999), pp. 25–49. See also Eltis (ed.), *Coerced and Free Migration: Global Perspectives* (Stanford: Stanford University Press, 2002).

12. An overview of developments in the Netherlands can be found in Gert Oostindie, "History Brought Home: Postcolonial Migrations and the Dutch rediscovery of Slavery," in Wim Klooster (ed.), *Migration, Trade, and Slavery in an Expanding World: Essays in Honor of Pieter Emmer* (Leiden and Boston: Brill, 2009), pp. 305–327; Oostindie, *Dutch Colonialism, Migration and Cultural Heritage.*

13. A corrective to this assumption has appeared in the last decade, see Rik van Welie, "Patterns of Slave Trading and Slavery in the Dutch Colonial World, 1596–1863," in Oostindie, *Dutch Colonialism, Migration and Cultural Heritage*, pp. 158–164.

14. Gert Oostindie discusses "Slavery as a non-problem in the Dutch world" in the chapter "Slave, Black; Human?" in Gert Oostindie, *Paradise Overseas: The Dutch Caribbean: Colonialism and its Transatlantic Legacies* (Oxford: Macmillan, 2005), pp. 24–51. See also the seminal article by Seymour Drescher, "The Long Goodbye: Dutch Capitalism and Antislavery in Comparative Perspective," in *American Historical Review* 99, no. 1 (February 1994), pp. 44–69, and the essays collected in Gert Oostindie (ed.), *Fifty Years Later: Antislavery, Capitalism and Modernity in the Dutch Orbit* (Pittsburgh, PA: University of Pittsburgh Press, 1996).

15. Ian Buruma, *Murder in Amsterdam: The Death of Theo van Gogh and the Limits of Tolerance* (New York: Penguin, 2006).

16. Johanna C. Kardux, "Monuments of the Black Atlantic: Slavery Memorials in the United States and the Netherlands," in Heike Raphael-Hernandez (ed.), *Blackening Europe: The African American Presence* (New York: Routledge, 2007), pp. 87–105.

17. For Crown Prince Willem Alexander's declaration, Gert Oostindie, "The Slippery paths of Commemoration and Heritage Tourism: The Netherlands, Ghana, and the Rediscovery of Atlantic Slavery," in *New West India Guide / Nieuwe West-Indische Gids* 79, nos. 1 & 2 (2005), pp. 55–77 at 66.

18. Oostindie, *Paradise Overseas*, p. 160.

19. Oostindie speaks of the "uncritical tone and even sheer exaltation characterizing many contemporary Brazilian renderings of Dutch colonialism," Oostindie, "The Slippery paths of Commemoration and Heritage Tourism," p. 74.

20. Ibid.

21. Russell Shorto, *The Island at the Center of the World: The Epic Story of Dutch Manhattan and the Forgotten Colony that Shaped America* (New York: Doubleday, 2004). See also Joyce D. Goodfriend, "Review of Russell Shorto, The Island at the Center of the World: The Epic Story of Dutch Manhattan and the Forgotten Colony that Shaped America," in *New York History* 86 (2005), pp. 298–301.

22. Jacobs, *New Netherland: A Dutch Colony in Seventeenth-Century America.*

23. Jacobs, *The Colony of New Netherland: A Dutch Settlement in Seventeenth-Century America* (Ithaca and London: Cornell University Press, 2009).

24. Mark Peterson, "Cities on the Margin: Boston and New Amsterdam," *de Halve Maen* 78, no. 2 (2005), pp. 32–35.

25. On New Amsterdam's European population, see Joyce D. Goodfriend, "Foreigners in a Dutch Colonial City," in *New York History* 90 (2009), pp. 241–269. On the background of immigrants to New Netherland, see Oliver Rink, "The People of New Netherland: Notes on Non-English Immigration to New York in the Seventeenth Century," in *New York History* 62 (1981), pp. 5–42, and David S. Cohen, "How Dutch were the Dutch of New Netherland," in *New York History* 62 (1981), pp. 43–60.

26. Johannes Postma, *The Dutch in the Atlantic Slave Trade* (Cambridge: Cambridge University Press, 1990); P. C. Emmer, *The Dutch Slave Trade, 1500–1850*, Chris Emery, trans. (New York: Berghahn Books, 2006).

27. Director-General Stuyvesant to the Directors at Amsterdam, 10 June 1664, in O'Callaghan, *Voyages of the Slavers St. John and Arms of Amsterdam*, p. 206.

28. The records of the Dutch Reformed Church have been analyzed in Joyce D. Goodfriend, "Black Families in New Netherland," in *Journal of the Afro-American Historical and Genealogical Society* 5 (1984), pp. 95–108; Linda M. Heywood and John K. Thornton, *Central Africans, Atlantic Creoles, and the Foundation of the Americas, 1585–1660* (New York: Cambridge University Press, 2007).

29. Joyce D. Goodfriend, "The Souls of African American Children: New Amsterdam," in *Common-place: The Interactive Journal of Early American Life* 3 (July 2003) [www.common-place.org].

30. Heywood and Thornton, *Central Africans, Atlantic Creoles, and the Foundation of the Americas.*

31. "Novum Belgium, By Father Isaac Jogues 1646" in *NNN*, p. 259.

32. Jan Lucassen, "The Netherlands, the Dutch, and Long-Distance Migration in the Late Sixteenth to Early Nineteenth Centuries," in Nicholas P. Canny (ed.), *Europeans on the Move: Studies on European Migration 1500–1800* (Oxford, U.K.: Clarendon Press, 1994), pp. 153–191.

33. For an overview of migration from the Netherlands to America, see Victor Enthoven, "Dutch Crossings: Migration between the Netherlands and America, 1600–1800," in *Atlantic Studies* 2 (2005), pp. 153–176.

34. "Passengers to New Netherland," *Holland Society Year Book, 1902*, p. 5.

35. Arnold Wiznitzer, "The Exodus from Brazil and Arrival in New Amsterdam of the Jewish Pilgrim Fathers, 1654," in Abraham J. Karp (ed.), *The Jewish Experience in America: Selected Studies from the Publications of the American Jewish Historical Society*, 5 vols. (New York: KTAV, 1969), 1:19–36; Leo Hershkowitz, "New Amsterdam's Twenty Three Jews—Myth or Reality?," in Shalom Goldman (ed.), *Hebrew and the Bible in America: The First Two Centuries* (Hanover, NH: University Press of New England, 1993), pp. 171–183.

36. On religious toleration in New Netherland, see Joyce D. Goodfriend, "Practicing Toleration in Dutch New Netherland," in Chris Beneke and Christopher S. Grenda (eds.), *The First Prejudice: Religious Tolerance and Intolerance in Early America* (Philadelphia: University of Pennsylvania Press, 2011), pp. 98–122; Jaap Jacobs, "Between Repression and Approval: Connivance and Toleration in New Netherland," in *de Halve Maen* 71 (1998), pp. 51–58.

37. On Lutherans in New Netherland, see Harry J. Kreider, *The Beginnings of Lutheranism in New York* (New York, 1949) and Joyce D. Goodfriend, "Stuyvesant en de luthersen van Nieuw Amsterdam. De uitdaging aan het ideaal van een calvinistische maatschappij," *Transparant: tijdschrift van de Vereniging van Christen-Historici* 17, no. 2 (April 2006), pp. 4–8.

Contributors

Leslie P. Choquette is Professor of History, L'Institut français Professor of Francophone Cultures, and Director of the French Institute at Assumption College. She is the author of *Frenchmen into Peasants: Modernity and Tradition in the Peopling of French Canada* (Cambridge, Mass: Harvard University Press, 1997), the 1998 winner of the Alfred Heggoy Book Prize of the French Colonial Historical Society, as well as many articles and essays on New France.

Willem Frijhoff is Professor Emeritus of Early Modern History at the Free University of Amsterdam and a member of the Royal Netherlands Academy of Arts and Sciences, the Royal Flemish Academy, and the Academia Europa (London). The author of many books, articles, and essays on religion in early modern Europe and New Netherland, his *Fulfilling God's Mission: The Two Worlds of Dominie Everardus Bogardus, 1607–1647* (Leiden and Boston: Brill, 2007) won the 2008 Hendricks Manuscript Award of the New Netherland Institute.

Joyce D. Goodfriend is Professor of History at the University of Denver. She is the author and editor of numerous works on New Netherland and colonial New York, including *Before the Melting Pot: Society and Culture in Colonial New York City, 1664–1730* (Princeton, NJ: Princeton University Press, 1992), the winner of the 1991 Hendricks Award of the New Netherland Institute, *Going Dutch: The Presence in America, 1609–2009* (Leiden and Boston: Brill, 2008), and *Revisiting New Netherland: Perspectives on Early Dutch America* (Leiden and Boston: Brill, 2005).

Lauric Henneton is Maître de Conferences en Anglais at the University of Versailles—St. Quentin, France. He is the author and editor of numerous works on American history, including *Liberté, Inégalité, Autorité: Politique,*

Société et construction identitaire du Massachusetts au XVIIe siècle (Paris: Honoré Champion, 2009) and *Histoire religieuse des Etats-Unis* (Paris: Flammarion, 2012).

Jaap Jacobs is the author of *The Colony of New Netherland: A Dutch Settlement in Seventeenth-Century America* (Ithaca, NY: Cornell University Press, 2009) and many essays and articles on New Netherland and the overseas expansion of the interests of the Dutch Republic. The 2005–2006 Doris Quinn Visiting Professor at Cornell University and the University of Pennsylvania and Erasmus Visiting Lecturer in Dutch Civilization and Culture in 2011–2012, he is presently working on a new biography of Petrus Stuyvesant, Director-General of New Netherland from 1647–1664.

Paul Otto is Professor of History and Chair of the Department of History, Politics, and International Studies at George Fox University and his research focuses upon European-Native American relations. His first book, *The Dutch-Munsee Encounter in America: The Struggle for Sovereignty in the Hudson Valley* (New York: Berghahn Press, 2006) was based upon his 1998 Hendricks Award-winning PhD dissertation and he is presently writing a history of the use and development of wampum in the colonial northeast in the seventeenth and eighteenth centuries.

Jon Parmenter is Associate Professor of History at Cornell University. He is the author of *The Edge of the Woods: Iroquoia, 1534–1701* (East Lansing, MI: Michigan State University Press, 2010) and many essays and articles on seventeenth- and eighteenth-century Iroquois history.

L. H. Roper is Professor of History at the State University of New York–New Paltz. He is the author and editor of a number of works on Anglo-America in the "long" seventeenth century, including *The English Empire in America, 1602–1658: Beyond Jamestown* (London: Pickering & Chatto, 2009) and *Conceiving Carolina: Proprietors, Planters, and Plots, 1662–1729* (New York: Palgrave Macmillan, 2004).

Claudia Schnurmann is Professor of History at the University of Hamburg, Germany. She is the author and editor of numerous books, articles, and essays on the history of the Atlantic World, including *Europa trifft Amerika: Zwei alte Welten bilden eine neue atlantische Welt, 1492–1783* (Berlin [u.a] 2009), *Vom Inselreich zur Weltmacht: Die Entwicklung des englischen Weltreichs vom Mittelalter bis ins 20. Jahrhundert* (Stuttgart [u.a.] 2001), *Atlantische Welten:*

Engländer und Niederländer im amerikanisch-atlantischen Raum, 1648–1713 (Cologne, 1998), and *Atlantic Understandings: Essays on European and American History in Honor of Hermann Wellenreuther* (Hamburg, 2006).

Timothy J. Shannon is Professor and Chair of History at Gettysburg College. He is the co-author (with David Gellman) of *American Odysseys: A History of Early America*, forthcoming from Oxford University Press, and is the author and editor of many works on the history of Native-European interactions in colonial America, including *Iroquois Diplomacy on the Early American Frontier* (New York: Viking Penguin, 2008), *Atlantic Lives: A Comparative Approach to Early America* (New York: Pearson Longman, 2004), and *Indians and Colonists at the Crossroads of Empire: The Albany Congress of 1754* (Ithaca: Cornell University Press, 2000).

Kees Zandvliet is Head of Research, Exhibitions, and Education at the Amsterdam Museum. In addition to curating numerous exhibits on the history of early modern Dutch overseas activity, including most recently "De Gouden Eeuw: proeftuin van onze wereld" at the Amsterdam Museum, he has published many essays and catalogue entries on the early modern history of cartography.

Index

Albany, NY. *See* Beverwijck

Acadia. *See* Samuel Argall; New France

Algonquian Indians: and fur trade, 171; production of wampum by, 88, 94, 179, 226–231; relations of with Dutch, 75; relations of with Iroquois, 122, 137; relations of with French, 137–138, 141. *See also* Esopus Wars; Long Island; Mahican Indians; Munsee Indians

"Amboyna massacre" (1623), 29, 186

Amsterdam, 120, 154, 159, 242; as cartographic and commercial center, 55–56, 148; iconography of, 35–38, 40, 43; patronage in, 38–40, 53–54, 57–59; religious character of 203–204, 211. *See also* Joan Blaeu; Willem Blaeu; Baltasar de Moucheron; Cornelis Claesz; Dutch East India Company; Dutch Republic; Dutch West India Company; Frederick Henry, stadholder: circle of; Gerard Hulft; Pieter Evertsz Hulft; Pieter Isaacsz; Maurice, count of Nassau and Prince of Orange; Gerard Mercator; Petrus Plancius; Pieter Reael; Werner van den Valckert

Anabaptists, 205

Antwerp. *See* Dutch Revolt

Argall, Samuel, 21, 26, 172, 178

Arminianism. *See* Dutch Republic: religion in

Atlantic world: as historiographical perspective, 86, 95–96, 113, 161, 187, 226, 240

Barentsz, Pieter, 90

Barentsz, Willem, 37, 47

Bast, Pieter, 36

Batavia. *See* East Indies

Bayle, Pierre, 204

Bermuda. *See* Somers Islands Company

Beverwijck, 72, 74, 76, 118, 154, 156

Blaeu, Joan, 39, 40, 57, 61, 62

Blaeu, Willem Jansz, 39, 47, 49, 51, 57–59, 62, 172–174, 180

Block, Adriaen Captain, 169, 175; map of (1616), 51, 89, 172. *See also* New Netherland: relations of with New England

Block Island (R.I.), 172, 175

Bogaert, Harmen Meyndertsz van den: observations by of Oneida Indians, 73, 88, 114

Blommaert, Samuel, 61, 178. *See also* Dutch West India Company

Bogardus, Rev. Everardus, 153, 161

Bradford, William, 182; correspondence of with Isaac de Rasière, 171, 173, 176–181. *See also* Plymouth Colony

importance of to Dutch colonial historiography, 239–241. *See also* "Amboyna massacre"

Dutch Republic: as basis for consideration of American colonies, 159–161; as model for New Netherland, 155–156; as perceived model of toleration, 160, 199–205; institutional character and overseas activities of 5–9, 13; political changes in, 154; relations of with England, 29, 157–158, 185–186; religion in, 198, 205–212. *See also* Amsterdam; Anabaptists; Confession of Heidelberg; Dutch Revolt; Frederick Henry; Maurice, count of Nassau and Prince of Orange; Mennonites; New Netherland; Toleration; William II

Dutch Reformed Church. *See* Reformed Church (Dutch)

Dutch Revolt, 4–7, 19; and toleration, 205–206; and Dutch cartography, 45; effects on English economy of, 19

Dutch West India Company (WIC), 27, 67, 173, 178, 237; and Dutch-Spanish relations, 6–8, 148; as patron of cartography, 59–63; colonizing approach of, 74–76, 90–91, 113–115, 148–149, 151–152, 160–161, 198, 213, 215, 216, 227; governing structure of, 9–10; relations of with New Netherland colonists, 10–13, 153–154, 156–157. *See also* Joan Blaeu; Willem Blaeu; Brazil; Cornelis Claesz; Hessel Gerritsz; Evert Gijsbertsz; Henry Hudson; Willem Kieft; Peter Minuit; Mahican Indians; Mohawk Indians; New Netherland; Patroonships; Augustijn Robaert; Slaves and slave trade; Petrus Stuyvesant; Toleration; Wampum

Edam, Dutch city: and overseas navigation, 55–56

Eelckens, Jacob/Jacques, 107–109, 111

Elizabeth I, queen of England (r. 1558–1603), 17, 173

English Civil Wars (1642–1651), 7, 18, 25, 29

English East India Company, 19, 29

Erie Canal, 81

Esopus. *See* Wiltwijck

Esopus Wars, 157

First Dutch-Munsee War ("Kieft's War"), 93, 152–153

Flinck, Govert, 38–41

Flushing, NY. *See* Vlissingen

Flushing Remonstrance (1657), 209, 213

Formosa, 12

Fort Massapeag (Massapequa, NY), 93

Fort Nassau (near Beverwijck), 107, 111

Fort Nassau (Delaware/South River), 152

Fort Orange, 10, 11, 12, 72, 74, 90, 111, 113, 114, 115, 116, 117, 118, 119, 144, 149, 150, 154, 173, 179. *See also* Wampum

French and Indian War (1754–1763), 80

Frederick Henry, stadholder: circle of, 58–59

Fredericks, Alfred: painting of *The Purchase of Manhattan Island* by, 68–69

Fresh River. *See* Connecticut River

Fur trade. *See* Connecticut River; Delaware River; Fort Orange; Hudson River; Massachusetts Bay; New France; New Amsterdam; New Netherland; New York; Plymouth Colony; St. Lawrence River; Wampum

Geopolitics: as scholarly concept, 170–171
Gerritsz, Hessel, 50–51, 55, 57–58, 60, 61–62
Gijsbertsz, Evert, 53–54

Hakluyt, Richard (the younger), 17, 19–20, 21, 44
Hall, Edward Hagaman. *See* Hudson-Fulton Commemoration (1909)
Hamilton, Dr. Alexander: observations of New York (1744), 78–80
Harvey, Sir John, governor of Virginia, 25
Hudson, Henry: as employee of the Dutch East India Company, 15, 17, 44, 49, 148, 172, 225 226; encounters with Indians of, 67, 69, 85–86, 89, 106, 110, 148; quadricentennial celebration of, ix–x, 120, 137. *See also* Mahican Indians; Wampum
Hudson-Fulton Tricentennial Commemoration (1909): portrayal of Indians at, 103–107
Hudson River: as commercial route, 72, 171; Dutch cartographic depictions of, 73. *See also* Lake Champlain
Hudson Valley: after American independence, 81–82; as focus of Indian and European imperial rivalry, 71, 74, 76–77, 79–80, 111–120, 169, 172–173; Atlantic world context of, 96, 112 113, extension of slavery into, 78; Indian-European relations in, 75, 85–86, 110–111, 152–153. *See also* Algonquian Indians; Dr. Alexander Hamilton; Henry Hudson; Hudson River; Huguenots; Iroquois League; Mahican Indians; Iroquois League; Munsee Indians; New France; New Netherland; Palatines; Patroonships; Plymouth Colony; Slaves and slave trade; Wampum

Huguenots, 17, 76, 143, 217
Hulft, Gerard, 40–42. *See also* Govert Flinck
Hulft, Pieter Evertsz, 37–38
Huron Indians, 137, 141–142

Indonesia. *See* Dutch East Indies
Irving, Washington, 81–82, 157
Iroquois Confederacy. *See* Iroquois League
Iroquois League, 77, 86; Covenant Chain between and English, 69, 71, 80; oral tradition of, 69 71, 88; relations of with Dutch, 110–120; relations of with French, 117, 137, 144; relations of with other Native nations, 111–116. *See also* Canasatego; Hudson-Fulton Tricentennial Commemoration; *Kaswentha*; Mahican Indians; Mohawk Indians; Oneida Indians; Onondaga Indians; Two Row Wampum Belt; Arent van Curler; Wampum
Isaacz, Peter, 35–36

James I, king of England (1603–1625), 18, 19, 23, 149
James II, king of England (1685–1688), 76; as duke of York (1660–1685), 75, 158, 186
Jamestown. *See* Virginia
Japan, 13, 40, 42, 54
Jogues, Fr. Isaac, S.J., 115, 217–218, 246
Johnson, Sir William, 77, 80

Kahionni. See Wampum
Kaswentha, 103, 106, 107–109, 110–111, 113–122
Kieft, Willem, 152, 153, 201, 214, 217, 246–247
Kieft's War. *See* First Dutch-Munsee War

Kingston, NY. *See* Wiltwijck
King George's War (1744–1748), 79
Kongo, kingdom of: forced migration
    of people of to New Netherland,
    245–246
Koninck, Abraham de, 37
Krieckenbeeck, Daniel van, 113, 149

Lake Champlain, 80, 137, 141, 174, 182
Langren, Jacob Florisz van, 43, 53
Le Moyne, Fr. Simon, S.J., 117
Lescarbot, Marc, 143
Lichthart, Admiral Jan Cornelisz,
    60–61
Linschoten, Jan Huygen van, 35, 43–44,
    46, 47, 48, 56
Livingston, Robert, 77
Locke, John, 204
Long Island, 74, 161; as site of
    wampum production, 87–91, 94–95.
    See also Connecticut (colony);
    Munsee Indians; New Haven
    Colony; Treaty of Hartford
Louis XIV, king of France (1643–
    1715), 76, 77, 140, 204
Lutherans. *See* Dutch Republic:
    religion in, and New Netherland:
    religion in

Mahican Indians: cultural characteristics
    of, 85–88; meeting of with Henry
    Hudson, 89, 225–226; relations of
    with other Native nations, 111–113,
    115–116, 118, 119, 144, 229. *See also*
    Hudson Valley; Mohawk Indians;
    Wampum
Manhattan, 172, 176, 244; purchase of
    by Dutch, 68–71, 149–150. *See also*
    Dutch West India Company; New
    Amsterdam; New Netherland
Martha's Vineyard: claimed by Dutch,
    175

Massachusetts Bay Colony, 68;
    expansion of, 71, 170, 181–183,
    185–186; fur trade and, 94; "Great
    Puritan Migration" (1629–1640) to,
    26. *See also* Pequot War; Plymouth
    Colony; Wampum; John Winthrop
Maurice, count of Nassau and Prince
    of Orange, stadholder, 35–38, 44, 49,
    53–54, 58, 201; use of name of on
    Dutch maps, 172–173
Medici, Marie de', 38, 49
Medici, Grand Duke Ferdinando de', 49
Mennonites. *See* Dutch Republic:
    religion in
Mercator, Gerard, 43–45, 51
Minuit, Pieter: and purchase of
    Manhattan, 68–69; as founder of
    New Sweden, 152
Mohawk Indians, 73, 80; relations of
    with Dutch, 75, 90, 103, 107–121,
    227; relations of with French, 231;
    relations of with other Native
    nations, 85–86. *See also* Iroquois
    League; *Kaswentha*; Mahican Indians;
    Schenectady; Wampum
Mohawk River, 72
Mohawk Valley, 106; British expansion
    into, 77–78, 80, 81; extension of
    slavery into, 78. *See also* Palatines
Moody, Lady Deborah, 247
Monts, Pierre de, 138–139
Moucheron, Balthasar de, 43, 47, 57
Mughal Empire, 29
Munsee Indians, 85–87. *See also* First
    Dutch-Munsee War; Second Dutch-
    Munsee War; Tackapousha; Third
    Dutch-Munsee War; Wampum

Nantucket, 175
Narragansett Bay. *See* Wampum
Narragansett Indians, 86, 87, 93, 185.
    See also Wampum

United Provinces. *See* Dutch Republic

Valckert, Werner van den, 37–39
Venezuela: as source of salt, 8; as source of tobacco, 22
Vingboons, Johannes, 61–62
Virginia, 178, 182; government of, 20–21, 23; indentured servitude in, 23–24; population of, 74, 139; relations of with Indians, 21; relations of with New Netherland, 24–25, 155, 157; slavery in, 26–28, 78. *See also* Samuel Argall; William Claiborne; Sir John Harvey; Powhatan Indians; Plymouth Colony; John Rolfe
Virginia Company, 18, 19, 22, 148, 176. *See also* Virginia
Visscher, Nicolas, 73, 175
Vlissingen (Flushing, NY), 56

Waghenaer, Lucas Jansz, 43
Wahunsonacock. *See* Powhatan Indians
Walbeeck, Johannes van, 60
Walloons, 139, 149–150, 210, 214, 217
Wampum: and fur trade, 71, 90, 94, 95, 114, 140, 178–179, 227, 229–231; as currency, 90, 94–95, 228–229, 230; as instrument of geopolitical relations, 181, 228–230; cultural importance of, 88, 90–92, 226; economic importance of to Indians, 88, 91, 92–93, 114, 178–180, 186, 228, 230–231; importance of to Dutch, 89, 91, 139,

227, 229–231; production of, 85, 87 88, 90, 91–94, 95, 96, 112, 226–229; women's involvement in production of, 94, 95. *See also* Atlantic world; Jacob Eelkens; *Kaswentha*; Long Island; Pequot War; Two Row Wampum Belt; West Indies
West, Benjamin, 68–69
West Indies, 27, 171, 186; as location of shells for wampum, 95; maps of, 46, 47, 57; slavery in, 140–141, 143. *See also* Atlantic world; Netherlands: post-colonial historiographical perceptions in the
William II, stadholder, 154
William of Orange (1533–1584), 5, 205. *See also* Dutch Revolt
William of Orange (1650–1702), 76
William III, king of England, Scotland, and Ireland. *See* William of Orange (1650–1702)
Williams, Roger: observations on Native-English trade, 91
Wiltwijck (Kingston, NY), 74, 76, 156, 157. *See also* Esopus Wars
Winslow, Edward, 181. *See also* New Netherland, relations of with other colonies
Winthrop, John, 100, 181, 191
Winthrop, John, Jr., 184. *See also* Saybrook (CT)
Wright, Benjamin, 48
Wytz, Jacob, 58–59. *See also* Frederick Henry

Brian Ensworth
952 - 937 - 9127